Evaluating and Improving Written Expression

A Practical Guide for Teachers

SECOND EDITION

JANICE K. HALL

ALLYN AND BACON, INC.
Boston   London   Sydney   Toronto

Copyright © 1988, 1981 by Allyn and Bacon, Inc.
A Division of Simon & Schuster
7 Wells Avenue
Newton, Massachusetts 02159

Library of Congress Cataloging-in-Publication Data

Hall, Janice K.
  Evaluating and improving written expression.

  Bibliography: p.
  Includes index.
  1. English language—Composition and exercises—Study and teaching.   I. Title.
LB1576.H22   1988   372.6'23   87-12417
ISBN 0-205-10548-3

Printed in the United States of America
10 9 8 7 6 5 4 3 2   91 90 89

CONTENTS

Preface   v

CHAPTER 1   Introduction   1

CHAPTER 2   Check Their Writing   11

CHAPTER 3   Get Them Writing!   47

CHAPTER 4   Use the Computer   59

CHAPTER 5   Let Them Write Creatively   75

CHAPTER 6   Write for a Reason   101

CHAPTER 7   Get It Organized!   119

CHAPTER 8   Use the Right Word   137

CHAPTER 9   Build Sentence Sense   157

CHAPTER 10   Tackle the Troublespots   179

CHAPTER 11   Check Their Spelling   193

CHAPTER 12   Improve Handwriting   199

Bibliography   **209**

Directory of Publishers   **217**

Index   **221**

PREFACE

This resource manual is designed to give teachers and students an overview of "what makes good writing." The concepts and activities are designed for use by regular classroom teachers, resource room teachers, and anyone else interested in helping students improve their writing ability. Informal evaluation procedures and numerous student writing samples assist teachers in analyzing student writing for pinpointing strengths and weaknesses.

The Introduction, Chapter 1, reviews the factors that cause writing to be a complex process; then it surveys methods and tests currently available for evaluating writing ability. Chapter 2, "Check Their Writing," presents informal evaluation procedures encouraging teachers to look at six areas that together contribute to writing competency: ideas/content, organization, vocabulary, sentence structure, spelling, and handwriting. Charts highlight three levels of performance in these six areas. Checklists for these areas also help identify levels of development in student writing ability.

Chapter 3, "Get Them Writing!" discusses important considerations when setting up the classroom writing environment using the writing process model: prewriting, writing, proofreading and editing, revising, and publishing. Writing is seen not just as an end-product but also as a development of ideas through the stages of the writing process.

Chapter 4, "Use the Computer," surveys current and future uses of computers in classroom and laboratory settings and reviews computer software related to writing instruction. Computers are changing the way people write, and this chapter points out the benefits of using word processing for writing purposes.

Chapters 5 and 6, "Let Them Write Creatively" and "Write for a Reason," begin the activity section of this manual. These activities provide an integrated language arts approach to improving writing skills. They emphasize thinking, listening, speaking, reading, writing, and rewriting as interrelated components of the total writing process. The teacher has several goals: to encourage students to increase their writing productivity, to identify their levels of performance and pinpoint areas of difficulty, and to set priorities, based on specific manageable objectives, for helping students improve their writing skills. Total correction of daily writing assignments is deemphasized as students follow goal-setting procedures and focus on improving one aspect of writing at a time.

Chapters 7 through 12 feature skill building activities in the areas of organization, vocabulary, sentence structure, mechanics, spelling, and handwriting. These sections also emphasize proofreading and editing skills. Instead of working on textbook exercises, students proofread their own writing to find and correct one specific error pattern at a time. When students have difficulty identifying errors in their own writing, activities from this section that isolate error patterns will help them. Placing responsibility for identification and correction of errors on the students helps to increase student awareness and to eliminate some of the persistent problems in writing.

Ideally, the total writing program should provide positive reinforcement for all student writing, regardless of errors. Written expression will improve gradually as students gain more experience with peer and self-evaluation, goal setting, isolation of error types, revision, and publication.

The revisions for the second edition of this book were completed on Apple II + and Apple IIe computers with a variety of word processing programs (AppleWorks, AppleWriter, Bank Street Writer, MECC Writer, and Milliken Word Processor).

CHAPTER 1

Introduction

The Complexity of the Writing Process

Why is writing such a complex process? This question has been the topic of many studies in recent years. Cooper and Odell (1977) have described the writing, or composing, process in the following manner:

> Composing involves exploring and mulling over a subject; planning the particular piece (with or without notes or outline); getting started; making discoveries about feelings, values, or ideas, even while in the process of writing a draft; making continuous decisions about diction, syntax, and rhetoric in relation to the intended meaning and to the meaning taking shape; reviewing what has accumulated, and anticipating and rehearsing what comes next; tinkering and reformulating; stopping; contemplating the finished piece and perhaps, finally, revising. This complex, unpredictable, demanding activity is what we call the writing process.

Many other factors contribute to the complexity of the writing process: the high level of abstract thinking required, the increased level of self-responsibility, the maturity of self-motivation, and the completeness that is required in the written form of language (Lundsteen, 1976a). Difficulty with these may result in a lag in writing skills of as much as six to eight years. In writing, students must translate their own inner language (which is often condensed and abbreviated in a form of verbal shorthand) into appropriate words, sentences, and paragraphs that accurately convey an intended message. Writers do not have the benefit of immediate feedback in the form of questions or other verbal or body language from a listener. Instead, the writer must anticipate the questions and other responses and account for them during the actual writing process. In other words, students must analyze their writing and clarify their ideas as they go along. See Table 1-1.

A large number of constraints must also be satisfied at the immediate time of writing. The writer must deal with content constraints (purpose, ideas,

TABLE 1-1
The Complexity of the Writing Process

Stage	Skills	Tasks
Prewriting	Thinking	decide to communicate in written form
		explain the matter to oneself
		form tentative plan for writing
		identify target audience
		identify style or writing necessary for purpose (narrative, expository, persuasive)
		discover ideas, generalizations, theme, topic
		narrow topic appropriately
		develop topic sentence or main ideas
		select relevant facts, examples, details from experience or research
	Organization	sequence general content of message
		group related ideas
		omit irrelevant ideas
		sequence ideas (chronological, spatial, logical, etc.)
		state conclusion or summary
Writing	Language Skills (Vocabulary and Sentence Structure)	choose appropriate vocabulary for purpose and audience level
		arrange vocabulary in meaningful sentences using correct grammatical relationships
		vary selection of sentence types
	Spelling Skills	discriminate the sounds and sequence of sounds in words
		recall the shape and form of letters
		recall the shape and form of non-phonetic words
	Handwriting	sequence the appropriate motor movements to write letters and words
	Mechanics	include proper punctuation, capitalization
Post-Writing	Editing and Revising	*content editing*
		read the written message
		identify gaps in presentation
		identify need for additional facts, details, examples
		clarify main idea and relationships between ideas
		delete irrelevant material
		add appropriate transitional phrases
		refine word choice
		structure editing
		revise awkward sentences
		combine simple sentences
		correct tense use

Note: Table 1-1 presents a summary and graphic display of the complexity and interrelation of the skills required in the writing process. Writing truly is not a linear process as the task analysis suggests. It is one of many stops and starts, of many readings and rereadings, of much movement back and forth from the first stages to the last as ideas are crystallized, reformed, and revised, and the structure is shaped, modified, and polished until, at last, the writing is done.

organization) and structure constraints (sentence and paragraph construction), all the while keeping in mind the need for comprehensibility, enticingness (keeping the reader's attention), persuasiveness, and memorability (writing so that the key points will be remembered) (Bruce, 1978). The necessity for keeping all of these constraints in mind at one time increases the difficulty in writing.

Different purposes for writing and different audiences require different styles of responses (Britton et al., 1975; Kinneavy, 1971, Moffett, 1968). Writing styles and purposes range along a continuum on which distance and time between the sending and receiving of the message increase. For example: The shortest distance from a message sender to a receiver is a *speaker* talking about a *familiar subject* with a *listener*. The longest distance is a writer writing a message about an *unfamiliar or theoretical topic* for a person who will *read* the message at a much later time (as in published writing) and who will provide no feedback. As the distance and time from the message sender to the message receiver increase, the demands placed on the writer increase: vocabulary, style, allusion, rhetoric all have to be geared to the intended audience (Moffett, 1968). A personal note to a friend, for example, requires different style, vocabulary, and organization than does a theoretical paper on the effects of nuclear warfare.

Evaluation of Writing Skills

For many years researchers and educators have been concerned with developing an efficient and reliable method for evaluating written language. One controversy has centered on the analysis of the qualitative versus the quantitative features of writing. Quantitative measures such as vocabulary knowledge, usage, capitalization, punctuation, and spelling can be measured with machine-scored, standardized measures; but qualitative features, especially style, organization, and level of abstraction in writing, cannot be measured so objectively. Analyzing qualitative features of writing requires the use of actual student writing samples. Even the use of student samples, however, has not solved the problem of evaluation, since there are numerous approaches to analyzing writing, ranging from simple error counts to any of the many forms of holistic scoring.

Different types of testing and scoring procedures are needed for different purposes. The selection of a particular test or testing process will depend on the kind of results desired and how these results are to be used. Generally, test results can be used in the following ways:

1. To report student progress to administrators;
2. To report progress to parents;
3. To identify the progress that students make over a period of time;
4. To determine levels of student ability in order to place students in appropriate classes;
5. To diagnose specific strengths and weaknesses of individual students as a preliminary to providing individual or small group remedial instruction;
6. To determine the effectiveness of a particular program or instructional method that is used; and
7. To identify the actual steps that students use as they prepare to write, then write, and revise their work.

Most authorities on writing express discontent with the type of evaluation measures used in the past. Even so, several different kinds of assessment strategies and devices have been used with varying degrees of success: formalized evaluation, such as in standardized achievement tests and diagnostic tests; informal teacher evaluation; rating scales; peer evaluation; and self-evaluation. This chapter will review a variety of these evaluation methods and measures.

Teacher Evaluation of Student Writing

Until recently, teachers have received little formal training in evaluating and teaching written expression. One research study using fifty-three evaluators identified five distinct approaches to grading writing samples. Some evaluators focused primarily on ideas in writing (the richness, soundness, clarity, development, and relevance to the topic and the writer's purpose); while others focused on mechanics (errors in usage, sentence structure, punctuation, and spelling); organization; vocabulary (the choice and arrangement of words in phrases); or, finally, flavor (the personal qualities revealed in writing style, individuality, originality, interest, and sincerity) (Diederich, 1974). The evaluators in this study received no training in grading procedures but reacted to the papers using their own standards.

In one common approach, teachers give assignments that emphasize ideas, but return students' papers with numerous red marks for poor spelling, punctuation, and grammar errors. Braddock, Lloyd-Jones, and Schoer (1963) summarize the results of a number of studies of teacher evaluation of writing with the following statement: "It has not been proved that the intensive marking (of student writing samples), with or without revision, is the best procedure to use with upper elementary or junior high (students)." Other researchers, in fact, note that only positive comments written on students' papers produce any positive effects (Beaven, 1977; Lundsteen, 1976b).

Holistic Evaluation of Writing

Holistic evaluation uses actual writing samples to get an overall impression of student writing ability, rather than a detailed analysis of errors. This technique gives a school district a reliable method for evaluation of large numbers of student writing samples by trained school personnel. It is most often used on a school-wide or district-wide basis at the secondary level, although it can be used at elementary and junior high levels as well.

In this process, students in all grades to be evaluated write on an assigned topic in a supervised writing session for a specified period of time. Evaluators, generally teachers excused from classroom responsibilities for the day, are trained to read each paper quickly (approximately one paper every two minutes) and score the papers according to a previously discussed rubric, scale, checklist, or graded series of samples. The reader does not take time to identify or count errors but rather reacts to the writing based on overall impression, then quickly moves on to the next paper. Two evaluators read each sample. If their scores differ substantially, a third reader is used to obtain a balance or consensus.

Holistic evaluation provides a rank ordering of scores. These results can be used for placement purposes and for reporting to administrators. Teachers receive the scores of students in their classes, but not the reasons a student received a particular score. In some cases the students with the lowest scores are identified for remedial services, and their papers may be returned to teachers for detailed analysis; otherwise, there is no other feedback to the classroom teacher. However, teachers trained in holistic scoring usually have internalized the features of good writing and use this evaluation method on a daily basis.

An excellent summary of the variations of holistic scoring is provided by Cooper and Odell in *Evaluating Writing: Describing, Measuring, and Judging* (1977).

Analytic Evaluation

The analytic method of evaluating written expression and composition is similar to the holistic method in that several readers rate each writing sample and then average the individual scores to obtain a final score. In analytic scoring, however, each rater assigns points in each of a number of specific aspects of the writing sample. Often the raters use a checklist or rating scale that lists features such as quality of ideas, organization of material, expression (diction and sentence style), grammar, punctuation, spelling, handwriting, and so on. This procedure takes more time than the holistic assessment because it requires multiple readings by each rater to analyze each item on the rating list. On the positive side, it does produce more usable results in the classroom, since teachers can use results to identify specific instructional objectives. Training is required for analytic scoring in order to eliminate as much rater variability as possible.

Text Analysis

Research studies have attempted to look at specific aspects of writing in careful detail in order to identify underlying rules for structure, and hence possible implications for teaching. Sentence structure has been the focus of a number of studies, primarily because sentences can be quantitatively analyzed by counting words and clauses. Strickland (1961), Loban (1963), Hunt (1965), and O'Donnell, Griffin, and Norris (1967) have identified sentence length and complexity as one indicator of syntactical maturity.

Hunt uses the T-unit as the research unit related to the sentence and defines it as "one main clause plus the subordinate clauses attached to it." In Hunt's method, writing samples are divided up into the smallest possible T-units, regardless of punctuation. Compound sentences are treated as two T-units because both parts are equal main clauses. The average number of words per T-unit is then computed. Hunt found that main clauses in sentences increased in length as students increased in age and that more subordinate clauses were attached to the main clause. Thus, T-unit length is an indication of syntactical maturity. Lundsteen (1976a) suggests one caution regarding sentence length: "It is not 'how long you make them, but *how* you make them long.'" In other words, run-on sentences can be very long, but they are very immature. Sentences that have a lot of description can be awkward and phony because they are overloaded with unnecessary detail. Complex sentences in which dependent clauses are attached to the main clause are more mature than the previous two examples.

Based on syntactic maturity studies, Mellon (1969) developed instructional strategies designed to train students to combine sentences and thus increase sentence length and complexity. While this is a part of writing competency, it is by no means the only answer to assisting writers in producing better reports and compositions.

Recent advances in technology have enabled researchers, educators, and students to analyze written text in a relatively easy manner. Now computerized writing analyzers can identify and compare sentence length throughout a writing sample. In addition, these analyzers can evaluate common writing errors in punctuation, capitalization, word usage, and spelling. Chapter 4, "Use The Computer," describes various computer writing analyzers.

Rating Scales

A rating scale is an organized list of factors to be considered when evaluating student writing. Diederich (1974) developed one scale that included four of the most commonly identified components (ideas, organization, wording, flavor) on the scale and subdivided one other, mechanics, into usage (which includes sentence structure), punctuation, and spelling. Since most teachers emphasize ideas and organization in their classes, these two components were double-weighted. Diederich provided a written description of three levels of performance (high, middle, and low) in these categories. The resulting scale is a means of systematically evaluating the qualities of writing without having to make detailed notes. After teachers had received training in the use of this scale and had used it over a period of time, they found that they could judge papers more quickly on general impression.

A second scale, the Carlson Analytical Originality Scale, focuses exclusively on the creative aspects of story writing. This scale contains five major categories: story structure, novelty, emotion, individuality, and style of stories. Items in each category are rated on a zero to five scale. Scale Division A, Story Structure, evaluates any unusual handling of basic story elements (title, beginning, dialogue, ending, plot) and gives points for originality or creativity. Scale Division B, Novelty, also looks at originality of approach with different story features (uniqueness of expression, ingenuity in solving problem situations, picturesque speech, humor, and unusual ideas). Three other scale divisions evaluate use of emotion in story individuality (unusual sensitivity, unique philosophical thinking, unusual sincerity in expressing personal problems), and style of stories. Each category is defined in a descriptive listing of samples in Carlson's book *Sparkling Words* (1973). While this scale focuses only on creative writing, it helps teachers pinpoint specific indications of originality in all student writing.

Peer Evaluation and Self-Evaluation

A number of researchers and teachers have found peer evaluation successful, and it is popularly used in writing workshop settings. Sager (1973) developed a program called *Reading, Writing, and Rating Stories* in which students learn to evaluate short samples of writing using descriptive scales for vocabulary, elaboration, organization, and structure. Sager's research, as well as others', indicates that improvement resulting from peer evaluation techniques may equal or even exceed that resulting from teacher evaluation (Beaven, 1977).

Peer evaluation techniques require that students read their stories or reports to small groups to get reactions and suggestions for improvement. Students may use rating scales or specific guide questions at first to help them focus on relevant concerns in writing samples. After students receive feedback from other students, they incorporate the suggestions in revised drafts. These techniques encourage students to think of writing as a multi-stage process.

Students can easily be trained to identify the positive aspects in the writing of others. This means that teachers must emphasize identifying positive qualities and giving suggestions in a positive manner without negative comments. Students quickly learn to start their comments with such phrases as "I really like . . .", "The most interesting part was . . .", "I could really see what you were describing." Students (and teachers) can give suggestions by saying, "Tell me more about . . .", "What did he/she/it look like?" or "I think something might be missing." The whole cooperative learning atmosphere in peer conferencing builds positive feelings among students and self-esteem for individuals.

Using this cooperative learning approach, students also learn to evaluate their own writing. Recalling comments given by their classmates on various writing samples, they strive to incorporate those ideas in their original drafts. Self-evaluation of writing also places responsibility for improvement on the student. Most often the student uses guide questions suggested by the teacher to review his or her own writing. Beaven (1977) asks the student to respond to questions related to the amount of time spent on the paper, the strengths and weaknesses of the paper, and how the paper will be changed in the next draft. Rating scales, such as Sager's (1973), have also helped students in evaluating their own writing.

Standardized Achievement Tests

Standardized achievement tests measure discrete subcomponents of writing, most commonly vocabulary knowledge, grammatical usage, capitalization, punctuation, and spelling. Occasionally, achievement tests include items on topic sentences, sequencing sentences, and eliminating irrelevant sentences. These skill areas are tested by proofreading and editing tasks in multiple-choice format. Students are asked to pick the correct word to complete the meaning of a sentence, to choose the best sentence from a group of sample sentences, to supply the correct capital letter or punctuation symbol, or to choose the correct spelling of a word. These subcomponents of writing have been selected because they can be easily standardized and scaled in relation to representative populations. Test results, therefore, appear in the form of grade equivalents and percentiles, allowing the teacher to compare each student's performance with standardized norms. Results are used to compare students' progress in specific subskill areas from one year to the next and to report progress to parents and administrators.

Currently there is general agreement that standardized achievement tests do not provide enough information about students' actual writing ability (Cooper, 1977). Furthermore, achievement tests are considered inadequate measures of writing ability because students do not produce a complete writing sample using their own choice of words, sentence structure, ideas, or organization; nor do they produce writing for different purposes or different audiences. (Braddock, Lloyd-Jones, and Schoer, 1963). A final weakness of achievement tests is their failure to provide diagnostic information about specific strengths and weaknesses in student writing ability. Any useful testing program should provide information to help the classroom teacher develop individual or group lesson plans that meet specific needs of the students.

Standardized Diagnostic Tests

Standardized diagnostic tests attempt to identify specific strengths and weaknesses of student writing ability. Although these tests provide more specific information than standardized achievement tests do, they take longer to score and interpret because they require the use of student writing samples. Three tests for intermediate students that fall into this group are the Myklebust *Picture Story Language Test, Test of Written Language* by Hammill and Larsen, and *Diagnostic Evaluation of Writing Skills* by Weiner.

The *Picture Story Language Test* (PSLT) features a picture stimulus to elicit writing samples from students aged seven to seventeen. Scoring on the PSLT requires the use of three scales: the Productivity Scale (to measure and compare the length of the writing sample, the number of sentences, and the number of words per sentence); the Syntax Scale (to measure correctness of word usage, word endings, and punctuation); and the Abstract-Concrete Scale (to measure the level of idea content). Evaluation of spelling and handwriting is not included in this test.

Reviewers have generally criticized this test for its complicated scoring procedures, its low interest picture, and its standardization information (Anastasiow, 1972; Hammill and Larsen, 1978; Poteet, 1979).

The *Test of Written Language* (TOWL) was designed for students in grades three through eight. The test has two evaluation components: a spontaneous student writing sample and three objective subtests in the areas of spelling, word usage (measuring such skills as forming tenses, using correct word endings), and style (measuring the correct use of punctuation and capitalization). The writing sample, based on a sequence of three related pictures (a group of people preparing to leave a parched, barren planet, the space flight, and finally the settlement on a new planet), is analyzed for thematic maturity, vocabulary, and sentence structure (thought units).

Thematic maturity on this test refers to the ability of an individual to write in a logical, organized fashion and in a way that will easily convey meaning. Each writing sample is evaluated through the use of twenty questions related to paragraph format, story parts (beginning, ending), naming of characters, invented vocabulary, development of a theme, and sequence of ideas. Scoring is based on the evaluator's judgment of whether these items are absent or present in the student's writing. Because it gives results in terms of scaled scores and grade equivalents, the authors suggest that additional informal diagnosis of student writing samples be completed.

The *Diagnostic Evaluation of Writing Skills* (DEWS) uses the assigned writing topic "My Favorite Activity" as the stimulus for writing. Each writing sample is assessed on forty-one separate items in six categories of writing errors: graphic (handwriting), orthographic (spelling), phonologic (spelling), syntactic (grammatical), semantic (vocabulary), and self-monitoring skills. The examiner reads the student writing sample and tabulates the number of errors made in each category. This test has been used to select students requiring special remediation in both reading and writing (Weiner, 1980).

Two additional diagnostic tests that use student writing samples have been developed for use with older students. *DI-COMP, A Diagnostic System for Teaching Composition for Grades 10–14*, uses a checklist to tally errors in ten categories concerned with spelling, organization, punctuation, grammar, and sentence structure. The *Test of Everyday Writing Skills* (TEWS) contains both objective and subjective measures. The objective measures utilize practical writing samples (e.g. letters, telephone messages) as stimuli for multiple-choice questions. The student is also asked to write an eyewitness report of an accident. This writing sample is then scored by the holistic procedures described earlier in this chapter.

Conclusion

If writing is a complex process, then evaluating writing is even more complex. While there are advantages and disadvantages to each of the described methods, some form of evaluation is desirable and necessary. The current emphasis on gathering student writing samples under test conditions, along with the use of holistic and analytical scoring methods, is a positive move. Peer and self-evaluation techniques are also important steps in the process. These methods are promising for classroom instruction in writing.

The evaluation procedures in this book are of an analytical nature and are designed to help the teacher evaluate and identify levels of performance in student writing. While there are distinct disadvantages with this method—most notably the amount of time it takes—the major advantage is that it gives the teacher specific direction in teaching writing. The next chapters will outline informal evaluation procedures and then will suggest instructional activities to meet specific instructional goals based on the informal evaluations.

CHAPTER 2

Check Their Writing

One purpose of this manual is to provide guidelines for a careful review of student writing ability. Part One, Informal Evaluation, Levels of Performance, presents student writing samples from grades four through twelve and special education, and discusses them in terms of three levels of performance. Part Two, Informal Evaluation Procedures, presents Informal Evaluation Activities, Evaluation Questions, and Student Writing Checklist I.

Part One, Informal Evaluation, Levels of Performance

Informal evaluation of written expression focuses on six areas of performance:

A. Ideas/content (level of abstraction)
B. Organization skills
C. Vocabulary usage
D. Sentence structure
E. Spelling
F. Handwriting

Each of these writing areas is subdivided into three levels of performance: *Low, Middle,* and *High*. See Table 2-1 for charts that outline the key factors of these levels for the six categories mentioned above. The next few paragraphs present a brief summary of these levels, followed by an in-depth treatment using student writing samples from both regular and special education classes.

In general, writing at the Low level is unfocused. Students do not have a clear sense of purpose, a sense of audience, or the skills and techniques necessary to write stories or reports that are coherent, complete, and interesting. Usually, written productivity is quite low—sometimes less than five or six short, simple sentences.

TABLE 2-1
Levels of Performance in Writing Ability

	Ideas/Content	*Organization*

Low	Writing is basically immature and exhibits one or more of the following characteristics:
	
	• unintelligible responses
	• "stimulus-bound" writing:
	    simple naming and/or describing
	    no original ideas
	    lists of words or phrases
	• single-event personal experiences,
	    or groups of events with no generalization
	    rambling, "on and on" stories
	• simple thought sequence
	• egocentric
		Writing lacks a specific organizing theme or purpose; overall organization is poor, and sequencing is generally inaccurate or absent.
		
		• simple thought sequence
		    ideas may be out of order, or written as they
		      occur to writer
		    unrelated ideas may be grouped together
		• irrelevant details

Middle	Writers *begin* to relate and classify experiences and/or facts and make generalizations. A definite storyline or theme is evident although it may not be completely developed.
	
	• relevant generalizations included
	• descriptive detail added:
	    character, setting, mood detail, emotions
	    sensory details: sight, sound, smell, taste,
	      touch
	    character interaction
	    character dialogue or monologue
	• sequence of events is clear
	• personal style evident
	    original ideas expressed
	    use of humor, imagination
		Organization skills show improvement —but inconsistency in handling generalizations, details, and conclusions is evident.
		
		• lack of overall planning
		• paragraph structure may not be adequate
		    overgeneralizations and unsupported
		      opinions
		    abundance of detail without summarizing
		      statement or appropriate conclusion (main
		      ideas omitted)
		    poor introductions to paragraphs or reports
		      (lack of topic sentence or topic paragraph)
		    inappropriate or omitted conclusions
		    poor transitions between paragraphs
		• topic development may not be complete
		    content may be copied from one source
		    topic choice may be too broad or too narrow
		    shifts in point of view
		    shifts in train of thought

High	Writing is CLEARLY and CONSISTENTLY purposeful. Ideas and details are selected for specific purposes and generally involve analysis, synthesis, or interpretation.
	
	• judgments made: stated or implied
	• morals suggested: stated or implied
	• consistent point of view supported by facts,
	    reasons, examples
	• deliberate selection of information:
	    some points emphasized, others ignored
	    appeals to readers's emotions
	    persuasion
		Writing is CLEARLY and CONSISTENTLY organized. The writer organizes his work for specific purposes and carefully selects relevant information.
		
		• topic appropriately narrowed and focused
		• adequate planning and preparation
		    use of notetaking and outlining skills
		• accurate paragraph structure
		    generalizations and summaries with relevant
		      supporting details
		    opinions supported by relevant facts, details,
		      examples
		    appropriate paragraph breaks and transitions
		    appropriate conclusions

TABLE 2-1 *(continued)*

	Vocabulary	Sentence Structure

Low	The writer OVERUSES the following kinds of words:
	
	• common nouns: the man, the thing, something, the dog, people, place
	• common verbs: is/was, are/am, go/went, do/did, see/saw/look, want/have, get/got, make, said, like
	• general adjectives: good/nice, big/little, funny, pretty
	• general adverbs: many, some, very, really, too
	• articles, prepositions, conjunctions
	• pronouns without clear referents
		The writer does not have good "sentence sense" and is unable to arrange words to form complete sentences. Some of the following characteristics may be seen.
		
		• lists of words and/or phrases (no sentences at all)
		• sentence errors
		  run-ons: overuse of *and, and then, and so*
		  sentence fragments
		  syntax errors: words omitted or word order inaccurate
		• overuse of short, choppy simple sentences
		• omitted punctuation, or totally inaccurate punctuation

Middle	The writer *begins* to play with words and introduces *some* of the following elements in the writing:
	
	• specific nouns, verbs, adjectives, adverbs
	• imaginative use of words
	  invented words
	  alliteration, rhyming, repetition
	  original similes, metaphors, analogies
	
	As students experiment in vocabulary use, the following kinds of errors may be made:
	
	• word selection errors
	  word form substitution
	  preposition errors: "regardless to"
	  clichés: "pretty as a picture"
	  overly elaborate, flowery words/phrases
	  excess words/phrases: "the reason is because"
	• word formation errors
	  prefix/suffix errors: "beautifulest"
	  inflectional ending errors
		The writer experiments with different types of sentences:
		
		• expanded sentences: *when, where, how* phrases added
		• compound sentences, complex sentences
		
		However, awkward constructions may appear with the use of longer sentences:
		
		• verb errors
		  subject-verb agreement errors
		  shifts in tense in sentence, paragraph, story
		  nonparallel constructions
		• noun/pronoun agreement errors
		• punctuation errors

High	The writer ACCURATELY and CONSISTENTLY selects words that convey the intended message. Word selection is appropriate for style of writing.
	
	• precise vocabulary: deliberate word choice
	  abstract nouns: *truth, hope, alternatives*
	  cognitive verbs: *understand, support*
	  judgmental adjectives: *adequate, controversial*
		The writer has clear "sentence sense" and manipulates words to form all types of sentences ACCURATELY and CONSISTENTLY.
		
		• variety of sentence structures and lengths used
		• all forms of punctuation are consistently and accurately used
		• stylistic features used
		  questions
		  exclamations
		  repetition of words or phrases for effect
		  deliberate use of sentence fragments

TABLE 2-1 *(continued)*

	Spelling	*Handwriting*

Low	Comprehension of story or report may be difficult because of frequent spelling errors. Possible error patterns may be
	
	• errors on both sight words and phonetic words
	    spelling may be bizarre and totally unrelated to either phonetic or visual elements
	• errors primarily on basic sight words (e.g., *went, want, where, work, walk, play, etc.*)
	    spells words phonetically, or
	    adds, omits, substitutes, or inverts letters
	• errors primarily on phonetic words:
	    adds, omits, substitutes letters, inverts letters
	    errors mostly on vowels; or
	    errors mostly on consonants; or
	    errors on both consonants and vowels
	• common substitutions
	    their, there, they're
	    your, you're
	    its, it's
	    to, too, two
	• errors on contractions
		Handwriting at the low level does not present an overall neat appearance. The following problems may be seen:
		
		• poor or inaccurate letter formation
		• letter substitution: *m/n, u/v, b/d*
		• poor spacing between letters and words
		• poor spatial organization (inconsistent letter size, inconsistent use of guidelines)
		• smudged erasures or write-overs
		• illegibility
		• letter reversals and inversions
		• slow, laborious writing or fast, careless writing

Middle	There are some spelling errors, but the words are readable. Errors occur on longer words and may be due to misapprehension or incorrect pronunciation.
	
	• phonetic spelling of misspelled words
	• word endings added or omitted incorrectly
	• syllables in words may be omitted
	• homonym substitution
		Middle level writing shows improvement. Overall handwriting is adequate, although there may be some awkward letter formations, especially if the student is just learning cursive writing. Students may need to work on overall neatness and margins. Some problems might be:
		
		• inconsistent slant
		• inconsistent size
		• careless letter formations: *a, d, b, h, k, r, s, g*
		        m, n, w, u
		        upper loops too
		        short
		        a, o, b, d not closed

High	There are relatively few errors and the student is working at or above grade level in spelling skills. Errors are generally made on difficult words (multisyllable words or words with unusual spellings). Only a few errors are found in first drafts of longer compositions and reports. Final drafts are generally error free.	High level writing is carefully done and is very legible. Final drafts of papers are very neat. Students use consistent slant, size, and style. Some elements of personalized style appear.

Writing at the Middle level shows signs of growth or maturity. The writer begins to focus on the purpose for writing and the audience for which the writing is intended. Students at this level explore and experiment with different styles of writing, different writing techniques, more specific vocabulary, and a variety of sentence structures. Overall productivity (total number of words and sentences) increases as students write with more fluency. However, because students are experimenting with new styles, structures, and vocabulary, they may make more sophisticated kinds of errors, such as awkward sentence constructions and inaccurate word choice. These types of errors indicate that the writer has some grasp of writing skills and a basic understanding (conscious or unconscious) of different purposes for writing.

High level writing is *clearly focused*. The student has a clear sense of purpose and audience and consistently chooses writing styles and techniques that are appropriate for the purpose and audience. These writers have mastered the skills and techniques for producing writing that is coherent, complete, and interesting. This includes the use of precise vocabulary, varied sentence structure, and careful organization of ideas appropriate for the style of writing.

High level writing is rarely seen in the student's first draft, but it emerges as students proofread and revise; add precise vocabulary; select appropriate details, facts, examples; vary sentence structures; and generally avoid grammatical or structural errors.

These three levels—Low, Middle, and High—represent *broad* levels of writing performance. Growth in writing does *not* necessarily occur evenly across the six skill areas (ideas/content, organization, vocabulary, sentence structure, spelling, and handwriting). Rather, evidence of varying ability within the six areas is often seen. A writer may exhibit evidence of higher levels of abstraction yet continue to use limited vocabulary or faulty sentence structure. Furthermore, writing may exhibit characteristics from more than one level of performance within a particular skill area. Thus, it becomes quite evident that it is necessary to look at writing performance in all six skill areas to identify particular strengths and weaknesses.

Low Level: Ideas/Content

Of all the facets of writing, ideas, content, and level of abstraction are the hardest to measure. Many variables (such as oral language, experiences, school opportunities, personal interests, and motivation) affect the students' actual written output. Evaluation of this area is very subjective and sometimes is influenced by the reader's own interests, motivation, and experiences. Characteristics of limited writers are described below, with samples of writing taken from special education resource programs and regular classes grades four through twelve. The abbreviation *L.D.* refers to learning disability.

1. **The writing may be totally or partially incoherent,** possibly because of serious spelling deficiency or garbled thinking.

   The wiet pelb kel The Indians to tak the besrbawuy.
   (The white people kill the indians to take the buffalo.)
   Grade 4 L.D.

2. **The poor writer may be stimulus-bound.** Writers simply make lists of words, phrases, or short, choppy sentences that relate only to obvious aspects of

the stimulus. There are no original ideas, and topic or picture stimulus is not used as a starting place for a more elaborate story.

> The man is walking on the moon. He walk around the moon. He had some rocks. Then He take a picture from the moon. He went back into the rocket. He go back to earth.
>
> *Grade 4 L.D.*

> If I won a trip I would go to Africa because I have special interest in African animals like the lion, elephant, cheetah, Giraffe, leaperd, Rhino, Hyena and so on. Well I also like to go there to see natives how they survive and I just like to be out in the wild and I like to Study animals.
>
> *Grade 5*

3. **The poor writer may write a single-event, personal experience or a series of events with no details.** Writing at this first level is very often self-oriented, presenting reports of single-event, personal experiences. At times students transcribe their own spoken language and produce rambling stories that have no true beginning, middle, or end. Some of these personal stories turn into "on and on" pieces that go on for pages. At other times these limited writers transcribe conversations with other imaginary or real persons without identifying the participants and often without including appropriate punctuation.

> I want to play No you can't go out to play You were a bad girl You have to stay inside OK I'll stay inside.
>
> *Grade 3 L.D.*

> The next day I got up and had breakfast and then I went to school and we did some work and played a game. Then we went outside and played some games and then I went home and then I went to bed.
>
> *Grade 4 L.D.*

> On Saturday mom, Dad and I went to the circus. The ring master announced the acts. We saw a lion tamer put his head in the lion's mouth. Then some acrabats swung on the trapeze up in the air. My favorite act was the one where the clowns ran around and tripped each other.
>
> The End
>
> *Grade 4 L.D.*

4. **The poor writer begins to write but stops when tired** or when enough paper has been covered. Occasionally, an inappropriate ending is tacked on as the student nears the bottom of the page. Trite endings, such as "And then I woke up" and "They lived happily ever after" are frequently used to finish the story.

Two little Black Grils
There was to grils. They were playing. They were jumping up and down. They playing whit a rhope. It was a grimy rhope. It was a grimy green rhope. I hate Jump rope. It really stinks. They were cute. But the rhope was ugly. They lived happily ever after.

Low Level: Organization

A student with poor or limited organizational skills has generally not identified his/her purpose for writing. Overall organization is weak, and sequencing is inaccurate or unclear. Specifically, poor writers exhibit the following characteristics.

1. **Poor writers do not have a plan for their writing.** They start to write with the first thought that pops into their head, and they continue to write until they think they have covered enough paper or time has run out. In this sample the student simply listed a group of totally unrelated sentences in a stream of consciousness style.

> I Learn Math.
> My friend Bob learns tricks.
> People all over the world love
> to shoot deersI like to see
> sound of music. Theres a lot of
> danger of going over train tra-
> cks. Wene I go to school I
> go through the front door.
> A bird stood there.when I g
> ot home I hid in my bed r
> oom.I kept my turkey in the
> cage Do you know anyone thats
> af raid of a dead animal?
> > *Grade 5 L.D.*

2. **Poor writers lack a specific organizing theme or purpose.** While this next sample has a clear sequence of events, the writer has made no generalizations to pull the events together or to show their relevance to each other. Many irrelevant details are also included, and a general statement of the importance of the trip is never made. Audubon Canyon Ranch is a sanctuary for egrets, yet the poison ivy and the woman running down the path receive as much attention as the birds. The problem results from a topic that is far too broad and not focused on the importance or relevance of the ranch.

Field Trip

At 8:35 Tuesday morning room 2 and 3 were Planning for a bus to be at school, because both rooms were ready to go to Audubon Cayon Ranch. But some paper work didn't go through yet.

Finally at 9:30 the bus came. So at 9:45 we left. It took us an hour and a half to get there, the ranch is in marin. Both classes were divided up into groups, then our guides were assigned to us.

Then we started the long climb up the hill. We climbed for about five minutes then we came to a look out on the marsh. After we looked at the marsh we started climbing again. As soon as we took about 15 steps we saw poison ivy, everyone said that They're not going to let any leaf of Plant tooch them. About five minutes later we saw a woman with a camera running down the path. Then we found a strange looking Plant and our guide said "You can eat this it's minors lettuce, it tastes just like lettuce."

Everyone ate then we hiked to a lookout point with binoculars
we looked at the birds called Egret. Then we at lunch after words
we caught a snake, then we hunted newts in the marsh after five
mins. we came home

Grade 5

3. **Poor writers do not present a clear or logical sequence of events or ideas.**
The writer stops and starts on a sequence but shifts to different lines of thinking as random ideas occur. In some cases students may be unable to identify the facts, details or main ideas, or other important considerations
necessary to respond to assignments with complete information. Others can
identify the information but present it in awkward fashion (for example,
sequence of ideas out of order, irrelevant details added, some important
information missing).

My friend John is afraid because he thinks that, the boat
will crash on the rocks.Big waves are sending the boat to the
rock.When he's scared he walks around. the boat. and his face
turns red. His crew as afraid to.He has a large boat.He loves the
sea so much, he fishes 4 times a week.

Grade 7

4. **Poor writers add irrelevant details.** Forgetting their original line of thinking, they move off into splinter thoughts connected only to their last
sentence.

A Mother and her child
There is a mother walking her little daughter in the park. The
girl is really enjoying. Her mother loves her a lot. and cares. that
is why she took her to the park on a nice day. I sometimes go to
the park with my auntie and her baby. At home I babysit for her
while she is doing something. And it will be her Birthday on
Nov. 11 will be 1 year old.

Grade 4

Overall, the poor or limited writer lacks planning skill, which includes the ability to make relevant generalizations and to select the appropriate supporting details that would help develop the personal narrative
or story. Ideas are handled in expected patterns, evidencing little, if any,
originality or personal style. Having written the story, the writer feels that
it is complete and does no further work on it.

One last example of this Low level of ideas/content shows a combination of the above-mentioned characteristics.

One day I went over to my firends house and I ask If he
could spend the Night with me. So his mother said yes and I
went and ask my mother. She said yes so I went to his house
and we went to my house and played some games with him.
And the next morning we went over to his house and he asked if
I could spent the night and she said yes. So me and him went to
my house and ask my mother. She said yes. I went over and his
mother said do you want to go play a game. The next mornign I
said that I had to go home now and I left and went But I stop at

my other friends house said do you want to play a game with me and he said yes. I said let play hin sece. I said I will be it . . . .

(and so on for two more pages)

Grade 6 L.D.

Low Level: Vocabulary

1. **Poor writers overuse high frequency general nouns and verbs and adjectives.** Function words, such as prepositions, pronouns, articles, and conjunctions, are also very heavily used.

    There are two men on a raft. One men is in the raft. the other is in the water. The color of the water is green and white. The color the raft is yellow They are on the ra pids It is in the summer The men a recold

    Grade 5 L.D.

2. **Poor writers use their own oral language patterns in their writing.** Students may write down the spoken version of a word, phonetically spelled, even though the word is a mispronunciation of the word they really need. While this is perfectly normal for young children such as first and second graders, it is not normal for students in grade four and above. By fourth grade, students should have enough spelling skills to avoid basic spelling errors. Misspelling occurs as students fail to notice the separateness of words in oral language: they either reduce words to abbreviated forms (*'em* for *them*); separate them incorrectly (*a nother* for *another*); combine them with other syllables (*hasta* for *has to*, *sposto* for *supposed to*, *wanna* for *want to*); or completely substitute them for more commonly known words ("The boy lives next *store*"). These errors are basically language errors rather than spelling errors because they relate directly to the way the student pronounces the words or uses them in oral language. Frequently they are spelled correctly phonetically.

3. **Poor writers frequently make homonym substitution errors and contraction errors.** *Their*, *they're*, and *there* are among the commonest homonym substitution errors. *To, too, two* are also especially confusing for poor writers. Contraction errors center on incorrect placement of apostrophe and addition or omission of letters.

Low Level: Sentence Sense

1. **Poor writers write short, choppy sentences** because they do not have a well-developed sentence sense, and they tend to omit required capitalization and punctuation. Another type of limited sentence structure is the repetition of simple sentence patterns.

    A Story about camp wing.
    Once I went to a camp. The camp was fun. I rowed a Boat. The Boat was a canoe. I rowed The canoe to The pond. and The pond had a Turtle named Big Mike. Big Mike tipped a row boat

over.a Boy was in The Boat. The man came to Help The Boy.
The boy was safe. The Boy's name was Anthony.

Grade 4 L.D.

He will fall and hurt him Self?
He will hit a rock.
He will hit a wille and fall?
He will have a soreleg.

Grade 4 L.D.

2. **Poor writers have many sentence errors.** Run-on sentences are quite common and normal in the work of young writers. As they rush to tell their story, they link each sentence with *and, and then,* or *and so* following the pattern used in oral language. Gradually, with more exposure to reading and more practice in writing, the average writer learns to eliminate this pattern. Some writers, in the fourth grade and above, persist in writing run-on stories after it is developmentally normal. In the following example, the writer demonstrates awareness of punctuation but still essentially writes a run-on story.

One day a big Dog come up *and* scared my cat the Dog.
Chase The cat up the tree. *And* he started to cry. *And* when I
came home I See a big Dog! *and* I scared hime away of the tree.
and my cat came down. I Love you cat somuch.

Grade 5 L.D.

3. **Poor writers have many punctuation and capitalization errors.** Poor writers write in short, choppy sentences and totally ignore punctuation and capitalization errors.

(My Dog Name is king) (he a German shepherd) (I take him
out a lot of time) (he Bit My Brother) (he want to the hospital)
(he was all right) (then I got Bit to and I wasall rigt to)

Grade 5 L.D.

Low Level: Spelling

Students in fourth grade and above who make spelling errors on basic sight vocabulary and on one and two syllable phonetic words have limited ability in spelling. At times the student misspells so many words that reader comprehension of the message is difficult.

Teachers should analyze spelling errors to determine whether an error pattern exists and to identify learning styles for specific spelling remediation strategies. The following error patterns may be evident.

1. **Errors on basic sight words and other phonetically irregular words.** Students may have difficulty in recalling or "revisualizing" the correct letter for a given sound. They may also be unable to identify whether a word has been spelled correctly once it has been written. Words may be spelled several different ways within the same paper.
2. **Errors on phonetic words.** Students may have difficulty analyzing words into separate sounds and syllables. While poor auditory discrimination is a major cause of spelling problems, inaccurate pronunciation, poor articula-

tion or other speech problem, or poor hearing acuity may also interfere with spelling ability. Students may spell words as they pronounce them. Example: *Enemy* may be pronounced as "emeny" and may also be spelled *emeny*.

3. **Errors on both phonetic and sight words.** When students have difficulty with both auditory and visual skills in their spelling, written production may be difficult to comprehend. The spelling may be totally unrelated to the sounds in the words, as if the student had just made a random guess.

> Thar having a wor and that cachered wun nashinlspi and
> the maricins have 17 tanks and the murincis have 7 rmechuks
> and a mrinkis 1001 men. and the a merinkuns wun.

> (They are having a war and they captured one national spy
> and the Americans have 17 tanks and the Americans have 7 army
> trucks and Americans 1001 men. and the Americans won.)

In this sample, the student seems to have some ability with auditory skills as he was able to phonetically analyze the words *Americans* and *national spy*; however, each time he came to the word he analyzed it a different way. He spells words as he pronounces them as in the words *cachered* for *captured*, and *chuks* for *trucks*. The pronunciation problem is directly related to his auditory discrimination of the word. On a spelling test this student was generally able to spell phonetically regular words at lower levels but had difficulty on longer phonetic words and the majority of sight words.

Bizarre spelling is generally found in the writing of students who have poor auditory or visual skills. Some of these students gradually learn basic sight words and short phonetic words, but their spelling of longer words is sometimes incomprehensible, such as in the following student sample taken from a spelling test using Morrison-McCall Spelling Scale.

arrange/awwathe   celebration/clerbreick
search/shuck   career/cousered
interest/enrtsen   acquaintance/oupites

Computer Games

Computer games come in all tipes. For exsapl, you may be in a flit semulatr for a F.15. Or you may be flying a hilowcaptor to desrowe Frotapculeps. Ther is more aventr tipe gemes too. Like Jumpman and Load runer. Load runer for exsapl, you are in a casil being cast by robots. You have to get all the crasers and get out befor the robots get you. Ther is agucasl games like games to help you play the peanow. But my favrit is F.15 Strik eagle.

Grade 6 L.D.

4. **Vocabulary errors.**
   - Homophones: Children may substitute the spelling of one homophone for another, as *here* for *hear*; *there* for *their*; *to*, *too*, and *two*.
   - Unknown vocabulary: Students may have difficulty spelling words they have never seen in print and/or whose meaning is unclear.
5. **Poor proofreading skills.**
   - The student has not learned to monitor his or her own writing by proofreading to spot errors.

Low Level: Handwriting

Low level handwriting has many errors and may be difficult to read. This may be a result of visual perceptual and/or visual motor integration difficulties. The following specific problems may be found in handwriting samples.

1. **Poor or inaccurate letter formation.** Students who have experienced motor awkwardness in manuscript writing will probably have difficulty with cursive writing unless the motor patterns are carefully taught and sufficient supervised practice is provided.

   The most common error in cursive writing is the failure to close letters properly. The letter *a*, for instance, may be formed like a *u*, *i*, *ci*, or like an *o*. Failure to dot *i*'s and cross *t*'s is responsible for another group of errors. The letters *r* and *s* also cause considerable difficulty.

   Some students form letters incorrectly because they have not had enough practice with the specific motor patterns required to produce different letters, or because certain letters require several changes in direction while being written (*g, h, z, j, q, p, y*). Because they cannot remember letter formations or the sequence of movements to use in writing the letters, they frequently look to wall charts for help. Students occasionally visually analyze letter formations and attempt to reproduce the letter in segments rather than in a continuous motor pattern.

2. **Letter substitution.** Substitution of rounded strokes for straight strokes (*m* for *w*, *n* for *u*, and vice versa) and substituting a short loop for a short straight stroke (*e* or *i*) adds to illegibility of handwriting. Lower case letters may be substituted for capital letters when students have not had enough practice on capital letter formations. Some students may continue to substitute *b* and *d*.

3. **Spacing problems.** Words may be jammed together and difficult to read. Spaces may be placed inappropriately within words or between words.

4. **Spatial organization.** Words may not be written on lines, and writing may go uphill or downhill regardless of lines and spaces. Letter size may be inconsistent.

5. **Slant.** Letters may be written in varying mixed slants: leaning backward, forward, and up straight.

6. **Illegibility.** Carelessness or rushed words with many erasures or writeovers produce a messy-looking paper. Occasionally, the student writes one letter over another, hoping the teacher will choose the correct spelling.

7. **Speed.** Some students may write very slowly and may produce very little because of their speed. When rushed, they become frustrated and make more errors. As students move into upper grades, they must write faster to complete assignments and tests in allotted time periods. The following Zaner-Bloser scale determines whether students are writing at an appropriate speed for their grade level.

Grade	4	5	6	7
Rate (letters per minute)	45	50	67	74

Middle Level: Ideas/Content

At this second level of idea generation, students show clear signs of growth and begin to focus more clearly on the purposes for writing. Writers generally experiment with different types of writing and begin to develop their individual styles, increasingly using imagination and originality; however, at this level the stories and reports are not completely developed or free from mechanical error. Writing samples at this level typically include some organizational difficulties, vocabulary choice errors, awkward sentence structure, and spelling errors. Students could improve these writing samples by selecting one or more specific problems to work on, then writing additional drafts. Peer editing with suggestions for revision would also be valuable.

Several specific characteristics mark the transition from the Low level to the Middle level, but all these characteristics will not be found in each piece of writing. Even one, though, indicates some progress.

1. **The middle writer has a definite theme or topic but does not develop it.** Writing may fall into predictable, uninspired patterns and contain little more than surface level discussion. Not really getting involved in the writing, the student writes just to complete an assignment. At times the writing will start with "There are many kinds of . . ."

Games to Play

There are many different kinds of games to play like aggravation, or even a game of go fish. If you don't have board games you can play a game of hide-and-go seek. You can even play tag or relay races.

There are many board games like monopoly or Stay a live. Some games are real fun like battleship, Pac-Man, Clue, and Life. Some can take an hour or so and some can take just fifteen minutes.

There are hundreds of word and letter games. Like crosswords puzzles or kryptograms.

Some of the card games are lots of fun such as go fish, war, blackjack and cribbage. Some of them you can play with teams, and some you can only use two people.

There are many different kinds of games to play just use your imagination.

Grade 6

At other times the topic is very clear and the writer has many good points, but he or she could use more facts, details, or examples to support the topic.

Strengths

Strength and weekness plays a very important part in a persons life. Someday in everyones life they will be faced with a situation where they have to decide whether to have strength or whether to show weakness. for example if you were stranded on an island with no food how would you survive? Would you show strength or would you show weakness?

Having strength doesn't always mean being strong and muscular. Strength is something a person must have to be able to survive in the wilderness in a native country and many other places.

Getting stressed out to a point where your just about to go crazy is a excellent example of weakness. On the other hand keeping your cool and dealing with the problem wisely is an example of strength.

Having strength isnt always easy. Some times it takes all you have to develop that strength. Strength takes courage and a will to be able to deal with any situation that comes in your way.

Grade 6

It's Not Easy Being a Teenager

Its not easy being a teenager. There are endless changes and conflicts to deal with as I grow up. Things that have worked for me in the past do not work now. I have to change, again, to deal with conflicting situations.

I need to feel acceptance from my peers almost to a point where I bend over backwards just to get it. Then I find out this is the wrong way about it. I should be accepted for just being me but I don't even know who I am at times. I am in a constant dilemma trying, searching for answers, experimenting with different ideas, being responsible and just growing up.

Grade 12

2. **The writer provides descriptive details.** This includes expressions of feeling or emotion, comparisons, opinions, or additional examples that support the writer's generalizations. Adding details to the story or paragraph, the writer uses, perhaps, materials from personal experiences and memories or factual details and descriptions. This next sample includes specific descriptive details but has weak sentence structure.

Sun Beginning to Set

The sun is beginning to set. The sun looks like a diamond with a glowing halo around it. The sun set seems to be going in to the mountains. There is a rushing river in front of the mountains. As the sun is going down it makes the river sparkle and gleam. Trees sit behind the river. The delicate leaves are blowing off the thin branches. The sun adds a glow to everything on earth.

Grade 5

3. **The middle writer tries different approaches and tries to write to the reader.** One approach is to include questions to the reader. The first sample attempts this but does not completely finish off the topic. The second sample has a better introduction and closing paragraph to round off the topic.

Games

Dont you hate the games that people play? For instance someone might be pretending to be your friend but realy is not. They are just using you for money or to get popular or even they like the boy your going with. You know if you think about it its realy kind of mean. Im not saying Iv never done it but really Im sure!

Or maybe its like this. You have all your friends and your kind of popular and you like someone that is not verey popular. Your friends start hating you. What should you do? or maybe they like you but there friends dont so then there friends make the person that likes you hate you so you don't have any friends. But im not saying i have any friends.

Grade 6

Rejections

Have you even been rejected? It hurts doesn't it? I know when I got rejected from a group it really hurt me.

What do you think about when you think of rejection? I think of how and why the clique or group kicked out a person. Many groups kick people out because the way they act or how the person dresses, the color of their skin, they style of their hair, or maybe just because they don't like him or her.

Their hair may look different or it may not always look perfect but your not suppose to like someone for their looks or hate them for their looks. Your suppose to like somebody for what they are and for whats inside them. And thats the only thing that counts about someone.

Many people are rejected and many people might always be rejected we can't stop that. But we can try!!

Grade 6

4. **The middle writer begins to develop a personal style and begins to show more originality in thinking.** This is seen in the invention of words or names, humor, dialogue, and original punctuation for added effect.

The Frog War

It was May 24, 1978, when the first hints of a frog versus toad war was started. It had been a hard winter for the toads and they had stooped to stealing rations from the frogs and the frogs suspected it. The frog king, a tough old army sergeant from the anteater wars, was preparing to declare war on the toads. The toads were not prepared.

On May 27, the frogs declared war on the toads. At the toad village there was near panic. It was a pell-mell of preparing for an attack. In the king's underground mansion, there was a meeting being held between the king and the heads of the war department. The king was young and inexperienced. He had the throne heired to him when he was young and evil toads had corrupted him.

And now, the meeting. The young king's name was Paul and his evil advisor, Ivan (the terrible) who directed him to do dastardly deeds. They were sitting at the head of the table, smiling menacingly, for they had an ingenious idea. They and their evil war department had bribed a king cobra snake into fighting for them in the war, which they *thought* would solve all their problems. Note, *thought!*

The food messengers sent word out all across the kingdom which relieved all the toad's tensions about losing the war. By and by word got around to the wizard who all his life wanted to be a frog, but alas, he was a toad. So the wizard got an idea. He set off across the toad-frog border with his hands up. Some frog soldiers captured him and took him to the king. The wizard told the king about the snake.

The king promised to make the wizard an honorary frog if he would tell him how to get rid of the snake and also give him a magic ticker-tape machine which would give reports on the toad's battle manuvers. The toad thought about it for a while and finally agreed. Then the wizard said some mystic words and the magic ticker-tape machine appeared. Then the crafty wizard told the king of his plan to get rid of the snake.

The plan was to have the best ax-man in the kingdom come and stand behind a tree while a frog would be set out for bait near the ax-man. When the snake stuck out its deadly tongue, the ax-man would come and chop it off. Whact! Meanwhile, tree frogs above would be dropping razor sharp spears directly through the snake and lodging themselves directly in the ground, rendering the snake powerless.

And so, the plan was carried out, and if I do say so myself, it was executed quite well. Then the wizard suggested that the frog king send a note of terms to the toads by carrier-mosquito and they did.

The note read:

June 6, 1978

Sirs,

We have rid ourselves of your so-called menace. We will let you surrender. We do not want to have a war. We will send a treaty over to be signed. We will help you during the winter. These are our terms. Take them or leave them.

Sincerely,

Jack Ribbit
King of the Frogs

And so the note was delivered and it came to the toad's palace. There was a great festival following the signing. The evil Ivan the Terrible skulked away when the festivities started, never to be seen again. After Ivan left, formerly wicked toads saw the light, and the two kingdoms came together and formed the Kingdom of Croak, ruled in joint throne by Jack Ribbut and King Paul. Their relationship grew strong and their reign was a long and happy one. As for the wizard, he became the royal alchemist and wizard. And they all lived Happily ever after. Ha, ha.

Grade 7

Middle Level: Organization

1. **The writer does not develop a well thought-out plan for writing.** Writers begin to sort and group information and to sequence ideas and details appropriately; however, their overall lack of planning at this level still results in an incomplete written product. While the organizing theme may be sufficiently clear, it is generally not well developed. Book reports, essays, and larger papers present considerable difficulty for middle writers. Papers tend to be uninspired because only obvious, superficial information is included.

Whales
There are many different kinds of whales. For instance, sperm whale, blue whale, humpback whale, and Right whale. They are

different shapes and colors. Whales are the largest living things in the world. The largest of all whales is the blue whale. The blue whale is 80–100 feet long. The smallest whale is 9–13 feet long. Its name is pigmy sperm. Whales are warmblooded. They can swim in cold water. Warmblooded means that the inside of the Whale stay the same temperature no matter what's the temperature outside. Some whales are different from each other. Only the sperm whale has teeth on the bottom. All whales eat their food whole. All whales are harmless except for the Killer whale. Killer whales like to eat whale, blue whales, dolphins, sleas, porpoises, Penguins, peoples, any thing that moves. Lots of Killer whales circle around the prey so it can't move. One Killer whale goes in and Kills him. They bite the mouth, the tongue and the fin, making him lose blood.

Grade 8

2. **Students may write adequate generalizations but fail to provide enough facts, details, or examples to support the topic sentence.**

Many influences are causing American youth to growth up fast. One of these is the large number of divorced parents. Children are forced to make more important decisions for themselves. Because the parent is working.

This fast growth creates problems. One of these is the child misses out on a lot of instruction from the parent.

One solution to this problem is the parent making more time to spend with their child. By cutting down on working extra hours.

Grade 10

3. **Middle level writers may write a clear sequence of events but may fail to write a good topic sentence.** They may also omit conclusions. Notice that this writer had difficulty with pronoun consistency.

Yesterday me my Mom, Doug, krystal, wanted to give Shadow a bath we hade to get the hose to wash her and the brush, tub and the dog. My dog did not want to take a bath like all dogs don't. My dog ran all around in the basement. We couldn't find her she poped out from nowhere. I had to jump on her because my sister sad to so I did. We got her and my mom came for her to put her in the tub. We washed her my sister is kid of wierd so she gave my dog and my mom a wash to. I started to laugh and giggle at him. We had to wash her with a brush, scrub her hard that is a lot of work and we had to but the soap on her, flea powder and the medicine. It is time to pit the dog in a towel and take him out when you take him out he runs all around the basement and goofs aroud and bugs people who are washing there clothes. She pops up out of no where again and then we dry him off all the way. He felt all better and started to kiss us.

Grade 5

Middle Level: Vocabulary

1. **Writers begin to experiment with new words in their writing** and begin to substitute specific nouns, verbs, adjectives, and adverbs for vague or over-used words of the Low level. At first, writers include specific proper nouns and verbs directly related to their own experiences or to the writing topic. The following two examples are based on a story starter. The first student includes words that would be expected when discussing a canoe trip: *swim, canoe, current, shore,* and *paddle.* The writer overuses the verbs *got* and *tried* and uses no adjectives at all. *Current* is the most sophisticated word used in the sample, but even it can be considered a topic imposed word.

> "Jerry! I can't swim!" cried Frank. Then the canoe tipped over Frank kept on yelling "help!" "help!" Jerry tried to swim by him put the current kept on pulling him back. Jerry got to him after he tried a couple of times, Jerry tried to hold Frank up and then turn the canoe backover, then he did He got Frank back into the canoe then Jerry got in it and tried to paddle to shore. They got to shore and went home and told their parents all about what happened.
>
> *Grade 6*

By contrast, the next example based on the same story starter shows greater maturity in vocabulary use. The writer uses specific verbs (*thrashing, drifting, clinging, grasped, gasping, oozing, grinding, ripping*); specific adjectives (*dazed, bruised*); and specific nouns (*flesh, bolt of lightening* [lightning], *downstream, splinters*).

> "Jerry! I can't swim!" cried Frank. Just then, a bolt of lightening struck the canoe. The boys were thrown out of the canoe. Frank and Jerry were thrashing their arms and trying to get to the canoe which was drifting downstream. Then Jerry looked in horror as a huge tree came crashing down on Frank. For a moment, Jerry thought he might never see his friend again. But then Jerry saw Frank clinging to the log. Frank was dazed and bruised, but he was alive. Jerry fought the waters with every ounce of strength that he had left in him to get to the log and Frank. A few moments later, his bare hands grasped the log. His hands were bleeding from the splinters of the log and he was gasping for air. "Frank! Frank! You've got to help me! Wake up!" cried Jerry. It was no use. Then Jerry felt mud oozing up through his toes and rocks grinding and ripping at the flesh of his bare feet. He realized he was on the other shore! So he dragged the log up on the shore and he and Frank just layed their gasping for breath. Then help came and all would be well, but Frank and Jerry would never forget that day.
>
> The End
>
> *Grade 6*

2 **Writers begin to use words in imaginative and inventive ways.** They may invent words to go along with their storyline, and they may try wordplay with alliteration, rhyming, or repetition. They also begin to replace some trite expressions with original similes, metaphors, and analogies. The following segments come from "The Frog War in the Kingdom of Croak" presented in the "Middle Level: Ideas/Content."

"Ivan (the terrible) . . . directed him to do dastardly deeds."
"The frog king, a tough old army sergeant from the anteater wars. . . ."
". . . the toads had stooped to stealing . . ."
"It was a pell-mell of preparing. . . ."
". . . the ax-man would come and chop it [snake's head] off. Whact!"
". . . send a note of terms . . . by carrier-mosquito."

3 **Middle level writers may make word selection errors while attempting to improve their level of vocabulary use.** As students strive to include more sophisticated words and word arrangements in their writing, they do begin to make additional kinds of errors. Students may inappropriately add or omit inflectional endings, prefixes, or suffixes. Occasionally, they may invent new words by combining incorrect prefixes or suffixes, or they may choose a very similar sounding word to the one they really need.

". . . The bewildered adolescent seeks escape through the consumation of alcohol."
". . . One reason that kids are growing up so fast is that they are more nutritioned."
"Many influences are causing American youth to growth up fast."

Middle Level: Sentence Structure

1. **The writers experiment with different types of sentences.** They begin to use a variety of sentence types: expanded (*when* and *where* phrases added), compound, complex, and compound/complex sentences.

   At first, they write expanded sentences with modifying phrases (*when/where*) as in the following examples.

The girl walks	<u>to school</u>.
There's a little white house	<u>in the garden</u>.
The man is walking	<u>on the moon</u>.
The man is riding	<u>on a horse</u>.
I was walking	<u>in the woods</u>.

   Simple sentences with compound subjects or compound predicates are used.

   Compound Subjects
<u>A boy and his father</u>	went skiing.
<u>Tina and Geraldine</u>	were playing.

   Compound Predicates
The racoons	<u>come out and eat</u> the garbage.
The boy's mother	<u>came out and told</u> the police.

   There are more of the complex sentence structures that the writers use in oral language. The subordinating conjunctions *because, if, so,* and *when* appear frequently.

When I stand up on the dirt road, I can see all the colors.
We don't have a washer or dryer so my mother has to wash the
clothes by hand.
All the people are screaming and clapping because they want the
fight to start.

2. **Middle level writers may write awkward sentence constructions as they experiment with a variety of sentence types.** As they begin to write longer sentences with more complex structures, they occasionally write awkward or incorrect sentences, sometimes because of inadequate punctuation. They sometimes shift their line of thinking in the middle of the sentence and then fail to proofread to catch the errors. Excess wordiness also becomes a problem. Words and punctuation may be added or omitted inappropriately, and subject-verb agreement errors creep into the writing. Nonparallel constructions occur in compound and complex sentences and in sentences containing a series of phrases separated by commas.

"He had the throne heired to him when he was young and evil toads had corrupted him."
"The young king's name was Paul and his evil advisor, Ivan (the terrible) who directed him to do dastardly deeds."

3. **Middle level writers may make verb tense shifts within their story or paragraph and may make noun-pronoun referent errors.**

Babe Ruth
Here we are at yankee stadium. The players are taking their positions. The first pitch came in—strike one! The pitcher got the ball. He takes a puff of air, he throws the pitch—strike two! The crowd has a puzzled look on their face because they know it was going to be a strike or a home run. He throws the baseball in for a foul ball. The next pitch is a blazing fast ball. He rips a home run. The yankees are now the champions.
Grade 5

Middle Level: Spelling

Spelling of basic sight words and short phonetic words is generally correct, but misspelling does occur on multisyllable words and words with unusual spellings. Some misspelled words may be phonetically correct, while other words may have been misunderstood or mispronounced. Endings may be dropped on words with inflectional or superlative endings, and syllables may be dropped or sequenced incorrectly on multisyllable words. When word endings are dropped, a teacher should notice the student's oral language pattern to see whether endings are dropped in normal speech. Students whose native language is not English may also drop endings (especially verb tense endings), since their own native language may not indicate tense by verb form changes.
Homonym errors continue to be a problem.

Middle Level: Handwriting

Overall handwriting is adequate and readable, although there may be a few awkward letter formations and/or inconsistent letter slant, especially if the student is just learning cursive writing. Students may use margins inconsistently and may present papers that are not always totally neat in overall appearance.

High Level: Ideas/Content

Idea development at the High level is marked by consistency between purpose and content. At this level, besides exhibiting mastery over the writing process, the student also has a distinct point of view and uses information to support that view.

1. **The writer maintains consistent point of view supported by details, facts, reasons, and examples.**

     Ideas, generalizations, and supportive details are deliberately selected for a specific purpose—to entertain, to present an argument, to persuade, or to build upon a specific theme. The selected generalizations are consistently appropriate and are supported by sufficient relevant examples, facts, or other descriptive details. This also implies that the writer consciously selects, eliminates, and possibly manipulates information in an attempt to influence the reader.

     Drinking and Driving
          There is an increasing problem concerning drinking problems and drinking related deaths on highways in the United States. For example there is the fact of 3.3 million youths with alcohol problems in the U.S. today, 6% of all high school seniors drink daily. Alcohol related motor vehicle accidents are the leading case of death in this age group also. In general Alcohol related driving accidents are the #3 killer in the nation (behind heartdisease and cancer).
          A lot of the drinking drivers of today were once the teenage alcoholics of yesterday. There should be some way teenagers could be more aware of these alarming facts than just publishing them in newspapers and magazines. Classes should be taught on this subject and be required from grade 6 on up. This would help in preventing the problem before it gets a chance to get deeply rooted in the susceptible personalities of our youths.
          Stiffer laws for repeat offenders in alcohol related accidents and problems could also help to remedy the situation. Instead of just slapping the violator on the hand and letting him off sentences should include attendance in Alcohol Abuse programs of some sort. Knowledge of the problem is just one way to hopefully help to stop it.
          No one benefits when a person that abuses alcohol is given freedom and license to possibly kill someone. No one benefits if an alcoholic is locked up and the key is thrown away either. Counselling and awareness of the problem is the only way to combat the problem and prevent it.

Grade 12

2. **Judgment and/or morals are either stated or implied.** This next sample shows originality in approach as well as other features of the High level. In addition, mechanical elements show mastery.

Hello Mirror. It's me again. You know that you are the only friend I have, so I know you will be honest with me. Tell me. Why don't other worms like me? Is it because my skin is brown? Lots of worms like me have brown skin. Do they hate all of us?

I thought Myrtle liked me. She's green. She's a nice shade of green. She looks something like a lily pad. I liked her anyway. But today, when she was talking to her friends and I went by, she looked the other way like she didn't even know me.

You know mirror, even worms have some kind of feelings. If old green Myrtle walked by and I was talking to Felisha, I would stop and talk to her.

Maybe Myrtle doesn't like me because I have a long tongue. Long tongues are good for catching flies though. I can't cut it!!

Some days I just feel like getting eaten by something! I must be different in some way. I have got it!!! I must have bad breath! I will go use some *SKOPE*. (That's Scope in our English). *AHHHHHH!!!* (blows on mirror) Hows that smell???

Well, if it's not that, what can it be? My skin is brown, but that doesn't matter. My skin has grooves, but that doesn't matter. My hair isn't long, but that doesn. . . .I don't have any hair at all!!!

Oh mirror, I just can't understand it. Once, when I was little, a wise old man told me to treat others as you want to be treated. I guess nobody ever told Myrtle that. Her friends too. I suppose if I told her, she would just say brown worms don't know anything! *IT'S NOT TRUE!!!* Is it???

Well, mirror, I guess I will just have to be satisfied with just having you for a friend. You still like me don't you? By the way, mirror, why don't you ever answer me?????

The End

Grade 6

3. The High writer uses a clear sequence of ideas and does not distract the reader with irrelevant facts, details, or examples.

Father Jim

I approached him and he took my hand to shake it and as he did so I felt his warmth and love running through myself and lightening my heart. He was an older and wiser man with deep commitments and an inner glow which pulled me towards him.

As we sat down I noticed the several bags and articles he carefully placed upon the table and I saw him look carefully at the items as if they were part of a sacred offering. He looked at me and looked around the room commenting playfully on his hasty arrival and the sequence of events leading to his visit. He quickly sat up, pulled out his book and started to read.

The mood of the people in the room changed instantly from laughs and jokes to attentiveness. Again he joked on something trivial and put everyone at ease. He controlled the air with carelessness and ease, seriousness and concern.

If his rounded frame and comical face were placed in a different attire he might even had been a clown. His humility

would even had permitted him so. His openess, straightforward-
ness and playfulness took me over and I believed in his words. I
listened to Father Jim spread his love and the love of God to me,
for me and everyone else.

Grade 12

Plot development is very clear and effective: the main character is
faced with a crisis or challenge requiring specific planning and action to
resolve. Information is included that develops characters' personalities and
provides background for the crisis or challenge. The writer may also inter-
ject judgmental elements with a moral that is either stated or implied. Not
following an expected pattern, story endings sometimes have unusual twists.

4. **The High writer has a clearly developed personal style** reflected in originality of thinking, use of humor, effective use of structural and mechanical
elements (sentence structure, paragraph structure, punctuation, and
capitalization), and mature vocabulary choice.

High Level: Organization

Writing at this level is clearly and consistently organized. The writer shows
evidence of notetaking and/or outlining skills in the preparation stage and is
able to select and narrow a topic appropriately and to state relevant generalizations about the topic. Facts, details, and examples are carefully selected to provide sufficient support for all generalizations, opinions, and judgments.
Paragraph breaks and transitions are appropriate.

High Level: Vocabulary

Vocabulary choice and use on the High level is the most sophisticated. Students
have learned to make subtle distinctions between closely related words and consistently choose words that most accurately convey their intended message. Finn
(1977) suggests three categories of words that appear to reflect maturity of word
choice:

Abstract nouns	*alternatives, efforts, evils, menace, reasons, suicide*
Cognitive verbs (as opposed to action verbs)	*abuse, blame, complain, investigate, manage, support*
Judgmental adjectives	*adequate, controversial, drastic, genuine, potential, unnatural*

In addition to mature word *choice*, students at the High level demonstrate
mature word *use*. They select words that are appropriate for the style of writing,
and also select words to create special effects (alliteration, rhyming, repetition)
when appropriate. Overall, the student writing at the High level has complete
control over vocabulary choice and arrangement.

High Level: Sentences

1. **The writer has clear sentence sense** and manipulates words to form all types
of sentences accurately and consistently. Longer sentences reflect the increased ability to handle more complete syntactical arrangements and to

clearly represent thought through language structures. Sentence length increases through the use of descriptive words, phrases, and clauses. The writer also uses all forms of punctuation correctly and uses a variety of sentence types.

2. **The writer also uses stylistic features:** deliberate sentence fragments, questions, dramatic punctuation, and the repetition of words and phrases for impact. Hunt (1965) points out that mature writers also use clauses, infinitives, and gerunds as subjects in place of the more common nouns and pronouns. These writers also eliminate wordiness by reducing clauses to phrases and embedding them in the sentence.

Complexity for its own sake is no mark of maturity (Moffett and Wagner, 1976). The writer at the High level has a well-developed sentence sense and consistently and deliberately uses sentence types that are appropriate for the writing purpose—whether they be fragment, simple, expanded, compound, complex, or compound/complex sentences.

High Level: Spelling

There are relatively few errors on the working drafts. Errors may occur on difficult words (multisyllable words, or words with unusual spellings).

All final drafts are free of spelling errors.

High Level: Handwriting

Completed writing assignments (final drafts) exhibit carefully produced, readable handwriting and an overall neat appearance. All letters, both upper and lower case, are written accurately. Personalized handwriting style may be evident on some letter formations.

Part Two, Informal Evaluation Procedures

Part One of this chapter reviewed student writing samples in terms of three levels of performance (low, middle, and high) in six skill areas (ideas/content, organization, vocabulary, sentence structure, spelling, and handwriting). Part Two provides guidelines for identifying strengths and weaknesses in your students' writing ability, and outlines informal evaluation procedures. Refer to Table 2-1, Levels of Performance in Writing Ability, as you begin to evaluate student writing samples. Use the following steps for your informal evaluations.

1. *Review all evaluation procedures,* (Informal Evaluation Activities, Evaluation Questions, and Student Writing Checklist 1). Give special attention to the charts and checklists that summarize the three levels of performance in the six skill areas. Review the specialized checklists for the skill areas (Tables 2-3 through 2-8).

2. *Schedule specific sessions for collecting writing samples.* Do not attempt to collect all writing samples in one day, since student writing varies ac-

cording to many considerations such as type of assignment, time of day, interest, and motivation.

The following writing samples would be useful:

- A narrative written from personal experience
- A story written from a picture stimulus
- A handwriting sample

Note: It may also be useful and/or necessary to collect oral samples from students who exhibit moderate or severe writing problems. To collect the oral samples, repeat informal evaluation activities 1 and 2 but let the student dictate responses. Tape record and/or write out the student's response. Use these oral stories and paragraphs to compare with the student's written sample. If the oral language samples show weakness in level of thinking, organization of ideas, vocabulary usage, and sentence structure, the student probably needs intensive work at an oral level. Progress in oral expression must precede progress in written expression.

3. *Quickly review a random sampling of papers* (at least one-third) from a particular evaluation activity before you begin to evaluate them. This will help you get an idea of the range of possible responses. Sorting papers in rough piles of high, middle, and low performance will also help you to classify the features most prevalent at each level.

4. *Use the Student Writing Checklist I (Table 2-2), guide questions, and specialized checklists as you evaluate writing papers.* Gradually, as you practice and become familiar with the checklists and guide questions, you will internalize the questions and you will be able to judge writing papers more quickly. The Student Writing Checklist I has three levels of performance in six skill areas. Note that point values have been assigned to low, middle, and high performance. Ideas/Content and Organization has been double-weighted to emphasize greater importance. If you use this scale on a regular basis, you may want to assign letter grades to total points accumulated (e.g., A = 35 to 40 points).

Put a check by items on the checklist that you notice in the writing samples, and select a point value based on your responses. You may want to read Part One of this chapter (Informal Evaluation Levels of Performance) before you begin evaluating writing samples.

5. *Have a second teacher go through this process and judge papers of your student in return for judging a series of papers for his or her students.* Follow this by a short discussion on those papers about which you disagree. This will definitely take additional time, but the results should yield more accurate information that you can then use to develop a valuable learning plan for students. Ideally, this self-training process, which emphasizes the need to consider all aspects of writing, will help you to internalize the features of good writing. Most important, it will direct you to look at strengths in student writing ability and, therefore, to deemphasize identification of errors or at least to put error identification in proper perspective. It is best to make complete notes on this first evaluation, since comparisons can be made at midyear and end of year.

TABLE 2-2
Student Writing Checklist 1

Name _____ Grade _____ Date _____

Title of writing sample _____ Draft # ___ / Final

	low		middle		high
1. Ideas / Content	2	4	6	8	10

_____ interesting title
_____ catch reader's interest
_____ clear topic, theme or storyline
_____ clear purpose (to entertain, to inform,
to report, to explain, to persuade)
_____ consistent point of view
_____ originality, creativity, imagination
_____ personal style
_____ humor
_____ unique features

	low		middle		high
2. Organization	2	4	6	8	10

_____ good introduction
_____ topic sentences . . . main ideas
_____ supporting information:
facts, details, examples
quotes, definitions, comparisons
observations using senses
(no irrelevant information)
_____ clear sequence of ideas, events or clear
story line
_____ paragraph format
_____ good conclusion

	low		middle		high
3. Vocabulary	1	2	3	4	5

_____ specific nouns
_____ specific adjectives and adverbs
_____ specific verbs
_____ imaginative use of words; orginality
invented words, puns, alliteration, similies,
metaphors
(no cliches, slang, or overused words,
no wordiness)

	low		middle		high
4. Sentence Structure	1	2	3	4	5

_____ complete sentences
(no fragments,
no run-ons,
no awkward constructions)
_____ variety of sentence lengths:
simple, compound, complex,
compound-complex
_____ variety of sentence types:
statements, questions, exclamations
_____ consistency of verb tense
_____ correct use of pronouns
_____ correct capitalization and punctuation

	low		middle		high
5. Spelling	1	2	3	4	5
6. Handwriting	1	2	3	4	5

Informal Evaluation Activity 1: Writing Sample Using Choice of Topics

Objective To determine level of performance in idea generation, organization, vocabulary, sentence structure, spelling, and handwriting.

Materials List of Short Topics

I Forgot	An Embarrassing Moment
All About Me	My Future Goals
Games	Problems at School
Friends	Parents
Pets	

Procedure 1. Explain to students that you need several writing samples for their writing folders before you can help them set goals for their writing.
2. Write the list of suggested topics on the board and suggest that they follow this procedure.
   a. jot ideas—*3 minutes*
   b. write first draft, double spaced—*12 minutes*
   c. edit and revise—*10 minutes*
   d. write final draft—*20 minutes*
   e. edit final draft
3. Do not *insist* that students follow these guidelines. Some students may need training in the writing process and may be willing to write only one draft.
4. Collect papers when done.

Evaluation Use evaluation questions and checklists following these activities.

Informal Evaluation Activity 2: Writing Sample Picture Using Picture Stimulus

Objective To determine level of performance in idea generation, organization, vocabulary use, sentence structure, spelling, and handwriting using a picture stimulus. (This second writing sample may determine whether levels of performance change when a different stimulus is used.)

Materials A large (at least 9″ × 12″) color or black-and-white picture that shows evidence of problem situation, several characters, and setting. It should be obvious that the illustration has a past, present, and future aspect. In other words, the student should be able to surmise what happened before the picture was taken and to draw some conclusions about what might happen next. Avoid cluttered pictures with too many irrelevant details.

Procedure 1. Say to students: "Look carefully at this picture. What is it all about? Think about it for a few minutes and jot down some ideas before you start to write."
2. Do *not* prompt the students in any other way, since it is important to establish an unaided level of response. (If you desire, for comparison's sake, repeat the activity on another day and ask specific leading questions to help the student in forming a response. This would be especially mean-

ingful for learning disabled students who may have some difficulty organizing their thoughts and getting started.)

3. Allow students a reasonable amount of time to complete the task. Encourage students to use the writing process (jot ideas, first draft, edit and revise, final draft—see Activity 1) but do not insist. Students may be willing to write only one draft at this point.

4. Collect papers when done.

Evaluation   Use evaluation questions and checklists following these activities.

Informal Evaluation Activity 3: Handwriting Samples

Objective   To gather three samples of student handwriting: fastest, best, and normal.

Materials   Sample sentences that contain all letters of the alphabet.

> The quick brown fox jumps over the lazy brown dog.
> Pack my box with five dozen jugs of liquid.
> The five boxing wizards jump quickly.

Procedure
1. Explain to students that you want to collect samples of their usual, best, and fastest handwriting. (This procedure was suggested by Otto, McMenemy, and Smith, 1973.)
2. Write one of the suggested sentences on the board and have students read it aloud.
3. Ask students to write the sample in their usual writing five times.
4. After a few minutes of relaxation, ask the students to write the sentence three times in their best writing. Do not put a time limit on this.
5. After another short period of relaxation, ask the students to write the sample as many times as they can in three minutes.
6. Have students look over their three samples and make any comments about differences between the three samples.
7. Ask students to identify their own trouble spots.
8. Observe students carefully while they write. (Students with numerous problems should be evaluated separately.)

Evaluation   Use the Handwriting Checklist (Table 2-8) to identify the specific handwriting difficulties. This checklist is concerned with overall legibility as well as with the following specific features in handwriting: letter formation (including reversals, inversions, or substitutions of letters); size of letters and writing in general; use of guidelines; slant; and speed.

Evaluation Questions

Ideas/Content

Different factors must be considered depending on whether the writing is narrative, descriptive, expository, persuasive, or personal expression. The main concern will be to determine how well the student is able to develop a theme, topic, or storyline. Use the following to assist you in evaluating ideas/content. (See Table 2-3.)

- Did the writer catch your interest with an unusual title, a question, or an intriguing beginning?
- Did the writer introduce and develop a theme, topic, or storyline?
- Was the writer's purpose clear?
- Did the writer keep a consistent point of view?
- Was there evidence of originality, creativity, and imagination?
- What was unique in the writing? Names? Locations? Dialogue? Descriptions? Unexpected or unusual beginnings or endings? Unusual sensitivity?
- Was humor used? Puns? Play on words?
- Was there any evidence of abstract thinking? Philosophical ideas? Moral issues? Unusual concepts? Opinions or judgments with reasons?
- Was there evidence of personal style?
- Did the writer appeal to the reader's emotions?

Organization

The focus of these questions is to determine the way that the student writer arranges information. (See Table 2-4.)

- Did student include a title?
- Did student have clear introduction to story (i.e., a statement of the problem or beginning of storyline)?
- Did student add relevant supportive information (facts, details, examples)?
- Did student avoid gaps in organization of storyline (or did student assume that the reader knew something about the topic)?
- Did student write more than one paragraph?
- Did student sequence information appropriately?
- Did student attempt any other form of sequencing of ideas other than narrative (such as spatial or logical)?
- Did student include only relevant information (or did student include irrelevant information)?
- Did student use paragraph format (i.e., indentation, beginning new paragraph at introduction of new idea or new topic sentence)?

TABLE 2-3
Ideas / Content Checklist

Name _____ Date _____ Grade _____

Writing sample title _____

_____

Directions: Put a check by items noted in writing sample.
Write in examples from writing sample.

		Examples

Low	_____ Writing is basically immature and exhibits one or more of the following characteristics:
	
	_____ • unintelligible responses
	_____ • "stimulus-bound" writing:
	     simple naming and/or describing
	     no original ideas
	     lists of words or phrases
	_____ • single event personal experiences, or groups of
	     events with no generalization
	     rambling, "on and on" stories
	_____ • simple thought sequence
	_____ • egocentric	

Middle	_____ Writers *begin* to relate and classify experiences and/or facts and make generalizations. A definite story line or theme is evident although it may not be completely developed.
	
	_____ • relevant generalizations included
	_____ • descriptive detail added:
	     character, setting, mood detail
	     sensory details: sight, sound, smell, taste, touch
	     character interaction
	     character dialogue or monologue
	_____ • personal style evident
	     original ideas expressed use of humor, imagination
	_____ • Writers begin to write to an audience for a specific
	     purpose
		Examples

High	_____ Writing is CLEARLY AND CONSISTENTLY purposeful. Ideas and details are selected for specific purposes and generally involve analysis, synthesis, or interpretation.
	
	_____ • judgments made: stated or implied
	_____ • morals suggested: stated or implied
	_____ • consistent point of view supported by facts, reasons,
	     examples
	_____ • deliberate selection of information:
	     some points emphasized, others ignored
	     appeals to reader's emotions
	     persuasion
	_____ • unusual concepts explained
	_____ • personal style clear throughout writing sample
		Examples

TABLE 2-4
Organization Checklist

Name _____ Date _____ Grade _____

Writing sample title _____

_____

Directions: Put a check by items noted in writing sample.
Write in examples from writing sample.

		Examples
Low	_____ Writing lacks a specific organizing theme or purpose; overall organization is poor and sequencing is generally inaccurate or absent. _____ • simple thought sequence, poor sequence of ideas, ideas may be out of order, or written as they occur to the writer unrelated ideas may be grouped together _____ • irrelevant details	
		Examples
Middle	_____ Organization skills show improvement—but *inconsistency* in handling generalizations, details, and conclusions is evident. _____ • lack of overall planning _____ • paragraph structure may be inadequate overgeneralizations and unsupported opinions abundance of detail without summarizing statement or appropriate conclusion (main ideas omitted) poor introductions to paragraphs or reports (lack of topic sentence or topic paragraph) inappropriate or omitted conclusions poor transitions between paragraphs _____ • topic development may not be complete content may be copied from one source topic choice may be too broad or too narrow shifts in point of view shifts in train of thought	
		Examples
High	_____ Writing is CLEARLY AND CONSISTENTLY organized. The writer organizes his work for specific purposes and carefully selects relevant information. _____ • topic appropriately narrowed and focused _____ • adequate planning and preparation use of notetaking and outlining skills _____ • accurate paragraph structure generalizations and summaries with relevant supporting details opinions supported by relevant facts, details, examples appropriate paragraph breaks and transitions appropriate conclusions	

Vocabulary

In evaluating vocabulary, notice how students use words and what kinds of words they use. Ask the following questions after you read the writing samples; or use the Vocabulary Checklist. (See Table 2-5.)

- Did the student use only limited vocabulary?
- Did the student use topic related words? List them. It is important to note whether writers use specific words spontaneously (without any stimulus) or whether students use some specific words because the subject requires their use.
- Did the student use specific nouns? List them. Did the student identify persons, places, or things by specific word choice? *Mr. Barnabas Quimley*, instead of *the man*? *Lincoln Elementary School*, instead of *the school*? *The automatic ice dispenser*, instead of *the thing*?
- Did the student use specific descriptive words? List them. Did the student use common adjectives such as *big, little, brown*; or more specific adjectives such as *monstrous, miniature, cocoa-brown*?
- Did the student use specific verbs? Or did the student overuse *is, are, have, make*?
- Did the student invent any words for names of people, places, or sounds?
- Did the student create any original comparisons?
- Did the student use any literary device? Onomatopoeia (such as *buzz, whack, swish*), alliteration, repetition?

Sentence Structure

The following questions focus on the types and variety of sentences used, as well as syntax and punctuation. (See Table 2-6.)

Sentence Types
- Did the student use:
  simple sentences exclusively?
  when and/or *where* phrases in simple sentences?
  descriptive phrases?
  any compound sentences?
  any complex sentences?
  a variety of sentence types and lengths?

Syntax
- Did the student use:
  correct word order in all sentences?
  consistent verb tense throughout story or report? (For example: Is past tense used consistently throughout story or report?)
  correct subject-verb agreement?
  correct noun-pronoun agreement?

Punctuation
- What forms of punctuation were used correctly?
- What forms were not used correctly or were omitted?

Spelling

Spelling may be checked using the Spelling Checklist. (See Table 2-7.)

Handwriting

Handwriting may be checked using the Handwriting Checklist. (See Table 2-8.)

TABLE 2-5
Vocabulary Checklist

Name _____ Date _____ Grade _____

Writing Sample Title _____

_____

Directions: Put a check by items noted in writing sample.
Write in examples of words used.

		Examples
Low	_____ The writer OVERUSES the following kinds of words: _____ • general nouns: the man, the thing, something, the dog, people _____ • general verbs: is/was, are/am, go/went, do/did, see/saw/look, want/have, get/got, make, said, like _____ • general adjectives: good/nice, big/little, funny, pretty _____ • general adverbs: many, some, very, really, too _____ • articles, prepositions, conjunctions _____ • pronouns without clear referents _____ The writer uses immature oral language patterns	
Middle	_____ The writer *begins* to play with words and introduces *some* of the following elements in the writing: _____ • specific nouns, verbs, adjectives, adverbs _____ • imaginative use of words invented words alliteration, rhyming, repetition original similes, metaphors, analogies puns _____ As students experiment in vocabulary use, the following kinds of errors may be made: _____ • word selection errors word form substitution preposition errors: "regardless to" cliché: "pretty as a picture" overly elaborate, flowery words/phrases excess words/phrases: "the reason is because" _____ • word formation errors prefix/suffix errors: "beautifulest" inflectional ending errors	Examples
High	_____ The writer ACCURATELY and CONSISTENTLY selects words which convey the intended message. Word selection is appropriate for style of writing. _____ • precise vocabulary: deliberate word choice abstract nouns: truth, hope cognitive verbs: understand judgmental adjectives: adequate	Examples

TABLE 2-6
Sentence Structure Checklist

Name _____ Date _____ Grade _____

Writing Sample Title _____

Directions: Put a check by items noted in writing sample.
                Write in examples of sentence structure.

		Examples

Low	_____ The writer does not have good "sentence sense" and is unable to arrange words to form complete sentences. Some of the following characteristics may be seen.
	
	_____ • lists of words and/or phrases (no sentences at all)
	_____ • sentence errors
	     run-ons: overuse of *and, and then, and so*
	     sentence fragments
	     syntax errors: words omitted or word order
	        inaccurate
	_____ • overuse of short, choppy simple sentences
	_____ • omitted punctuation, or totally inaccurate punctuation	

Middle	_____ The writer experiments with different types of sentences:
	
	_____ • expanded sentences: *when, where, how* phrases added
	_____ • compound sentences, complex sentences
	
	However, awkward constructions may appear with the use of longer sentences:
	
	_____ • verb errors
	     subject-verb agreement errors
	     shifts in tense in sentence, paragraph, story
	     non-parallel constructions
	_____ • noun/pronoun agreement errors
	_____ • punctuation errors
		Examples

High	_____ The writer has clear "sentence sense" and manipulates words to form all types of sentences ACCURATELY and CONSISTENTLY.
	
	_____ • variety of sentence structures and lengths used
	_____ • all forms of punctuation are consistently and accurately used
	_____ • stylistic features used
	     questions
	     exclamations
	     repetition of words or phrases for effect
	     deliberate use of sentence fragments
		Examples

TABLE 2-7
Spelling Checklist

Name _____ Date _____ Grade _____

Writing Sample Title _____

Directions: Put a check by items noted in writing sample.
Write in examples of spelling errors.

Low	*Examples* Comprehension of story or report may be difficult due to frequency of spelling errors. Possible error patterns may be: _____ • errors on both sight words and phonetic words: spelling may be bizarre and totally unrelated to either phonetic or visual elements _____ • errors primarily on basic sight words (e.g., went, want, where, work, walk, play, etc.) spells words phonetically, or adds, omits, substitutes, or inverts letters _____ • errors primarily on phonetic words: adds, omits, substitutes letters, inverts letters errors mostly on vowels; or errors mostly on consonants; or errors on both consonants and vowels _____ • common substitutions their, there, they're your, you're its, it's to, too, two _____ • errors on contractions
Middle	*Examples* _____ There are some spelling errors, but the words are readable. Errors are made on longer words and may be due to misapprehension or incorrect pronunciation. _____ • phonetic spelling of misspelled words _____ • word endings added or omitted incorrectly _____ • syllables in words may be omitted _____ • homonym substitution
High	*Examples* _____ There are relatively few errors and the student is working at or above grade level in spelling skills. Errors are generally made on difficult words (multi-syllable words, or words with unusual spellings). Only a few errors are found in first drafts of longer compositions and reports. _____ Final drafts are free of errors

TABLE 2-8

Handwriting Checklist

Name _____ Date _____ Grade _____

Writing Sample Title _____

Directions: Put a check by items noted in writing sample.

Handedness: right _____   left _____
Style: manuscript _____   cursive _____
Body Position: correct _____   incorrect _____
Paper Position: correct _____   incorrect _____

Low	_____ Handwriting at this level does not present a neat appearance. _____ • poor or inaccurate letter formation; letter substitution _____ • poor spacing between words and/or letters _____ • poor spatial organization (inconsistent letter size, or inconsistent use of guidelines; letters may be too large or too small) _____ • smudged erasures or write-overs _____ • illegibility _____ • letter reversals, inversions _____ • laborious, slow writing or fast, careless writing _____ • incorrectly formed letters (circle) i u w t j p s r e l b h k f m n c o a d g q v x y z C O A E M N W V U H P R B K F Q X Y Z T G S L I J D
Middle	_____ Overall handwriting is adequate, although there may be some awkward letter formations, especially if the student is just learning cursive writing. Student may need to work on overall neatness and use of margins.
High	_____ Overall writing is carefully done and is quite readable. Complete papers are very neat.

CHAPTER 3

Get Them Writing!

Current instructional theories emphasize a process approach to the teaching of writing. This means that teachers should concentrate more on the different stages of writing rather than just on the final written product. Students learn to write better by writing more and by receiving more evaluative feedback along the way from teachers and peers. Teachers provide guidance and instruction through the process rather than just at the final step in the process.

As mentioned in Chapter 1, the writing process is not totally linear or sequential but consists of moving back and forth through the stages of prewriting, writing, editing, rethinking, revising, publishing, and sharing. This chapter outlines these stages and suggests ideas for teaching writing using the process approach.

Setting Up the Writing Environment

Even though a complex process, writing is satisfying to the writer. Students enjoy sharing their writing and getting feedback from their peers at different stages of development. To encourage this enjoyment of writing, remember that the more attention you pay to the different drafts of writing, the better the final written product will be and the more satisfied and motivated the students will be. When setting up the writing environment, keep in mind the following points:

1. *Build a positive atmosphere.* A positive atmosphere provides encouragement, praise, motivation, and numerous opportunities to write. Students should feel free and safe enough to risk making mistakes—to express their thoughts without being criticized for making structural and mechanical errors. Supporting this view, Hillerich (1979) states that "the most outstanding and consistent finding in research literature is that children learn to write better when praised than when criticized." In a more relaxed atmosphere, with less emphasis

on absolute correctness of mechanics usage, students will develop a more positive attitude toward writing (Beaven, 1977), and they will also exhibit increased sophistication in language and style (Hillerich, 1979). Students should not have to concentrate on absolute mechanical correctness as they write; rather, they should focus on idea generation, vocabulary choice, and sentence variety.

2. *Keep an abundant supply of reading and writing materials in the classroom at all times.* Every writing program should be based on large doses of reading. This should be a combination of oral reading sessions in which the teacher, an older student from another grade, or a student from the classroom reads to the class; and individual reading done by students in regularly scheduled silent reading periods with material of their own choosing.

Identify series of books that are especially popular with students. You can do this in two ways: (1) talk to the school or community librarian and find out which books are most frequently read by students of different age and grade levels; or, (2) have students interview students in other classrooms to determine both the general reading interests of students and specific titles and series that students particularly like. Post a list of the most popular books on the bulletin board. Keep the names of various students who have recommended books and arrange an occasional cross-grade book discussion period for students to share viewpoints on selected books.

Try to identify the special interests of individuals by asking students to fill out a reading interest questionnaire (Table 3-1).

3. *Provide read-along or other audio-visual materials* for those students who are reluctant to read and write or whose skills are below grade level. Very often, this kind of material stimulates both reading and writing. Reluctant writers can make their own illustrated and annotated booklets to go along with the audio-visual material.

4. *Collect examples of published student writing* so that students may see what their peers around the country are writing. Use these to stimulate writing sessions. Students say "I can do that" and eagerly begin to write. Writing is not so formidable when they see what others their own age have published.

Collections of Student Writing and Thinking

Somebody Real: Voices of Real Children, 1973
   Nicholas Anthony Duva, editor
   American Faculty Press
Somebody Real is an anthology of writings by twenty-four minority students in a sixth grade class in Jersey City. The students write about their life in the city and their awareness of violence, drugs, school, neighborhoods, and their expressions of love, death, life, loneliness, and other abstract ideas. Pictures of the writers are included. Reading Level: 5–6. Interest Level: 5–12.

The Voice of Children, 1974
   June Jordan and Terri Bush, editors
   Holt, Rinehart and Winston
A collection of poetry and short prose pieces written by black and Puerto Rican children from Brooklyn about school, families, life in the city, and their feelings about themselves. Reading Level: 5–6. Interest Level: 5–12.

Listen to Us: The Children's Express Report, 1978
   Dorriet Kavanaugh, editor
   Workman Publishing Company
More than 2,000 children present candid views on such topics as family relationships, family problems, school, friends, children with special problems (handicaps), children in trouble, sex, TV, money, religion, feelings, adult treat-

TABLE 3-1
Questionnaire about Reading

1. Circle the kinds of reading materials that you like. You may circle as many kinds as you like.

about boys	cowboy stories
about girls	Indian stories
about family	pioneer stories
about friends	outdoor life
about growing up	racing (cars, motorcycles)
about school	sports
adventure	hobbies
sea adventure	how-to-make-it books
exploration	historical stories
space exploration	biography
science fiction	war stories
mystery	science
detective	inventions
animals	nature
cats	fantasy
dinosaurs	fairy tales
dogs	myths and legends
horses	humor
wild animals	jokes and riddles
others? _____	careers
_____	
_____	
plays	
poetry	

2. How many books did you read last year?

3. What are the names of the books that you have enjoyed the most? (You may look up authors' names if you have forgotten them.)

Title _____ Author _____

Brief Summary _____

_____

_____

_____

_____

Title _____ Author _____

Brief Summary _____

_____

_____

_____

_____

4. How many books do you think you will read this year?

5. What kind of book would you like to start reading? (*Choose one kind from the above list.*)

ment of kids, and others. The book was compiled by teenage editorial assistants who interviewed children all over the country.

"The underlying philosophy of Children's Express can be summed up in four words: 'Children Can Do It.'"

The Me Nobody Knows: Children's Voices from the Ghetto, 1969
Avon Books
Ghetto children write on such topics as "How I See Myself," "How I See My Neighborhood," "The World Outside." Some are poems, some are paragraphs, some are diary entries.

5. *Correlate writing instruction with other curriculum areas.* One useful technique is asking the students to summarize a discussion in science or social studies classes. This often helps teachers to identify those students who have not grasped the concepts discussed and who may need additional review. Students often have difficulty putting concepts they think they understand in written form.

Prewriting

1. *Schedule frequent prewriting and writing sessions.* To improve in writing, students need to write regularly and to receive frequent feedback from teachers and peers. Not every piece of writing has to go through the entire writing process to final draft. Some pieces may stay in the writing folder and never be touched again, while others will go through many drafts until the student is satisfied.

2. *Discuss purpose for writing and intended audience.* Ask students what they want to accomplish with their writing. Do they want to entertain? To give directions? To explain a process? To persuade? Or just give friendly news? Explain that different types of writing require different styles of writing. If, for example, you're telling someone how to catch a silver salmon, you don't need a lot of descriptive detail; instead, you need a series of clear step-by-step directions. If, however, you were trying to convince your friend to visit your campsite, you probably would want to include a lot of descriptive detail—including sights, sounds, smells, and tastes.

3. *Provide motivating prewriting experiences. Brainstorming, role playing, reading, listening, speaking, drawing* . . . all these help students to develop, expand, then organize their thoughts before writing.

Brainstorming is a popular technique for generating many ideas on a given topic in a short time. The process encourages divergent thinking and calls for random or unusual associations rather than just linear or sequential relationships. This process encourages students to stretch their imagination and play with ideas before writing instead of writing in the same old way.

Several important guidelines should be followed in this procedure.

a. *Anything goes!* Any idea expressed should be accepted without judgment of right or wrong, good or bad. Frequently, one person's idea can be expanded, developed, and refined into a totally new concept by another person. Each new idea then becomes a potential stimulus for further ideas.

One way to introduce brainstorming techniques is to use a nonserious topic as a stimulator so that all answers will be equally acceptable. One such topic could be, "What can you do with an alligator (or any other living or nonliving thing)?" See Alligator Antics in Chapter 5.

b. *Collect as many ideas as possible in a given time.* Limit the brainstorming session to a specific time, depending on the interests and attention span of students, but allow enough time to generate a variety of ideas. Five to ten minutes should be enough. Too short a period will not permit the expression of enough ideas, too long a period will produce boredom.

   Appoint one or two students to be notetakers to write down all ideas. Restate ideas after they have been given. Record each idea or statement where all participants can see it. (Use a chalkboard, overhead transparency, or large chart.)

c. *Encourage students to elaborate, combine, or expand ideas* as they are mentioned. Very often, the idea, suggestion, or word from one student triggers another idea, suggestion, or word from another student. This multiplies the number of ideas that an individual can draw upon for his or her own writing. Thus, instead of having only one idea (his or her own), a student can now combine and choose the best parts of many ideas.

   4. *Teach different methods of generating ideas.* Students can begin to plan their writing before they start to write. Brainstorming as a group is one way, but students need to organize their writing on an individual basis as well. After you have completed a number of group brainstorming sessions, schedule a few writing sessions and ask students to brainstorm on their own. Give students a topic or let them choose one of their own. Ask them to jot down ideas about the topic in brief phrases as they occur. After giving them several minutes to do this, ask students to read their jottings to themselves to see if the order needs to be changed or if they can add ideas. Use these jottings in writing sessions.

Writing

   1. *Get them writing!* Require that students write something, regardless of length, after each brainstorming or role playing session, whether they invent new material, elaborate on previously discussed material, or simply summarize what was presented in the prewriting sessions.

   Reluctant writers frequently write the minimum amount to complete the assignment—often using the shortest and simplest sentences and the most limited vocabulary. These students may increase their writing production if a minimum word count is set up for them. To begin, establish a base by counting the number of words a student uses in his or her writing assignments. Then determine a reasonable number of words that should be written. For example: A minimum for third grade might be thirty words; for fourth grade, forty words; and so on. When a student's amount of writing (fluency) is charted over a few weeks, writing production will be seen to increase gradually. Students will begin to write more fluently when they realize that they will not be penalized for spelling or other mechanical errors. Gradually, they become more involved in their writing rather than in counting words.

   Occasionally when students will write only the required number of words, but when peer competition becomes a consideration, they usually begin to write more and more. Eventually they won't need to use word counts.

   2. *Do "fast writes."* These are short, timed writings, usually five or ten minutes, in which students write without stopping on a given topic or on one of their own topics. The purpose is to increase writing fluency as well as to generate ideas on the topic that can be used later when editing and revising.

3. *Write with the class.* Let class members see that writing is important by doing it along with them; otherwise, they may be tempted to see writing as busywork. When it comes time to share, read your writing, too. Students enjoy hearing what you have to say.

4. *Call each paper a first draft.* Have students write on alternate lines of their paper to allow room for words to be inserted, notes to be added, or lines to be crossed out and rewritten. Calling each piece of writing a "first draft" acknowledges that the paper is not absolutely perfect and that it may be revised and rewritten. Point out, however, that not every piece needs (or deserves) to be rewritten. Keep all first drafts together in a writing folder until a later time when one or more may be expanded, revised, and rewritten. Emphasize that all writing is important even if it is never revised and rewritten.

5. *Encourage different types of writing.* Children in elementary grades enjoy writing and sharing creative stories. Story starters, pictures, and picture storybooks are good sources for imaginative writing, but students also have active imaginations of their own that can be tapped for topics. These students also enjoy writing about their own personal experiences. Elementary students, however, probably do not spend enough time with expository writing—that is, explaining a process, summarizing subject matter, or reporting events. In later school years and in adult life it is likely that they will need to produce expository writing more than creative writing.

Journal writing and letter writing are two other types of writing worthy of practice in school.

6. *Encourage small-group writing collaboration.* Collaboration is easily accomplished when students work at a computer, although it can easily be done with regular writing sessions. In group collaboration students generate ideas through conversation. This thinking aloud assists students in organizing ideas and also enables stronger students to work with weaker students. Students enjoy the ownership of the final product, and all the group members receive equal recognition regardless of skill level. Even in collaborative writings, though, the stages of the writing process should be followed so that all members experience the proofreading and revising stages.

Editing

1. *Schedule frequent periods for proofreading, editing, and revision.* Ask students to choose one story or report from their writing folder for review and revision; then have them read the papers aloud to a partner, small group, or tape recorder. Frequently, oral reading of written work helps students to identify their own errors more easily. Group members can also offer suggestions for addition or changes.

2. *Teach students to evaluate their own writing.* An informal Student Writing Checklist may be useful in helping students to begin to evaluate their own writing. (See Table 3-2.) One student stated confidently after going over the checklist, "I can do that! Now I know what to do!" Another stated that he could tell he was getting better in his writing because "I always reach my goal."

Different groups of students within the classroom may have different objectives depending on individual needs. It is very helpful to have students write their personal objective at the top of every paper (including science, social studies, and even math, when appropriate) so that student and teacher review may focus on the selected objective. State the objective in positive terms. (Some students seem to understand the word *goal* better than the word *objective*.) At

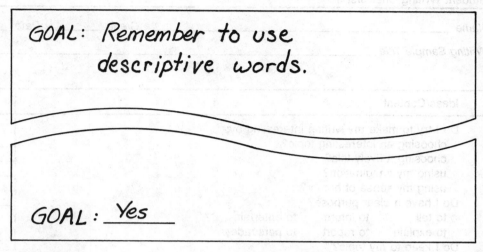

GOAL: Remember to use descriptive words.

GOAL: _Yes_

FIGURE 3-2
Goal Setting

the bottom of the paper have the student write the word *Goal* again, then draw a line.

When students have completed their asignment, ask them to proofread for their target objective and write *Yes* or *No* on the Goal Line to indicate whether they feel they have met the objective. Most students like to write *Yes,* so they quickly proofread and make corrections when necessary.

3. *Point out indications of strength in writing ability*—the choice of a specific word, an original comparison, an interesting sentence, or an unusual idea. This kind of acknowledgment of their ability encourages students, giving them increased pride and interest in writing. This does not mean that you should totally ignore mechanical errors. The next few points will elaborate on this idea. Too often, we try to encourage students by giving a general response such as "Your writing is improving." This kind of statement is useless unless you point out what it is that shows improvement. Make specific statements such as "You're using very specific verbs instead of the most commonly used ones" or "You're using a variety of sentence patterns." Try to offer at least one positive statement for every paper you read.

4. *Establish "teacherless writing groups" for peer editing and feedback sessions.* Form small groups for the purpose of oral reading and sharing of writing attempts. Establish ground rules that comments must be positive. Encourage students to identify and underline good phrases, specific vocabulary, or their favorite parts. Occasionally, trade papers within the group, with members writing comments on each paper and signing their names. Readers can also note any spelling or other mechanical error.

5. *Identify class experts in spelling and mechanics.* Every class has several students who are especially skilled in spelling and mechanics. Ask them to share their expertise by helping their peers correct all spelling before the writing of final drafts. Thus, students who do have poor spelling or difficulty with mechanics will also have the opportunity to hand in a corrected paper. After all, adults use this process; why shouldn't students?

6. *Use the Student Writing Checklist.* One way to involve students in the evaluation process is to use a checklist, such as in Table 3-2. Checklists can be varied according to the reading and ability levels of students by adding or deleting items. Use the following procedures with the student checklist.

a. Review a small collection of the student's writing with the individual student to identify specific strengths and weaknesses. (You may want to share

TABLE 3-2
Student Writing Checklist II

Name _____ Grade _____ Date _____

Writing Sample Title _____

		Yes	I need practice
I.	**Ideas/Content**		
	Do I try to make my writing interesting by:		
	choosing an interesting topic?		
	choosing a lively title?		
	using my imagination?		
	using my sense of humor?		
	Do I have a clear purpose?		
	to tell to inform to entertain		
	to explain to report to persuade		
	Do I keep to my topic?		
	Do I have my own personal style?		
II.	**Organization**		
	Do I have an interesting beginning?		
	Do I have enough		
	facts, details, examples		
	quotes, definitions, comparisons		
	observations using my five senses		
	Do I omit unnecessary information?		
	Do I have a clear sequence of ideas or events?		
	Do I have a good ending?		
	Do I use good paragraph format?		
III.	**Vocabulary**		
	Do I use		
	specific names and places?		
	specific descriptive words?		
	specific action words?		
	Do I avoid overusing the same old words:		
	nouns: man, people, thing, place, something		
	adjectives: nice, pretty, good, wonderful, big, little, funny		
	verbs: is/was, am/are, go/went, do/did, see/saw/look, want/have, get/got		
	make, said, like		
	adverbs: many, some, very, really, too		
IV.	**Sentence Structure**		
	Do I use complete sentences?		
	with capital letters?		
	and punctuation?		
	periods, question marks, exclamation marks, commas, quotation marks		
	Do I try to use a variety of sentence lengths?		
	some long, some short?		
	Do I avoid sentence fragments?		
	Do I avoid run-on sentences?		
V.	**Spelling**		
	Do I have correct spelling on my final draft?		
VI.	**Handwriting**		
	Do I use my best handwriting on my final draft?		

your evaluation notes made previously using the evaluation guidelines presented in Chapter 2.) If there are a great many errors in the student's writing, choose just one skill area to work on. Remember, the first important goal is to increase writing fluency (i.e., the quantity of writing a student does).

b. Review the items on the checklist and have the student mark the column that is most appropriate (*Yes* or *I need practice*). Occasionally, a student will check *Yes* when, in fact, he or she has not mastered the particular skill in question. A quick scan through some writing will help the student recognize the areas where help is needed.

c. Decide with the student which problem will be the focus of writing for the next week or two. Agree on a specific time period in which this goal is to be mastered. Often, the student masters the goal very quickly after focusing attention on that particular item.

d. Point out positive signs of growth whenever you see them.

Revising

1. *Collect a number of before-and-after versions of stories.* Display them on a bulletin board, and ask students to note the changes. Ask students to identify the better story and the qualities that make it better.

Students do not like to rewrite stories. They consider a story to be finished as soon as they put the pencil down. Since they often develop the story as they write, it may meander or change directions abruptly as the student becomes involved in a new train of thought. The younger student writes in verbal shorthand as if he or she assumes the reader will understand and fill in the information that is missing. Two approaches may be used to correct this problem. First, it is often best to ask these students to write something related to the story they have already written *instead* of revising their original story. For example: A student might be asked to tell more about one of the characters in the story, or to tell more about the setting, or more about the emotional climate of the story. How do the characters feel? What might happen next? In this way students can be encouraged to explore a topic without feeling that they are being asked to revise the original story.

If students have difficulty with proofreading, help them focus on one error type at a time by providing activities that isolate that error *pattern* only. (See Chapter 10, "Tackle the Troublespots," for specific suggestions and activities for developing proofreading and editing skills.)

2. *Use this "Six Square Activity" to identify good qualities in writing.* Ask the students to do a five minute fast write on the topic "What Makes Good Writing?" Next draw six large squares on the board to correspond to Table 2-2 in Chapter 2. Do not label the squares, but see if students can guess the category label based on the information you put in each square. Ask student volunteers to read their writing samples while you jot down selected phrases in squares that will eventually be labeled *Ideas/Content, Organization, Vocabulary, Sentence Structure, Spelling,* and *Handwriting*. See Table 3-3 for a "Student Generated Chart" on "What Makes Good Writing?"

3. *Suggest an objective for revision relative to the student's paper.*

Examples: Add more descriptive detail.
Add some character interaction.
Add some character dialogue.
Change overused words (such as *nice*).

TABLE 3-3
Student Generated Chart, "What makes good writing?" (grade 5)

Ideas/Content	Organization
tell people things use good ideas use creative ideas use your imagination entertain your readers enjoy writing express your feelings write scary things, adventures put a tad of humor in it give opinions write about interesting things ask a question write what you know about	plan before you write give lots of details prove what you are saying with examples or facts pick out facts and organize them have happy, scary, and spooky parts use good paragraphs remember to indent make sure your facts are true use 5 w's (who, what, when, where, why) tell what's going on (sequence) use showing writing (description)
Vocabulary	**Sentence Structure**

use good words
use interesting words
use down-to-earth words
use action verbs
use descriptive words
use some proper nouns
make comparisons
   (as brown as _____)
use big words and little words
	use good sentences
	use capital letters
	use punctuation (periods, question
	   marks, exclamation marks)
	put in quotation marks if necessary
	use different kinds of sentences
	don't use all short sentences
	don't have sentences that take a year to
	   read or people will get confused

Spelling	**Handwriting**
be careful with your spelling proofread your paper correct spelling mistakes	have good writing so people can read it slant your paper a certain way be neat

After students revise for the suggested objective, have them share their results with a small group. Encourage students to respond with positive comments on the style and content of the writing by asking questions such as "What was the most specific name or place? The most descriptive word?" or "How do you think the characters are feeling? What could be added to the story? What was the most interesting event? The funniest?"

4. *Do fast-write expansions.* Look over your students' collection of fast writes and identify some suitable for expansion. Since fast writes are limited in time, they are not totally developed. A few have many good topic sentences and need only facts, details, or examples to round them out. Put one of these barebones fast writes on an overhead transparency, writing each sentence separately and allowing space for information to be inserted. Have class members suggest supporting information and add it to the transparency. Compare the before-and-after versions and discuss.

5. *Do fast-write shrinkings.* Identify examples of wordy fast writes in which students have repeated words or phrases. Ask permission to use the papers for a demonstration; then copy the fast writes on a transparency or ditto and to discuss with the class. Have students identify the problem and suggest

changes. Have the class rewrite the same fast write and compare papers with one another. List the various changes that students made.

6. *Have students revise one another's first drafts.* Students sometimes don't notice their own mistakes. When a writing partner makes suggestions for revisions, the original writer receives new ideas and can make changes based on the suggestions.

7. *Recognize that some writing is not worth revising.* If a student hates a piece of writing, don't force him to rewrite it. The advantage of doing many fast writes and other types of writing is that there are many samples to choose from when revising. Do not, however, let students throw away their "junk" writing; at some later date it may generate another piece of writing. Allow students to start over completely with a piece of writing if they don't like their first attempt. First attempts are often the writer's way of clearing away the cobwebs and getting (finally) to the point of the writing.

8. *Recognize that some students may be capable of correcting surface errors only.* Over time, students will be more willing to make major changes (deletions, additions, rearrangements), but they need practice, experimentation, and demonstrations. If you do a number of revisions using whole class input, students will gradually carry this over to their own writing.

9. *Select interesting phrases from students' writing to put on overhead transparency or ditto.* Share these with the class and discuss what makes them interesting.

Publishing and Sharing

1. *Provide many opportunities for students to share their writing efforts.* Establish regular sharing periods when students pair up to read the results of their efforts to each other—or to a small group or even to the whole class. When stories or reports are read aloud, encourage students to respond with positive comments.

2. *Make collections of student writing.* Publishing, the final stage of the writing process, brings the purpose for writing into sharp focus. Writing is meant to be read and shared. As students become more involved in the publishing stage, they will expand their efforts and interest.

Publishing may be as simple as making a final, handwritten copy of the writing sample for display on a Writer's Bulletin Board, or it may be as sophisticated as a final print on a letter-quality computer printer. Students enjoy handcopying their stories or compositions on duplicating masters and then running off copies for classmates, parents, friends, or other important people in their lives. Sometimes their best efforts can be bound in a small book with such simple materials as cardboard and colored mystic tape or construction paper and yarn. Final bound copies can even be placed in the school library in a special student writer collection. Whatever the method, publishing allows the students to develop pride and satisfaction in their writing efforts.

Resources

Reading, Writing and Rating Stories, 1982
    Carol Sager
    Curriculum Associates
Reading, Writing and Rating Stories is a writing program designed to improve

the quality of writing in the middle grades. The program trains students to evaluate their own writing using a descriptive scale covering four areas: vocabulary, elaboration (the addition of ideas and details that enliven people, places, and events), organization, and structure (includes punctuation, sentence structure and variety). Students are asked to read short selections then to answer guide questions related to the four evaluation areas. The program employs a self-directing self-correcting approach although demonstration lessons by the teacher are encouraged.

CHAPTER 4

Use the Computer

A recent innovation in teaching writing is the use of microcomputers and word processing software programs. Word processing is the computer language term for writing on a computer, while keyboarding is the term for typing on a computer. As you type, your writing appears on the monitor screen; when you have finished and give the computer a print command, the printer prints out a copy on paper. Because of the ease with which a person can write, edit, and revise, word processing changes the way a person writes. Papers can be totally reorganized; revised by shifting the arrangement of words, sentences, or paragraphs; corrected; and totally reprinted in a manner of minutes. Writers of all ages quickly discover that they willingly put much more effort into their writing and revision when they don't have to laboriously handcopy or retype everything.

Computer Writing Is a Process

Word processing enables students to see more clearly that writing is a process and that it may take several drafts for them to organize their ideas in a clear and complete manner. This is contrary to the traditional view of writing as a one-step, one-copy activity. Handwriting generally is too slow and laborious for students to bother revising by adding lines or paragraphs, so they balk at editing, revising, and recopying their work. Sometimes, when they copy their papers by hand, they create new mistakes, such as skipping a whole line or misspelling previously correct words. Computer word processing eliminates this problem.

Computer writing also encourages collaboration among students, and with collaboration comes better writing. Providing peer support for one another, students assist each other with idea generation, sentence structure, vocabulary, and spelling. Enthusiasm and spontaneous sharing naturally result from collaborative writing using a computer.

Collaborative writing is especially helpful for students who have poor writing skills. Those students very frequently have good ideas, but have difficulty getting their ideas down on paper because of handwriting or a serious spelling problem. If a weak student pairs up with a stronger student, spelling and other mechanical problems decrease. In addition, because poor writers are generally unaware of their own errors, the better writer can provide assistance in identifying and correcting mistakes.

On the other hand, one major disadvantage in using computers and word processing programs is that, initially, keyboarding skills are weak and take as much time as handwriting. Training on specialized keyboarding software programs alleviates this problem and assists students in developing correct fingering, typing accuracy, and speed.

Advantages of Using a Computer for Instruction in Writing

A number of major advantages arise from using word processing programs on computers. These advantages will be reviewed using the writing process model sequence: prewriting, writing, proofreading and editing, revising, and publishing. The end of this chapter has a review of computer software programs that focus on writing skills and the writing process.

Prewriting

1. *Students can quickly type out their ideas* or develop a list of ideas, words, or phrases that might form a general guide or outline for their writing. Some students may still prefer to complete this prewriting stage with paper and pencil, but others like thinking things out in lists, jottings, or even "fast writes" on the computer. Fast writes are short, timed writings in which the student tries to jot down ideas in a specified time period (usually five minutes). Fast writes often become general outlines or starting points for more developed writing sessions. For fast writes, students do not need to worry about correctness in typing skills or in spelling, grammar, and punctuation. Fast writes simply gather ideas and become a starting point for writing.

2. *Students can often work in pairs*, and in this type of collaborative writing we often see rapid improvement. Instead of working in the vacuum created by the isolation of working with paper and pencil at desks, partners can talk, write, reread, and gradually develop their story or report. The partners can also share responsibility for identifying spelling errors, and those errors that go by unnoticed can be identified by a computer spelling checker (a software program specifically designed to identify misspelled words).

3. *Software programs specifically designed to assist the writer at this prewriting stage* aid students in planning their writing. These programs assist in developing listings of ideas, word or topic associations, or responses to prompts (questions) about their topic. The student can then analyze and categorize responses in order to form an outline or sequence of ideas for the writing assignment. Other software programs encourage students to respond to

story starters or picture prompts. See the Resource section of this chapter for software suggestions.

Writing

1. *Students write more fluently when using a computer and word processing programs.* After their first experience with printing out an assignment, they often express surprise at the brevity of their writing sample. Later writing samples increase in length as students become more comfortable with keyboarding (typing) and word processing.

2. *Students can add, delete, or change information at any point in the writing process* simply by moving the cursor to the spot needing information. No laborious handwriting or erasing and rewriting interfere with the creative thinking processes.

3. *Students feel positive about using the computer for word processing and writing.* One research study indicated that students believed they could write better on the computer and that writing seemed easier. Also, students were interested in what other students were writing and became more critical of their own efforts (Sommers and Collins, 1984).

Editing

1. *Computer printed drafts are easier to read* than handwriting; thus, it is easier for students to identify spelling and other mechanical errors. In addition, students working in pairs tend to read the writing samples aloud to one another and discover sentence awkwardness or other errors even before the writing sample is printed out. Because students don't have to struggle with their sometimes illegible or awkward handwriting, they tend to reread their own material more frequently. Computer printouts are especially beneficial for students with fine motor problems because handwriting awkwardness does not become a disadvantage; final written products look equal to those of classmates.

2. *Peer evaluation is easier* when first drafts are printed out by the computer. Peers can underline sentences, words, or ideas that they especially like and can also give suggestions on information or details that need to be added. Because multiple copies can easily be printed, first drafts can also be reviewed by several readers.

3. *Corrections, additions, or deletions are easy to make.* To correct spelling or other errors, the student has only to move the cursor to the error, delete the error, and type in the correction. Spelling checkers highlight or underline misspelled words, suggest the correct spelling, and ask the writer to make corrections.

4. *Software programs evaluate writing and point out common errors and possible errors.* Among the errors that can be identified by computer checking are capitalization and punctuation errors; split infinitives; passive voice on regular and irregular verbs; vague, overused, and slang vocabulary; wordy phrases and redundant expressions; and abbreviation errors. These programs also analyze sentence and paragraph length and suggest when they are too short (perhaps not enough information) or too long (possibly too much information or a paragraphing error). Error reports can be printed out or can be viewed on the monitor screen. If viewing errors on the screen, the student has the option of making corrections and getting another printout. Students quickly identify their own most common errors and try to avoid them in later writing efforts.

Revision

1. *Students accept suggestions and constructive criticism more willingly* when using computer word processing programs because they know that revision and reprinting are far easier than laborious handcopying. With a few strokes of the keyboard, they can correct any errors; can add and delete; and can print a new, clean, error-free copy. One danger, however, is that students may revise surface errors only (such as punctuation and capitalization) and fail to revise content and structure problems. As students receive more training in revising, they will learn to correct structure and content problems as well as mechanical problems. While the computer software programs can check common mechanical writing problems, they cannot check content, so students still need to have peer and teacher feedback on clarity of ideas and style of writing.

2. *Teachers and peers can make specific suggestions for improvement.* Since multiple copies of the writing sample are easily printed, several students and the teacher may read a clean copy and make suggestions right on the draft copy. None will be affected by the comments of the other. Thus, having the benefit of a number of suggestions, students can use all of them or choose only those that seem to fit the intent of the assignment.

Publishing

1. *Publishing a final draft is faster and more efficient with the computer* and is perhaps the most exciting part of the process for students. Students may easily print multiple copies of their writing to share with classmates, to take home to parents or friends, to post on bulletin boards, or to place in a class collection of student writing.

2. *Publishing completes the writing process and provides the reward for writing.* Students value neat final written products and express pride in their writing. They may also save their writing efforts and compare their progress over a period of time.

Other Computer Applications for Writing

Word processing is only one way of using microcomputers in the classroom writing program. Signs, banners, greeting cards, letterheads, award certificates, birthday wrapping paper, and many other writing applications can be made using the computer. In addition, on selected software programs, you can choose between type styles and sizes, borders and designs, and graphics. Students can use their imagination to combine any of the various possibilities for their specific purpose. Newsletters, flyers, and announcements are another important end product of writing applications programs. Never before has the publishing aspect of writing been so easy and so enjoyable for students and readers.

Another application with high potential for computers in the classroom is telecommunications. Telecommunications is the process of sending information (data) over telephone lines or satellite relays from one computer to another computer or to a network of computers. Telecommunications brings a whole new vocabulary to the world of computers in the classrooms: electronic bulletin board, electronic mail, modem, on-line networks, password, upload, download, query, host computer, connect time, and many others.

Several classroom applications are possible with telecommunications. One is the use of the bulletin board system that connects computers to one another by telephone lines and allows users to send public or private messages. The bulletin board is best used to share information on a topic of interest to many people, to share student-generated materials (stories, reports, letters) with other students at another location, to work on a cooperative project, or to ask questions. These items can be read at a later time by the receiving location.

In contrast to the message system, with on-line communications students can "talk" with one another directly and get immediate responses. For example, students in one computer group in Homer, Alaska, wanted up-to-the-minute news on the famous annual Alaskan Iditarod dog-mushers race, so they called up the on-line network on the computer, typed in a password, then typed their questions. Their answers appeared immediately on their monitor screen. Students then asked additional questions and carried on a conversation via computer telecommunications. They were thrilled when they realized that another person some distance away at the Iditarod Information Center was reading their message and responding directly to them.

Telecommunications systems are also in use in remote geographic areas with students who are unable to go to school because of vast distances. An instructor sends educational material to the student via telecommunications; the student works on it and sends back responses. Courses of study become very individualized, and students can progress at their own rate of speed. This system allows students to take courses that otherwise would be totally unavailable.

Another important use of telecommunications in education is research. With a computer link-up, students can search databases (computerized information storage systems) using key words, and can locate information on their topic or identify additional sources of information. This process, however, can be expensive and requires knowledge of search logic strategies. These searches can best be done by media specialists, but software is available to train students in on-line database searching. One such software program, *The Information Connection* by Grolier, demonstrates how a fictitious database search operation might take place. A tutorial leads students through the process of searching an encyclopedia database to find information on a basic research question.

To use the bulletin board system or the database search system, both the message sender and receiver must install a direct telephone line to the computer area; they also must purchase a modem to be connected with the microcomputer. The modem is a device that translates information (digital data) from the computer into analog tones that can be transmitted over telephone lines. A modem on the receiving end then reverses the translation, and the receiver answers the message. Communications software is necessary to use the bulletin board system, but it can be purchased in local computer stores for reasonable costs. For a local bulletin board system that uses local telephone lines, there is generally no charge. However, long-distance calls to commercial information systems increase telephone costs and incur connect time charges. The longer the connect time, the more expensive the costs; thus, efficient database search strategies are essential. National databases feature up-to-date information from stock and weather reports to medical information and encyclopedia entries.

Computer Labs versus Computers in the Classroom

Where should computers be placed in school settings? Opinions vary, but the answers all refer to the intended use of the computers. Some school programs emphasize computer assisted instruction (drill and practice programs) while others insist on having the computer used as a tool for learning in all areas of the curriculum. Word processing is one such tool that can maximize learning in all areas.

While students can learn word processing on a computer in the classroom, time constraints and number of students limit time available to practice. In addition, instruction in computer use is often limited to those teachers who are interested in using computers in the classroom. In a lab setting, students can work on a rotating schedule basis and acquire the necessary practice time for mastering keyboarding and word processing skills. In addition, the lab set-up, which also provides for greater computer security, could be available before school, during lunch, and after school for other enrichment activities. Trained personnel, though, are often not available to organize and manage a computer lab, and staff allocations may not include such a position.

Another alternative is to gather the computers in one area (the media center or library) for a specified period of time and train students on software programs, then disperse the computers back to the classrooms for follow-up practice. This method raises the level of students' understanding of computers and generally increases their enthusiasm for computers in the school.

Again, computer placement in schools really depends on the philosophy and objectives selected by the particular school.

Resources

Computer Software for Writing Activities

This resource section lists software in the following categories:

1. Keyboarding/Typing Tutorials
2. Word Processing Programs
3. Prewriting Helpers, Planners, Organizers
4. Postwriting Checkers and Analyzers
5. Spelling Checkers
6. Specific Writing Activities
7. Special Purpose Software

Software is listed in alphabetic order. A Publisher Directory, found after Chapter 12, lists publisher addresses.

1. Keyboarding/Typing Tutorials

Keyboarding simply means typing on a computer. Desirable features for keyboarding or typing tutorials include: clear, user friendly directions; graphics which show correct finger positions on keyboard; lessons and practice activities that increase in difficulty, focusing first on groups of letters, then words, then paragraphs; program controls in practice exercises that won't let the student continue until the correct key is typed; timed practice tests with correcting allowed; and a management system that tracks student speed and accuracy in typing. Game format tutorials, designed to increase speed, sometimes actually encourage hunt-and-peck typing rather than good keyboarding skills.

One distinct disadvantage of keyboarding tutorials is that students lose interest after a period of time. One way to avoid this is to have a variety of programs available and alternate their use. Since most keyboarding programs let you control the lesson level, you can alternate software with relative ease.

Mastertype
> Scarborough Systems, Inc.
> Available for Apple II, IBM PC and PCjr, Commodore 64, Atari
> Designed for ages 7 to adult

This game format typing program has sound, pacing, and allows change of speed as students master letters. The lessons provide practice in single letters, triple letters, groupings of unrelated words, and sentences. The computer tells you your speed after each practice. This program does not let you correct errors as you go along and it does not provide practice on paragraphs. Player must type letters or words before they get blown up.

MECC Keyboarding Primer
MECC Keyboarding Master
> MECC
> Available for Apple IIe and IIc
> Designed for grades 4 through 9

The *Primer* teaches correct fingering positions and provides practice exercises for increasing speed. The *Master* is a collection of games and drills designed to improve speed and accuracy of keyboarding skills. Both programs have classroom management features that keep records of student progress.

Microtype, The Wonderful World of PAWS
> South-Western Publishing Co.
> Available for Apple II and Commodore computers
> Designed for elementary grades

PAWS uses graphics to show keyboard and fingering positions for letters on the keyboard. It tracks speed and accuracy, keeps score, and prints out score results. It also has a sound on/off option. On practice sections, the program won't allow the student to continue after an error is made, but requires that the student type the correct key before moving on. Errors are ignored on the open paragraph section, thus giving reliable accuracy and speed results.

Microzine "Keyboarding"
> Scholastic, Inc.
> Available for Apple II computers
> Designed for grades 3 through 8

Displays graphic keyboard and highlights keys that would be typed from home row position. Shows fingering positions on keyboard and uses a bouncing ball technique to train students to use the home row keys. Once students master the home row keys, they can move on to practice on the keyboard "reaches". The program provides three levels of difficulty and several motivational games.

Stickybear Typing
> Weekly Reader Family Software
> Available for Apple II computers
> Designed for grades 4 and up

Stickybear Typing uses arcade type games to sharpen keyboarding skills.

Type-Hype
> Comp-Unique
> Available for Apple II computers
> Designed for grades 4 through 9

Type-Hype features twenty sequential keyboarding lessons with graphics that show keyboard and hand positions. The program will not allow errors, but will wait until the student types the correct key before it will go on. Students may practice with letter groups or words in a paragraph.

Typing is a Ball, Charlie Brown
    Random House
    Available for Apple II computers
    Designed for grades 3 and up
More practice on keyboarding. This program features selected key practice and speed option using games that feature the Peanuts gang.

Typing Tutor III and Letter Invaders
    Microsoft Corp.
    Available for Apple II computers
    Designed for elementary through adult
This program provides practice on single letters, random nonsense words, and regular words. It reports error and speed results after each drill. *Letter Invaders* requires players to blast letters off the screen before the time limit is up.

2. Word Processing Programs

Consider the following factors when choosing a word processing software program: ease of learning and using; use of editing, saving, and printing; availability of tutorial (on disk or in manual); availability of support materials; reasonable cost; availability of special features (underlining, bold type, large type option); and the ability to interface with other programs such as spelling checkers and writing analyzers.

Most word processing programs work best with two disk drives, although they will work adequately with one. Most word processing programs require eighty column cards for Apple computers and most will not work on Apple II + computers.

AppleWorks
    Apple Computer
    Available for Apple II computers
    Designed for high school students and adults
AppleWorks uses the ProDOS operating system, which speeds up text file management. It is an integrated wordprocessor-database-spreadsheet program that is most useful for older students and adults. It is also among the more expensive programs but it is also more powerful. A spelling dictionary is available for correcting errors.

Apple Writer II
    Apple Computer
    Available for Apple II computers
    Designed for high school students and adults
Apple Writer II is also among the more powerful, more expensive, and more difficult to learn word processing programs. The trade-off is that it has more capabilities than the simpler word processors and could be used with older students who may want more sophisticated writing features.

Bank Street Writer
    Broderbund Software
    Available for Apple II and IBM PC/PCjr
    Designed for grades 4 and above
A disk tutorial provides initial instruction in how to use this menu driven word processing program. Both 40 and 80 column display are available as well as underlining and boldfacing capabilities. Difficulties in using early editions of this program have been corrected. This program works with the *Bank Street Speller*.

Bank Street Writer III, School Edition
Scholastic, Inc.
Available for Apple II, IBM, Commodore, and Atari
Designed for grades 4 and above

The Scholastic edition of *Bank Street Writer* provides a loose-leaf notebook that includes a Student Guide, Student Activities, and a Teacher's Guide. BSW III has an integrated, 60,000 word spelling checker; a 50,000 on-line thesaurus; and a 20, 40, or 80 column option. This version requires 128K of memory. Earlier BSW versions require 64K of memory.

FrEd Writer
CUE Softswap Project
Available for Apple II computers
Designed for grades 3 to 12

This public domain word processing program is similar in difficulty to *Apple-works*. It does feature a teacher prompt capability which walks students step-by-step through a writing assignment. A manual is on the disk and can be printed out for reference. It uses direct commands for writing functions (loading, saving, printing) rather than an on-screen menu. On-screen tutorials and reference lists are accessible at any time in the writing process. It is available at very low cost from the CUE Softswap Project and may be copied without charge.

Magic Slate
Sunburst Communications
Available for Apple II computers
Designed for grades two to adult

Magic Slate offers three type sizes (20, 40, and 80 column) which makes it a desirable program for use with younger children. It has a three level format that provides additional writing features for older students.

MECC Writer
MECC
Available for Apple II computers
Designed for grades 4 to 12

MECC Writer does not have an on-screen menu but uses direct computer commands using the control key to move between writing tasks (writing, saving, loading, printing). For students familiar with word processing, this saves some time. *MECC Writer* works best with two disk drives and also works with several writing analyzer programs: *MECC Editor*, *MECC Ghost Writer*, and *MECC Speller*. These programs provide valuable assistance to students and make this series well worth purchasing. School districts that have licensing agreements with MECC may copy these programs for their own in-district use.

Milliken Word Processor
Milliken
Available for Apple II computers
Designed for grades 3 and up

This easy-to-use program features on-screen graphic menus to show the basic word processing commands needed to run the program. It also displays the final page format of the writing sample on-screen, thus enabling users to make format changes before the final print-out. This program works with *The Writing Workshop: PreWriting Module* and *The Writing Workshop: Post Writing Module*.

The Writer's Assistant
Brittanica Computer Based Learning
Available for Apple II computers
Designed for grades four and above

The Writer's Assistant is a word processing program which may be used by both students and teachers, but it is not totally user friendly and you will need to refer to the accompanying manual to get started. Help screens are available in three levels of difficulty; novice, intermediate, and expert.

3. Prewriting Helpers, Planners, Organizers

Prewriting helpers feature such activities as brain-storming, list-making, and other methods of generating ideas. They encourage students to plan before they begin to write.

Alaska Writer
　Yukon Koyukuk School District
　Nenana, Alaska
　Available for Apple IIe
　Designed for grades 4 and above

Alaska Writer is not a word processing program, but rather a series of user friendly activities designed to assist the writer in identifying subjects to write about, organizing information on the subjects, and finally analyzing writing samples for common errors. It is designed to be used with word processing programs that use DOS 3.3 text files (for example, *Bank Street Writer*).

"The Idea Bubbler," the first component of *Alaska Writer*, consists of three activities that help writers explore a topic: List Maker, The Questioner, and Fact Collector.

"The Essay Writer" has seven activities that help organize ideas for writing: Grouping Ideas, Making Comparisons, Ordering Events According to Time, Finding Contrasts, Writing an Essay, Telling a Story, and Working on One Paragraph.

After writers use these sets of activities and get a print-out of their notes, they switch to a word processing program to compose their story, essay, or report. Next, writers return to *Alaska Writer* and use "Analyzing Writing" to check drafts for accuracy, punctuation, grammar, and problem words (homonyms, words with apostrophes, common spelling substitution errors). One interesting activity, Compute Reading Level, analyzes word length and sentence length to determine whether writers might need sentence combining activities or vocabulary substitution activities. The "Analyzing Writing" component looks only at mechanical elements in writing—the content must still be checked and evaluated by a teacher or other reader.

A final selection of activities (Story Starters, Story Middles, and Letter Writing) provides suggestions for writers who are at a loss for ideas.

Alaska Writer is available at reasonable cost through the Yukon Koyukuk School District, APEL Project.

First Draft
　Scholastic, Inc.
　Available for Apple II, IBM PC/PCjr
　Designed for grades 6 to 12

This helper features step-by-step lesson plans that teach outlining, brainstorming, and other prewriting activities. The program has an on-screen help menu. *First Draft* can be used to prepare essays, stories, reports, or research papers.

MILLIKEN: The Writing Workshop, "Prewriting Module"
　Milliken
　Available for Apple II computers
　Designed for grades 3 through 10

The "Prewriting Module" assists students in planning using Brainstorming, Nutshelling, and Branching options. Nutshelling asks simplistic questions (prompts) related to types of writing: explanatory, persuasive, descriptive, letter, and story. Brainstorming asks you to list words on a topic and then to group them in categories. Branching asks you to fill in a title or topic, then two to four short main ideas, and at least ten short detail phrases about the topic. These ideas can be used as a starting point for writing assignments. *The Milliken Word Processor*, described earlier, provides the framework for entering, editing, and printing the text of the writing assignment.

QUILL
  DCH Software
  Available for Apple II computers
  Designed for grades 4 and above
This program, essentially a limited word processing system, views writing as a process and features four options to support this concept. The program is not user friendly and requires frequent reference to the manual for assistance.

  "The Library" stores writing and allows students to retrieve and revise previously written work.

  "The Mailbag" allows students to write messages to each other. Essentially it is an in-class electronic bulletin board.

  "The Writer's Assistant" is the word processing option.

  The user's manual provides excellent suggestions for computer writing activities.

Writer's Helper
  Conduit
  Available for Apple II computers and IBM PC
  Designed for grades 8 through 12
This planner helps students brainstorm and organize ideas for writing. It features twenty-two mini programs to help students practice prewriting and writing skills.

4. Postwriting Checkers and Analyzers
MECC Editor
  MECC
  Available for Apple II computers
  Designed for grades 6 through 12
MECC Editor is a series of five activities that focus on improving writing skills by analyzing writing samples created on *MECC Writer*, *Applewriter II*, or *Appleworks*.

  "Analyze Prose" searches the writing sample for specific errors in style, usage, and mechanics. For example, it identifies verb usage errors, punctuation and capitalization errors, and six categories of vocabulary choice errors (such as vague, overused, slang, and redundant).

  "Picture Paragraphs" displays sentences graphically and enables students to look for variety in sentence length and to identify run-on sentences and fragments.

  "Print Reports" prints out all information identified in the previous two activities.

MILLIKEN: The Writing Workshop, "Postwriting Module"
  Milliken
  Available for Apple II computers
  Designed for grades 3 through 10
The "Postwriting Module" features six disks with three basic activities.

  "Proofreader" allows a peer or teacher to read a writing sample and to insert comments at relevant points. It also suggests problems that should be evaluated, but expects students to find their own pronoun and verb errors.

"Mechanics Checker" focuses on word choice (tired or tricky words), pronoun problems, overuse of "and" and sentence fragments. This checker is quite limited in focus.

"Spelling Checker" scans the writing sample and identifies possible spelling errors (those words not on the computer spelling list) and enables the writer to correct them.

Ghost Writer
 MECC
 Available for Apple II computer (64K minimum)
 Designed for grades 6 through adult
This writing analyzer checks for sentence length, repetitive words, passive verbs, and reading level of the writing sample. If the reading level is low, the program gives suggestions for effective changes. Two versions (DOS 3.3 and ProDOS) allow this program to be used with most word processing programs. Students will be able to identify their most common errors and will be able to correct them using suggestions from the program. Students tend to watch for those specific errors in later writing samples.

5. Spelling Checkers
A spelling checker scans through a piece of writing and identifies words that do not match the checker's special dictionary. The non-matched word will be identified and a prompt will ask if you want to change the spelling. In some cases, the identified word is an uncommon word that is not included in the dictionary, but in most cases, the word is either typed or spelled incorrectly. Spelling checkers also identify homonyms and give definitions or samples of correct usage so that you may identify incorrect usage.

Bank Street Speller
 Broderbund
 Available for Apple II computers
Designed to work with the *Bank Street Writer*, this checker contains over 31,000 words in its dictionary. It scans and highlights possible errors and suggests correct spellings. You may add any specialized vocabulary, such as spelling lists or scientific terms, to the dictionary.

MECC Speller
 MECC
 Available for Apple II computers
 Designed for grades six and above
This spelling checker analyzes writing samples created on *MECC Writer, Appleworks, and Applewriter II*. The main spelling dictionary contains over 10,000 words, but the teacher can also add up to one hundred more words. If the same word is misspelled a number of times, the Find and Replace command can correct all of the errors at the same time. *MECC Speller* checks for probable misspelled words (those not found in the dictionary file) or confusing words which sound alike and are often confused. This program is somewhat awkward to use since you must save the typed material on a data disk, then boot the checker, then reload the typed material.

Sensible Speller
 Sensible Software
 Available for most computers
 Designed for older students, but could be used with elementary students with teacher assistance.

Sensible Speller comes in two versions so that it may be used with most processing programs. Check to see that you get the version compatible with your computer and word processing program. This checker uses an 80,000 word dictionary and also enables you to add specialized words of your own.

6. Specific Writing Activities

MECC Write Start
   MECC
   Available for Apple II computers
   Designed for grades 6 to 12
This user friendly program consists of ten separate introductory level word processing activities. Students can contribute segments to an existing story, or create a new one of their own. One activity helps students set up a database for book reports, while another helps students create their own ad lib type poems. Other activities emphasize sentence expansion, brainstorming, song-writing, and stream-of-consciousness writing.

Narrative Writing Tool: Writing Skill Package
   InterLearn
   Available for Apple II computers
   Designed for grades 3 to 12
"Science Fiction Story Maker", "Treasure Hunt", "Animal Dialog", and "A Fairy Tale" assist students in writing various kinds of narratives.

Super Scoop
   COMPress
   Available for Apple computers
   Designed for grades 9 and above
This high interest program simulates a news story in the works. A friendly caller gives a news tip and the news reporter then tracks down facts in order to write the story. The reporter must evaluate information sources and choose pertinent information to write a 500–700 word news article. Students must take notes during the computer interviews and use these notes to write the article.

Show Time
   MECC
   Available for Apple II computers
   Designed for grades 6 to 9
This program encourages students to write short plays by providing a choice of characters, backdrops, props, and music. *MECC Writer* is built into the program so students may write, revise, and print their scripts.

Story Maker
   Sierra-On-Line, Inc.
   Available for Apple II computers
   Designed for grades 2 to 6
Students create a picture using a joystick, Koala Pad, or mouse, then write a story about the picture. Or they may select a pre-existing graphic and develop a story about it.

Story Tree
   Scholastic, Inc.
   Available for Apple II, IBM, and Commodore computers
   Designed for grades 2 to 6

Story Tree helps students write different endings for interactive stories. Students read a story on-screen, then choose what might happen next. Stories can be printed out and compared with others written on the same topic.

That's My Story
Learning Well
Available for Apple II computers
Designed for grades 2 to 8

This program features story starters at different grade levels. Students begin writing, then choose from two story paths. After each segment, two new story paths help the student continue writing. Teachers or students can create additional story starters.

View and Write
MECC
Videocasette
Designed for grades 4 to 6

The objective of this videocasette is to show the different stages of the composing process using a computer. Short vignettes provide the discussion stimulus for the two writers portrayed. The writers then go through planning, writing with some collaboration, checking, and printing. Worksheets assist students in identifying sensory details to add to descriptive and narrative writing.

Writing Adventure
DLM
Available for Apple II computers
Designed for grades 4 to 8

Students use graphic story starters to develop a narrative. The program provides prompts to help students identify the structure of their story. The second disk features a word processing program that students can use to write, revise, and print their stories. The program also flags writing and spelling errors.

Writing a Character Sketch
MECC
Available for Apple II computers
Designed for grades 9 to 12

This user-friendly, interactive tutorial assists students in gathering raw data for writing first drafts of character sketches. Students can write about a fictional character, an historical character, or someone they know. The program enables students to list specific facts, details, anecdotes, or examples related to the character's external characteristics and behavior mannerisms.

A second part of the program, *Point of View*, shows how a character sketch can be written from three different points of view.

Writing a Narrative
MECC
Available for Apple II computers
Designed for grades 7 to 12

Using this program, students try brainstorming techniques to gather information for a narrative, then write and revise their own work based on responses from student readers. "Catch the Moments", one activity in the program, helps students develop a narrative based on an event in their own lives. "Point of View" emphasizes writing from the first and third point of view.

Writing an Opinion Paper
MECC

Available for Apple II computers
Designed for grades 10 to 12

After initial practice in making distinctions between fact and opinion, this program assists the writer in identifying what he/she already knows about the topic. Next, it asks the writer to narrow the topic by restating it in question format, and finally it asks for the writer's opinions and the reasons for the opinions. Students then use these notes to write a first draft of an opinion essay.

7. Special Purpose Software

Special purpose software encourages students to explore the graphics capabilities of computers.

Certificate Maker
Springboard Software, Inc.
Available for Apple II computers
Designed for all ages

This easy-to-use program enables you to create personalized certificates from over 200 humorous and serious samples.

Create with Garfield
DLM
Available for Apple II and Commodore computers
Designed for grades 1 to 9

Using a variety of Garfield graphics, students can create cartoons, posters, and labels with either a Garfield quote or an original quote. Kids love this one!

The Newsroom
Springboard Software, Inc.
Available for Apple II, IBM PC, IBM PCjr, Commodore
Designed for grades 6 and above

The Newsroom enables students, teachers, and others to create newsletters, brochures, banners, and flyers using graphics and variations in size and style of text. It is not totally user friendly and requires a fair amount of practice before it can be used with ease. It allows the editor to create segments of text or graphics and then to place those segments in a desired order. It eliminates the need to cut and paste individual blocks of text and makes newspaper production a faster process.

The Print Shop
The Print Shop Graphics Library 1, 2, and 3
The Print Shop Companion
Broderbund Software
Available for Apple II, Commodore, Atari

This series of software programs is very user friendly and generates high levels of enthusiasm on the part of all students and teachers who use it. The Print Shop enables you to make personalized greeting cards, invitations, letterheads, stationery, signs, and banners. The program features eight type styles and dozens of graphics, border designs, patterns, and a graphic editor that allows you to create your own designs.

The Graphics Library disks include 120 additional designs for holidays, special occasions, and special needs.

The Print Shop Companion allows you to make specialized calendars for your school that feature special events, birthdays, target dates, or whatever you choose to emphasize. This software also enables you to design monograms, T-shirt designs, and crazy creatures.

Walt Disney Comic Strip Maker
   Bantam
   Available for Apple II, Commodore
   Designed for grades 2 to 12
Students can create personalized comic strips, cards, or posters featuring characters from the Disney gang. Students can mix and match 180 graphics with backgrounds, props, and word balloons. Results may be printed in black and white or in color depending on your printer capabilities.

CHAPTER 5

Let Them Write Creatively

Students of all ages enjoy writing accounts of personal experiences and creating narratives of imaginary events. Television, radio, and a wide variety of reading materials influence students as they think and write. They like reading, watching, and writing fantasy, adventure, and science fiction because they have unlimited ideas and their imaginations can run free. They especially enjoy sharing these personal and creative narratives through oral reading, but also through display on bulletin boards or bound in student writing collections.

Creative writing (or expressive writing, as it is sometimes called) is important for all students. As students increase in writing fluency, they gain confidence in writing skills and in themselves. This fluency and confidence provides a strong basis for pleasure, practical, and academic writing.

Almost anything becomes a springboard for creative writing: a word, a title, a picture, a quote, a personal experience, a memory. The list could go on endlessly. The more students contribute to the list of writing possibilities, the more involved they will be with the whole writing process. In using the following suggested activities, remember to allow large doses of prewriting, brainstorming, and discussion time. Also provide frequent opportunities for students to share the results of their writing efforts.

Specific instructional objectives include the following:

1. Increasing fluency in writing;
2. Increasing use of descriptive detail;
3. Developing clear sequences of events; and
4. Increasing use of emotional responses.

Note: Consider using a word processing program for many of the following activities. For example, students could each have their own word processing data disk and could set up a journal on it. Each entry could be placed in a different file on the data disk, with new thoughts being added to the files at any time. Print out files for editing or final publication.

If only one computer is available in the classroom, students can collaborate more on writing activities. The possibilities for using a computer for writing purposes are almost unlimited. For more information on this topic, review Chapter 4, "Use the Computer."

Journals

Objective   To encourage personal writing through the use of a journal.

Materials   Looseleaf notebook, notebook dividers, notebook filler paper, copies of "Journal Topics".

Procedure
1. Ask students to purchase a looseleaf notebook, dividers, and paper. Explain that each student will start a journal that will be used *at least* twice a week for writing on different topics of personal importance. Each topic will have its own section in the notebook.
2. Have students label each divider with a topic category (see Journal Topics). Use fewer categories with younger writers, then add categories as needed. For older writers, use all categories. Have students keep all blank filler paper in back of notebook. Paper can be added to category sections when needed.
3. Give students a list of the categories and related questions. Ask them to complete the personal identification information for the front of the journal. Explain that writing in notebooks will not be graded but that it may be reviewed occasionally to be sure that students are writing.
4. Have students decide on a category to write on for the first journal session. (At first, schedule specific journal writing sessions. Later, as students become more familiar with the process, let them schedule their own writing time. Encourage students to write in journals as often as possible.)
5. Encourage students to use all their senses as they write on their topic.
   What sights do you see?
   What sounds do you hear?
   What smells do you smell?
   What textures do you feel?
   What tastes do you taste?
6. Encourage students to include emotional responses in their writing.
   How to you feel when _____ ?
7. Provide some time for students to share their writing with small groups.
8. Have students keep a log of entries (like a table of contents) in which they record the date and kind of entry. Keep this in the front of the journal.

Note: Too often, student journal writing falls into a tedious accounting of "what I did today." While this is occasionally acceptable, it is more important to have students think, review, and compare broader ranges of experiences. As they remember and sort ideas, reactions, and feelings about these suggested categories, they will uncover raw material for journal writing and for later writing activities. Duplicate this list of Journal Topics so that students may refer to it whenever they write. Encourage students to add other topics or questions to the list.

Extension   Some library books are written from the first person point of view. Have students identify some of these books and notice how the main character talks about his feelings and attitudes. Fill out the Character Description Worksheet, found later in this chapter, for the main character.

JOURNAL TOPICS

1. *About Myself*
   Who Am I?
      What do I look like?
      What do I like? Why?
      What do I dislike? Why?
      What do I like best about myself?
      What do I like least about myself?
      What things do I do well?
      What things are difficult for me?
      What are my good qualities?
      What are my weaknesses?

   _____

   _____

   My Feelings: What causes this feeling? What do I do when I have this feeling?
      Fear
      Anger
      Sadness
      Happiness
      Jealousy
      Pride
      Worry
      Hate
      Love
      Hope
      Sympathy
   Memories: What is the memory? How did I feel then? How do I feel about it now?
      My Earliest Memory
      My Happiest Memory
      My Saddest Memory
      My Angriest Memory
      My Biggest Decision
      My Biggest Mistake
      My First Punishment at Home
      My First Punishment at School
      When I Forgot
      When I Was Afraid
      My Favorite Childhood Toy
      My Baby Pictures
      Stories My Parents Tell about My Childhood
   Important Events
      First Day of School, Best Year in School, Favorite Teacher
      Birthdays
      Christmases
      Holidays
      Vacations
      Others?
   Leisure Time Activities
      My Hobbies
      My Favorite Activity

My Favorite TV Program, Movie, Book
My Favorite Sport
What Do I Do When I Am Alone?
Dreams: What dreams do I remember?
My Future
What I Will Be Like in the Future
My Hopes for the Future
My Education Plans
My Career Plans

2. *About My Family*
Who Are My Family Members?
What do they look like?
What kind of persons are they? Give examples of things they do that show what kind of persons they are.
What Lessons Have I Learned from Family Members?
Who Am I Most Like?
Where Were My Ancestors from?
Stories about My Parents When They Were Young

3. *About Others*
Important People in My Life and Why They Are Important
My Best Friend and Why I Like Him/Her
My Enemy
People I Admire
People Who Have Helped Me
What Qualities Must a Person Have to Earn My Respect?

Picture File

Objective   To make a picture file for use in writing activities.

Materials   Magazines; old calendars; scissors; posterboard, oaktag (9″ × 12″), or manila folders; stapler or scotch tape.

Procedure   1. Ask students to bring old magazines and calendars from home. Have them look through the magazines for pictures of interesting characters, settings, and situations to put in the picture file.
2. Have students cut pictures out. (You may want to straighten edges with a paper cutter.) Staple or tape pictures to posterboard or oaktag. Keep the size of posterboard or oaktag consistent so that the pictures can be filed easily.
3. Put the mounted pictures in a brightly decorated box in the classroom. Use larger pieces of oaktag as dividers, or use manila folders.
4. Sort the pictures as the collection grows. Ask the students to help you categorize the pictures. They can suggest the labels for the manila folder. Some labels might be Undersea Pictures, Cowboys, Vacations, Hobbies, Animals, Adventures, Dangerous Situations, Interesting Characters, Settings.
5. Use the pictures in the following brainstorming and writing sessions.

Extension   Continue to collect pictures throughout the year. Bring lots of magazines into the classroom. Students can look for pictures (and *read* the magazines) during free time.

Resources Several companies publish sets of photographs or illustrations that are excellent for use in brainstorming and writing activities.

Photogrammar
   DLM Teaching Resources
   240 color photo cards

All-Purpose Photo Library
   Sets 1 and 2
   DLM Teaching Resources

WH-Questions, 3 levels
   DLM Teaching Resources

Write Away (6–8)
   Joy Littell
   McDougal, Littell & Co.

Write to Spell
   Judith Schifferle
   Curriculum Associates

What's Wrong Here?
   DLM Teaching Resources

Scene I, Scene II, Scene III

Objective To write about a sequence of events.

Materials Newspaper or magazine pictures that show characters involved in an activity or problem situation, *Scene I, Scene II, Scene III* Format.

Procedure
1. Choose one picture to show to the students. Ask students to identify the main characters and the setting. Write this information on the board. Decide what must have happened *before* the picture was taken. Write students' comments on the board under the title "Scene I."
2. Discuss what was happening at the time the picture was taken. Write comments on the board under "Scene II."
3. Discuss what the *outcome* of the situation might be. Write comments under "Scene III."
4. Ask students to write a story based on the information discussed using the "Scene I," "Scene II," and "Scene III" format.
5. Or, have students choose a new picture and write a story using the "Scene I," "Scene II," and "Scene III" format.
6. Have students read their stories aloud.
7. Allow students to illustrate their stories.

Extension 1 Have students illustrate their scenes on three separate transparencies. Next have students read their narrative on a tape recorder. When both transparencies and tape are finished, let the students put on a transparency-tape show for their own classmates or another class.

Extension 2   Use this Scene 1, Scene 2, Scene 3 format to help students develop story outlines for longer stories. Encourage them to plan all parts of their story before they actually begin to write.

Scene I, Scene II, Scene III Format

Characters   Character Description and Role

_____   _____

                                                    _____

_____   _____

                                                    _____

_____   _____

                                                    _____

_____   _____

Setting   Setting Description

_____   _____

Scene I: _____

_____

_____

_____

Scene II: _____

_____

_____

Scene III: _____

_____

_____

Comic Strips

Objective   To sequence and write about a comic strip.

Materials   A collection of comic strips taken from newspapers or from comic books, writing paper, index cards or construction paper.

Procedure   1. Cut comic strips apart into individual frames and place each strip in an envelope.
2. Have each student choose an envelope, read the separate frames, then arrange the frames in the correct order. Paste, tape, or staple each frame to a separate sheet of paper.
3. Have students write a narration of the action in each frame of the comic strip underneath the individual frame.
4. Bind pages together in booklet form.
5. Or, put each frame on a separate 4″ × 6″ index card. Have the student write the narration of each frame underneath the comic frame.
6. Mix up cards and give to another student to read and arrange in correct order.

Extension   Remove "speech" part of cartoon. Have students write in new discussion between the characters in the comic strip.

Resources   See Chapter 4, "Use the Computer" for descriptions of the following computer software: *Create with Garfield* and *Walt Disney Comic Strip Maker*.

Storyboard Sequences

Objective   To recall a sequence of events.

Materials   Blank storyboard (see Figure 5-1), crayons, colored pencils, short story or play.

Procedure   1. Read a play or short story to a group of students. Have students retell the story orally, emphasizing the sequence of events.
2. Give each student a blank storyboard. Ask students to draw the main events of the story in the separate boxes, then to write a description of the action for each picture.
3. Have students read story sequences aloud to class members. Read the story a second time so that students can check their storyboard sequence.
4. Give students an extra blank storyboard and ask them to write and draw their own sequence story.
5. Have students cut each segment of their storyboards and pictures apart. Then switch stories between pairs of students. See whether the second student can match the picture with the matching sentences, then arrange pictures and sentences in correct sequence.

Extension   Illustrate a sequence from science class:
Stages of Plant Growth
How Volcanoes Are Formed
Complete Circuits
Phases of the Moon

*Name*_____*Title*_____*Page*_____

FIGURE 5-1 Storyboard

Slide-Tape Show

Objective   To develop a slide-tape show.

Materials   A selection of library books, storyboards (slide size frames), Kodak write-on slides, projection marking pens.

Procedure
1. Explain that students are going to make their own slide-tape show based on a children's storybook. (Later, students may want to use this format to do a book report on their own reading.) Plan to take several weeks to a month for this project depending on class size. Emphasize the need to have a clear plan and script completed before the slides and tapes are produced.
2. Let students choose a book for making a slide-tape show. The book may be a picture storybook on an easier reading level in which there is a clear sequence of events, or it may be grade-level reading material.
3. Ask students to read books and note sequence of events. For each main event, have the student draw one picture on the storyboard, then write the narration beside it. Have them read sequence aloud to another person to see whether it makes sense and enough information is presented.
4. Give blank slides to students and let them trace or draw the sequence of events following the storyboard plan.
5. Make the audio portion of the program. Include sound effects when appropriate. Sound effects records are generally available in the school or local library. After playing some introductory music, turn the music down as the student reads the narrative. Use a clicker to indicate when the slide should be changed. You may have to do the taping session two or three times to get the music and reading in the best form.
6. Show the completed production to the whole class. Invite other classes in to see the shows.

Extension 1   *Slide Tape—How To*
Ask several students to do a slide-tape sequence on how to make a slide-tape show. Use it as an introductory lesson for other students.

Extension 2   *Transparency-Tape Show*
Use overhead transparencies for students who have difficulty drawing on the small space of the write-on slides. Follow the same procedures as above, but let students use 8″ × 10″ blank drawing paper to plan their scenes.

Resources   *Animating Films Without a Camera*
Jacques Bourgeois
Sterling Publishing Co., 1974
Simple techniques for making animated films are described in detail in this book. Designs, characters, and sequences of events are drawn directly on ordinary movie film. Photographs and line drawings clearly illustrate the process.

Film Animation as a Hobby
Andrew and Mark Hobson
Sterling Publishing Co., 1975
This book takes you step by step through the planning and shooting of a complete animated film. Lots of helpful hints are provided along the way. Photographs throughout the book illustrate the process clearly. Andrew and

Mark Hobson started making animated films while they were doing a geometry project in high school.

Moviemaking Illustrated: The Comicbook Filmbook
   James Morrow and Murray Suid
   Hayden Book Co., 1973
This is a book about how films work. Comicbook style is used to explain different film techniques such as speed changes and picture size enlargement or reduction. This book would be interesting for older students who might wish to learn special effects and other filming techniques.

Classroom Projects Using Photography
   Vol. I, Vol. II
   Eastman Kodak Company, 1975
Many of the activities in these two manuals involve writing in some form: making notes on a problem, writing captions, writing out directions, writing dialogues, and others. Each activity is illustrated with color photographs.

Storybooks

Objective   To write original children's storybooks. (Sequence of events.)

Materials   Many samples of children's storybooks, drawing papers, crayons, or magic markers. (Or use storyboard format.)

Procedure   1. Tell students that they are going to write original storybooks for younger children. Have them look over a number of storybooks to see what they contain (many pictures, a few sentences on each page, easy words to read, an interesting story).
2. Ask students to think of a story that might interest younger children. It could be a personal experience that happened to a student at a younger age; or it might be a "how to" book telling children how to make something; or it might be a poetry book.
3. Have students draw the illustrations and write the first draft of the story.
4. Go over the first draft and have the students make necessary corrections. Copy the first draft neatly by writing a few sentences under each picture, or on a separate sheet of paper.
5. Bind all the pages of the book together.
6. Go to lower grade classrooms and read the books to children.

Extension 1   Look in the library for picture books without words. Have students write the narrative for each picture. Write the final draft on slips of paper that can be clipped to the pages; or have students draw pictures to go with the narrative.

Extension 2   Have students choose a picture, or a book with words, and take it to a lower grade classroom. There they can have a younger student dictate a story about the picture or book. The older student can write the story down as the child dictates it. The younger child can then draw pictures to go with his or her story. The story and pictures can be bound in a booklet. Read completed stories to both classes.

Resources See Chapter 4, "Use the Computer" for a description of *Writing a Narrative* and word processing programs that could be used with this activity. *Bank Street Writer III* and *Magic Slate* feature 20, 40, and 80 column options. This large-type feature is especially useful when creating storybooks for younger children.

"Stories without words" can be used to emphasize story sequence and to give additional ideas for story lines.

The following stories were illustrated by Mercer Mayer.
Bubble, Bubble
    Parent's Magazine Press
Mine
    Simon and Schuster
The Great Cat Chase
    Scholastic Book Co.
Two More Moral Tales
    Four Winds Press
What Do You Do with a Kangaroo?
    Scholastic Book Co.
You're the Scaredy-cat
    Parent's Magazine Press
A Boy, a Dog, and a Frog
    Dial Press
Frog, Where Are You?
    Dial Press

John S. Goodall also illustrates stories without words.
Creepy Castle
    Atheneum
Jacko
    Harcourt Brace Jovanovich
Naughty Nancy
    Atheneum
Paddy's Evening Out
    Atheneum
Paddy Pork's Holiday
    Atheneum
The Ballooning Adventures of Paddy Pork
    Harcourt Brace & World
The Midnight Adventures of Kelly, Dot and Esmeralda
    Atheneum

Other illustrators have also published stories without words.
A Flying Saucer Full of Spaghetti
    Fernando Krahn
    Dutton

April Fools
    Fernando Krahn
    Dutton

The Self-made Snowman
    Fernando Krahn
    J.B. Lippincott Co.

Drip-drop
Donald Carrick
Macmillan

The Dirt Road
Carol and Donald Carrick
Macmillan

Autobiography

Objective   To write an illustrated autobiography.

Materials   Writing paper and drawing paper, colored pencils, crayons, magic markers.

Procedure
1. Plan to do this activity after students have written a number of entries in their journals.
2. Discuss milestones in the lives of the students.

> Past: birth, first day at school, first birthday party
> Present: life at school, life at home, friends
> Future: graduation, occupation choice, marriage, children, future plans

3. Ask students to suggest other events that affect their personal lives. Add these to the list.
4. Ask students to illustrate these events and write a narration for each event. (Each event can be a separate chapter in the autobiography and can be done on a different day.) Some students may choose to use the storyboard format. Students may choose to revise something already in their journals, or they may write totally new pieces.
5. Have students put the events in order according to their life span and make a table of contents to go along with the sequence.
6. This activity will take several weeks to complete. Encourage children to make corrections as they go along so that the task does not become overwhelming at the end.
7. After revising and editing their autobiography, the students should make a book cover for the autobiography, then bind the pages together in book form.

Extension   Creating a fictitious character, write a biography for him or her. Include past events, present circumstances, and future hopes. These biographies can be realistic or they can be imaginary and humorous. The title of the book can be a reflection of the character's name.

> Suggestions: "My Life as a Chimney Sweep"
> by Charlie Broom
> "My Life as a Star of Stage and Screen"
> by Miss Star Let
> "The Life and Times of a Female Detective"
> by Ima Spy

Other possible characters:

Ima June Bug	Cal Q. Lator
Tillie Tightwad	Cal Lifornia
Mr. G. Whizz	Luke Warm
Lala Palooza	Ben E. Fit
Ima Phoney	Tom Ato
Sam Sonite	Rose Bud
Miss Ann Thrope	Neb Raska
Ella Fant	Ida Ho
Leo Pard	Carol Lina
Ana Mul	Connie Tecut
Brock Alie	Ari Zona
Lillie Tiger	Mary Land
Ann Teak	Minnie Apolis
Cora Apple	Fran Cisco
Ella Vator	Prince Apal
May O. Naise	

Characters I

Objective To listen for character detail as a descriptive selection is read.

Materials Selections from reading material with good descriptive character detail (see suggested books with good character description); "Character Description Worksheet" on overhead transparency.

Procedure
1. Review the items on the "Character Description Worksheet" so that students will know what to listen for.
2. Read a character description and have students listen for character details.
3. Ask students to recall details after the selection has been read. Write details on the worksheet as students suggest them.
4. Read the selection again if students missed some of the details. Have students listen specifically for the information needed.
5. Have students try to visualize the character and make suggestions about information that was not included in the reading selection.
6. Have students write a short descriptive paragraph about the character. Share paragraphs by reading aloud. The students may draw a picture of the character if they wish.

Extension Have students look for descriptive detail as they read their library books. Encourage them to use the Character Description Worksheet to collect information as it appears in different places in the book. Then have them write a descriptive paragraph about the main characters. Illustrate. Display final draft of description on bulletin board to show how details can be incorporated into descriptive paragraph.

Resources *Who's Who in Children's Books: A Treasury of Familiar Characters of Childhood*
Margery Fisher
Holt, Rinehart and Winston, 1975

Character Description Worksheet

Directions: Choose one character from your current reading selection and find as much detail as you can about the main character or another character. Fill in the Character Description Worksheet as you come across new information.

1. Name of character _____

   Age clues (young, old, teenage, etc.) _____

2. Family information _____

   _____

   _____

3. Size (height, weight, shape) _____

   _____

4. Hairstyle and color _____

5. Eyes (color, size, shape) _____

6. Style of dress (clothing) _____

   _____

   _____

7. Speech characteristics (accent, stutter, loud voice, etc.) _____

   _____

   _____

8. Manner of movement (graceful, clumsy, awkward, etc.) _____

   _____

   _____

9. Personality clues (friendly, mean, kind, etc.) — give an example

   _____

10. Hopes, desires, dreams _____

   _____

11. Occupation and work habits (always on time, hard worker, etc.)

   _____

   _____

12. Anything else? _____

The Mysterious Disappearance of Leon (I Mean Noel)
Ellen Raskin
Dutton, 1971

The Tatooed Potato and Other Clues
Ellen Raskin
Dutton, 1975

Harriet the Spy
Louise Fitzhugh
Harper & Row, 1964

Sounder
William H. Armstrong
Harper & Row, 1969

The Witch of Blackbird Pond
Elizabeth G. Speare
Houghton Mifflin, 1958

Tuck Everlasting
Natalie Babbitt
Farrar, Straus & Co., 1975

The Man Who Was Magic
Paul Gallico
Doubleday, 1966

My Side of the Mountain
Jean George
Dutton, 1959

Characters II

Objective To write a character description.

Materials A collection of character pictures gathered from magazines; "Character Description Worksheet."

Procedure 1. Ask students to cut out pictures of different people from magazines. Encourage students to look for a wide variety of facial expressions. News magazines (*Time, Newsweek*) and newspapers are a good source of candid photographs. *National Geographic* magazine and *Psychology Today* also have good character pictures. This could be done as a homework assignment or an in-class activity.
2. Review the information required on the character worksheet after a large number of pictures have been collected.
3. Choosing one picture, talk about the prominent features of the pictured character. Write students' comments on the worksheet (on chalkboard or overhead transparency).
4. Discuss other characteristics of the character that cannot be seen in the picture (for example, personality clues, mannerisms, speech patterns). Have students suggest additional information about the character (for example, family structure, home, location of home, occupation).

5. Ask students to write a short descriptive paragraph about the character, using some of the information listed on the character worksheet.
6. Have students read their descriptions to the rest of the class. Compare the ways that different students wrote their descriptions.
7. Do this activity with different pictures on other days. Continue to have students write a short paragraph after each brainstorming session.

Extension   After many brainstorming sessions, let each student choose a picture and do a character description on his or her own. Perhaps the students could involve the character in a sequence of events or a problem. Share descriptions with classmates.

Character Moods

Objective   To make a collage showing character moods.

Materials   Magazines, scissors, paste, construction paper.

Procedure   1. Have students collect old magazines at home and bring them into school. Again, encourage them to look for a wide variety of emotional response.
2. Ask students to look through the magazines for pictures of characters showing different facial expressions and cut them out.
3. Categorize these pictures according to the expression: Happy, Sad, Angry, Worried, Surprised, Fearful, etc. Make a collage for each expression.
4. Take one completed collage at a time and ask students to suggest words that describe this mood. List clues that helped determine the mood of each picture.
   Worried: eyebrows knit, frown, thoughtful look, intent
   Surprised: eyes open wide, mouth open wide
   Encourage the use of a thesaurus. Ask students to use suggested words in complete sentences.
5. Display the collages and word charts on the bulletin board.

Extension 1   Have students choose one character and mood, fill out a "Character Description Worksheet", then write a few paragraphs that describe the character and the reason for the mood. Display final drafts of the paragraphs with their corresponding pictures.

Extension 2   Have students role play an emotion. Have observers note what actions, mannerisms, and facial expressions aid in identifying the emotion portrayed.

First Person Point of View

Objective   To identify tone and style of books that use the first person point of view.

Materials   A collection of library books written with first person point of view. (See Resources in this activity.)

Procedure

1. Collect the suggested library books and place them in one spot in the classroom.
2. Read some beginning paragraphs of the suggested books to students. Ask them to identify the main character. (Most often the name of the character will not be given right away—so students will only be able to say, "I.") Point out that this kind of story is told from the first person point of view as if the main character is telling the story himself or herself. To point out the difference from other stories, read a few beginning paragraphs from several books that use the third person point of view.
3. Ask students to browse through the collection of first person books and select one for a book report.
4. Ask students to pay particular attention to the teller of the story. Have students complete a character worksheet (from Characters I Activity) as they read the story so they can get a complete picture of the main character.
5. Place all completed character worksheets on the bulletin board.
6. Focus on first person stories for at least a month. Ask students to identify the ages of the main characters. (They may make the observation that the majority of the stories deal with pre-teenagers and teenagers. Ask students to speculate on why that might be.) Ask students to identify any themes that might be common to the majority of the stories. Do these stories seem any more realistic than third person stories?
7. Ask the students to comment on their reactions to first person stories.

Resources   The following books are all written from the first person point of view.

The Great Brain (A series)
Jack D. Fitzgerald
Dial Press, 1967

Pinch
Larry Callen
Atlantic/Little, Brown, 1975

Sorrow's Song
Larry Callen
Atlantic/Little, Brown, 1979

The Muskrat War
Larry Callan
Atlantic/Little, Brown, 1980

My Side of the Mountain
Jean George
Dutton, 1959

My Brother Sam Is Dead
James L. Collier and Christopher Collier
Four Winds Press, 1974

Are You There God? It's Me Margaret
Judy Blume
Bradbury Press, 1970

Otherwise Known as Sheila the Great
Judy Blume
Bradbury Press, 1976

A Girl Called Al
Constance C. Greene
Viking Press, 1969

Summer of My German Soldier
   Bette Greene
   Dial Press, 1973

The King's Fifth
   Scott O'Dell
   Houghton Mifflin, 1966

Will the Real Monday Please Stand Up?
   Pamela Reynolds
   Lothrop, Lee & Shepard, 1975

Island of the Blue Dolphin
   Scott O'Dell
   Houghton Mifflin, 1960

Dorrie's Book
   Marilyn Sachs
   Doubleday, 1975

It's Like This, Cat
   Emily Neville
   Harper & Row, 1963

Berries Goodman
   Emily Neville
   Harper & Row, 1965

The Truth About Mary Rose
   Marilyn Sachs
   Doubleday, 1973

See Chapter 4, "Use the Computer", for a description of *Writing a Character Sketch*. It emphasizes point of view.

Settings I

Objective   To listen for descriptive words and phrases in setting paragraphs.

Materials   Selections from books or magazines that have good setting description, "Setting Description Worksheet".

Procedure
1. Review the items on the worksheet so that students will know what to listen for.
2. Read a setting description and have students listen for details.
3. Ask students to recall details after the selection has been read. Write details on the worksheet as students suggest them.
4. Read the selection again if students missed some of the details. Have students listen specifically for the information needed.
5. Have students try to visualize the setting and to make suggestions about information that was not included in the reading selection.
6. Have students write a short descriptive paragraph about the setting. Share paragraphs by reading aloud.

Setting Description Worksheet

Directions: Choose a setting from your current reading selection and find as much information as the book provides. Then use your imagination to visualize the rest of the details and fill those in on the worksheet. Be very specific.

1. General location: _____

2. Prominent features in the foreground (man-made or natural) size, shape, color, texture, composition, function, unusual detail, etc.

    a. _____ : _____
    _____
    _____
    _____

    b. _____ : _____
    _____
    _____
    _____

    c. _____ : _____
    _____
    _____
    _____

3. Prominent features in the background

    a. _____ : _____
    _____
    _____
    _____

    b. _____ : _____
    _____

4. Weather conditions, lighting, time of day, season, year

    _____

5. Sound effects _____

    _____

6. Smells _____

    _____

    _____

7. Textures _____

    _____

Extension 1   Have students use the Setting Description Worksheet to collect details as they read on their own. Have them write descriptive paragraphs about the settings that they have found. Ask them to illustrate their setting paragraphs.

Extension 2   Collect a group of setting pictures from magazines or calendars. Choose one picture and try to fill in the worksheet, taking suggestions from everyone in the class. When it is complete, ask students to write a short paragraph about the setting, using the information provided.

After a number of brainstorming sessions, let each student select his or her own picture and write a descriptive paragraph. Share all paragraphs by reading aloud.

Extension 3   Have students take photographs of different settings, then spend about ten minutes at the spot observing and jotting down descriptive details of the area. When this is complete, have students write a descriptive paragraph without naming the spot. Display the photographs without identifying the settings. Have each student read his or her description to the class without naming the setting. Ask classmates to identify the place from the descriptive detail given by the writer. Later, match descriptions with photographs and display on bulletin board.

Settings II

Objective   To identify sounds and smells in the environment.

Materials   Paper and pencils.

Procedure
1. Tell the class that you are going out into the neighborhood to make a list of sounds and smells in the environment.
2. Divide the class into small groups. Assign some groups to listen and write down all sounds that they hear. Ask other groups to notice different smells and write them down.
3. Return to the classroom after about fifteen minutes. List the different sounds and smells that students listed on their papers.
4. Take one sound or smell at a time and ask students to suggest and/or write sentences with more descriptive detail. Read results to class.
   Example: The sound of a truck going by.
          The huge moving van, with the red tractor and trailer, roared down the street.
          The muffler sound rumbled and echoed through the neighborhood.

Resources
Owls in the Family
Farley Mowat
Little, Brown, 1961

Julie of the Wolves
Jean Craighead George
Harper & Row, 1972

Call It Courage
Armstrong Sperry
Macmillan, 1961

The Wheel on the School
Meindert De Jong
Harper & Row, 1954

The Witch of Blackbird Pond
   Elizabeth George Speare
   Houghton Mifflin, 1958

Tuck Everlasting
   Natalie Babbitt
   Farrar Strauss & Giroux, 1975

The Man Who Was Magic
   Paul Gallico
   Doubleday, 1966

My Side of the Mountain
   Jean George
   Dutton, 1959

One-Eyed Cat
   Paula Fox
   Bradbury Press, 1984

How Do Stories Begin?

Objective   To identify various ways to begin stories.

Materials   A small collection of reading books from the library, an anthology of stories, or list of titles from previous activities.

Procedure   1. Explain to the class that you want them to notice how different stories begin. Read the beginning few paragraphs from the suggested books. After each selection, ask the students to identify the way the author began his or her story.
2. List suggestions on the board. Suggested categories might be:
      a description of setting
      a description of a character
      a description of the weather
      an action by a character
      a question to be answered
      a conversation
      a time
3. Continue reading the opening paragraphs of stories, and let the students identify the types of beginnings.
4. Ask the class to evaluate which beginnings were most interesting. Which beginnings tempted them to read the book?
5. Ask various students to read the beginnings of their own library books aloud. Count the number of beginnings that fall into each category. Were any additional categories added? Which categories were most common?
6. Have students look over their own file of stories. Ask students to notice what kinds of beginnings they used in their own stories. Do students use a variety of story beginnings? Or do they generally use the same pattern over and over?

Extension 1   Ask students to choose one of their previous stories, then to write two or three alternate beginnings for the story, using the list of story beginning types developed in the previous lesson. Ask students to share their different story beginnings with other students, and ask for comments regarding which beginning is most effective.

Extension 2   Ask students to write a different beginning to one of the stories read in the first activity.

Creatures, Monsters, and Dragons

Objective   To create an imaginary creature or monster.

Materials   List of creatures identified in *Kickle Snifters and Other Fearsome Creatures* or in *Professor Wormbog in Search for the Zipperump-a-Zoo.*

Procedure
1. Give a copy of the list to each student. Read over the names of the creatures. Have each student pick his or her favorite creature and tell what it might be like. Read a few sample descriptions from the suggested books.
2. Ask questions as students describe a creature.

   - What unusual features does this creature have?
   - Where does it live, and what does its home look like?
   - What kind of disposition does this creature have? (friendly, angry, moody, dangerous)
   - What does it eat?
   - What unusual habits does it have?

3. Have students choose one creature and write a newspaper report that provides information about the creature, where and when it was first identified, and what the local government plans to do about it.
4. Have students share their reports with class members. If students have used a creature name from one of the suggested resources, compare their description with the original description written by the authors. Which student came closest to the original description? How were student descriptions different? Explain that because all writers think differently, all descriptions will be different.
5. Make a creature and monster book complete with illustrations.

Extension 1   *Follow-up Installments*

Extend the lesson in following days by having students write follow-up installments about their creature or monster. Try some of these titles:

The _____ Is Captured

The_____ Escapes

The_____ Meets the President

The_____ Finds a Mate

The_____ Goes to School

The_____ Joins the Swim Team

Extension 2 *Creature Point of View*

Have students write a newspaper report from the creature's point of view.

Resources *Kickle Snifters and Other Fearsome Creatures*
Alvin Schwartz
J.B. Lippincott Co., 1976
Here's a sampling of Schwartz's fantastic creatures:

Snawfus	Glytodont
Squonk	Tripodero
Goofus Bird	Squidigicum-Squee
Rubberado	Hoopajuba
Lufferland	Kickle Snifters

Professor Wormbog in Search for the Zipperump-a-Zoo
Mercer Mayer
Golden Press, 1976

Alligator Antics

Objective To brainstorm uses of unlikely subjects or items.

Materials A selection from *100 Ways to Have Fun With an Alligator.*

Procedure
1. Ask students what they would do with an alligator if they had one. Encourage them to think of different or unusual responses. Read several examples to them from *100 Ways to Have Fun With an Alligator.*
   Examples: let him play first base on the Little League team
   tickle him with a long stick
   take him sky diving
   use him as a surfboard
   teach him to juggle in a circus
2. Write student suggestions on the board as they mention them. Accept all ideas. (Review brainstorming procedures suggested in the introduction to this chapter.)
3. Let students draw pictures of an alligator activity. Put them up on the bulletin board with short description of what is happening.
4. Or bind the pictures and the written descriptions in a book titled *100 Ways to Have Fun With an Alligator.*

Extension 1 Try to find other books on alligators or crocodiles. Many have interesting titles, and students might like to invent their own story for a title. Put several different titles on the board; let students choose one that interests them. They may choose to do a series of alligator or crocodile stories.

Extension 2 Have an "Alligator and Crocodile Week." Read lots of alligator and crocodile books, and have students write and illustrate stories about alligators and crocodiles.

Resources *100 Ways to Have Fun With an Alligator & 100 Other Involving Arts Projects*
Norman Laliberte and Richey Kehl
Art Education, 1969

Zany Stories

Objective	To write a story when character, setting, time, situation, and style are given.
Materials	Index cards (3″ × 5″) of different colors, list of characters, settings, time, events, and style.
Procedure	1. Choose five colors of index cards or construction paper. Write the suggested phrases for each category on a different color card. Do not mix the sets of cards. Include the style category when working with more sophisticated writers.
	2. Place cards on the table in the different groups. Ask each student to draw one card from each pile, read the card, then try to develop a Zany Story with the given character, setting, time, situation. All information on the selected cards must be included in the story. Develop several stories orally with the group so that students get the idea.
	3. Next, have students select one card from each category for their own written story. Provide any spelling words that students think they might need *before* they start writing.
	4. Allow students to choose an additional character to make the story even crazier.
	5. Have students share completed stories by reading to a small group of classmates.
	6. Continue working on the stories on another day. Ask students to proofread stories and make necessary corrections, then copy stories in preparation for making a class collection of Zany Stories. You may want to put these stories on duplicating masters so that each student can have his or her own collection of stories. Have students illustrate their Zany Stories, then bind stories and illustrations in a book form. Present a copy of the book to the school library.
Extension	Ask students to add other characters, settings, times, and situations to the card sets.

Characters	*Settings*
a timid muscleman	a mucky swamp
a lion tamer	a deserted island
Superman	an abandoned graveyard
Mighty Mouse	on another planet
a man of superhuman strength	in another galaxy
a frightened ghost	in outer space
a greedy goblin	in a rocket ship
an early pioneer	in a stage coach
a microscopic person	in a movie theater
an astronaut	on a safari
an elderly schoolteacher	on a movie set
a grumpy principal	in a hayloft on a farm
a mischievous child	in a space capsule
a mad scientist	in a playroom
a chemistry genius	on a hang glider
a whiz kid	in a skyscraper
a nosy reporter	on a mule caravan
an army sergeant	in a football stadium
a hobo	in a crowded department store

a sheriff
a pirate

on a sinking ship
in an imaginary world
in a foreign country

Time	*Event*
in the far future	being chased by a shark
in the year 2000	losing something valuable
in the year 1000	winning a prize
in the present	having a fight
in pioneer days	finding a million dollars
at midnight	flying an airplane
at high noon	being arrested
New Year's Eve	falling in love
Halloween	being robbed
April Fool's Day	hunting a lion
Christmas	having an accident
dawn	getting lost
at sunset	being trapped in a time machine
at dinner time	getting married
during prehistoric times	first day at school
at the Boston Tea Party	first day at work
on Election day	a birthday party
on your birthday	joining a parade
	going on a camping trip
	discovering gold

Style (optional)
drama
comedy
soap opera
narrative
play
newspaper report
poem
dialogue
interview
children's storybook
TV guide article

Story Starters

Objective To write original story starters.

Materials Several samples of story starters.

Procedure 1. Read a number of story starters to the students. (There are a number of different kinds of story starters. Some consist of only a sentence or two; others provide more detailed beginnings that include character and setting detail, as well as a problem. For this activity, use the longer variety.)
2. Ask students to note the common elements in the story starters.
   a. characters

     b. setting

     c. problem

3. Ask students to explain why the story starters ended where they did.
4. Ask students to make up a story starter on their own. Remind them to include a character, setting detail, and a problem situation in which the character or characters must make a decision. Do not have them complete the story.
5. Have students read their original story starters to the class. Have class members listen to see whether required elements are included.
6. Have students copy story starters on large index cards. Suggest that they illustrate the card, too. Put these in a class story starter box. On another day, let students choose a story starter from the box and write an ending.

Extension 1   *Stop the Action*

Read an exciting short story to the class. Stop at the point when the character or characters must make a decision that will affect the rest of the story. Have students write an ending to the story. Read students' endings and compare with original ending.

Extension 2   *Picture Story Starters*

Have students choose a picture from the picture file and write a story starter based on characters and action in the picture. Have students stop writing at the decision point in the story. Put these story starters on cards and clip them to the picture. Let other students choose the picture that interests them and finish the story.

Storybooks for Young Children

Objective   To write a story for young children.

Materials   Collection of children's storybooks.

Procedure
1. Write the titles of a number of children's picture books or short storybooks on the board. Try to find unusual and interesting titles that will spark students' imaginations. (Or, have students go to picture book section of the library and each find three titles that are interesting.)
2. Choose one title and ask students what they think the book might be about. Let a number of students volunteer about a title. Read the book to students and have them compare their own ideas with the author's ideas. Repeat this procedure with a number of books.
3. Let students choose a title and write a story or small book. Encourage them to draw pictures to illustrate their story. Bind the pages of the final draft together to make a storybook.
4. Have students find the original book in the library or classroom and compare the author's story to their own. Have students read stories aloud to class, then take their books to younger grades to read aloud.
5. Place the new books in the school or classroom library. Have students prepare a library file card and a sign-out card for their books.

CHAPTER 6

Write for a Reason

While students enjoy writing imaginary stories and can compose fantasy, adventure, or science fiction stories at length, they sometimes have difficulty with everyday writing, such as taking messages, giving directions, writing letters for a particular purpose, writing classified advertisements, and explaining a process. Handling factual information places constraints on writers: they must present information in a clear, logical manner so that the reader will understand and, if necessary, carry out a specific action.

A common weakness in this kind of writing is that students omit significant steps or pieces of information and assume that the reader will fill in the blanks. In addition, students may include irrelevant detail or arrange details in a confusing order, or they may confuse fact and fiction and thus give inadequate support for their topic.

Instructional objectives include the following:

1. To practice practical writing skills, such as taking messages, writing letters of various kinds, and writing classified ads;
2. To give clear, sequential directions;
3. To write about factual information; and
4. To identify fact, fiction, and opinion and when to use each in writing.

Additional activities related to organizational skills will be found in Chapter 7, "Get It Organized!"

Telephone Messages

Objective   To write down telephone messages. (To select specific details.)

Materials   Telephone message form (Figure 6-1).

101

```
TO: _____
DATE:_____ TIME: _____
              WHILE YOU WERE OUT
MR.
MS. _____
OF _____
AREA CODE _____ PHONE _____
```

TELEPHONED		PLEASE PHONE	
CAME BY TO SEE YOU		WILL CALL AGAIN	
WANTS TO SEE YOU		RETURNED YOUR CALL	

```
MESSAGE: _____
_____
_____
_____
_____
          MESSAGE TAKEN BY:_____
```

Figure 6-1
Telephone Message Form

Procedure

1. Ask students to develop a telephone conversation in which the person answering the phone has to take a message for someone else. Discuss what some possible messages might be.

   Examples: Father called to say he would be home late.
   Dentist called to cancel an appointment.
   Mother's friend called to talk to mother.
   Brother's friend called to plan a meeting time.

2. Review the items that a person taking a message should always write down. Give students a copy of the message form.

   who the message is for
   time
   who called
   expected response: return call or wait for another call?
   telephone number to call
   message

3. Have pairs of students choose a sample topic or make up one of their own to use in writing a sample telephone dialogue requiring that a message be taken down. Remind them that messages and telephone numbers should be repeated back by the message taker in order to check the information.

4. After students have finished writing the message dialogue, have them tape record it and play it back for other students. Ask students to fill in message form as they listen to tape. Compare results. Play tape a second time for those students who missed some information.

Writing Letters for a Purpose

Objective To develop letter writing skills by writing for free materials.

Materials *Free Stuff for Kids, The Whole Kids Catalog, 100 Valuable Free Things,* writing paper, stamps, envelopes.

Procedure
1. Place several copies of each book in the classroom. Let students look through the books to find items that interest them. (Many of the items are free; however, some require stamped, self-addressed envelopes; other items cost less than a dollar.)
2. Have each student compose a basic letter requesting the item. Or, compose a sample letter with the whole group together. Write the sample letter on the board.
3. Emphasize the parts and placements of a letter: the heading, the salutation, the body, the closing, and the signature. Place a sample letter on the bulletin board.
4. Have students complete their own letters.
5. Explain correct envelope addressing procedures. Post a model on the board. If students have difficulty with placement of address, draw pencil guidelines for them.
6. Mail the letters. Keep a record of responses.

Extension 1 Have students locate on a map the cities and states that their letters went to. Pinpoint the cities with markers. Keep track of responses. Warn students that sometimes companies run out of the material offered but that they usually answer the letter anyway.

Extension 2 Here are other letters that students can write. Collect magazine coupons that offer free material (e.g., travel information, recipes). Have students write for some of this material. Use postcards instead of letters when money or self-addressed envelopes are not required.

Extension 3 Collect a few humorous "Dear Abby" letters from the newspaper and read them to students. Have students make up a "Dear Abby" letter. Trade letters with students in another class. Ask them to respond with advice.

Extension 4 Write a letter to Guiness *Book of World Records* describing the new world's record that you have set. Make it outrageous.

Extension 5 Tell the students that they are away at camp for the summer. Have them write letters home to their parents about their activities, accommodations, likes and dislikes, friends and enemies, counselors, food, and so on.

Complain, Complain, Complain

Objective To write a complaint letter.

Materials Sample complaint letters, suggested problems for complaint letter.

Procedure
1. Look in newspapers for columns that print complaint letter from readers.
   Example: I ordered seat covers for my car from
               Sharsky and Company in Chicago. They
               cashed my check but they haven't sent
               the seat covers.
2. Read the sample complaint with students and decide on what course of action should be followed by this reader.
3. Review some basic rules for writing complaint letters:
   a. *Make your letter look professional.* Write or print the letter neatly. Or better yet, type the letter.
   b. *Be polite. State the facts clearly and without anger.* Avoid accusations and name-calling.
   c. *State your problem as clearly as possible.* Include important information. If your letter is about a product you have purchased, state the name of the product, the date and place you purchased it, and the price you paid.
   d. *State how you want the problem resolved.* (e.g., "I would like my money back, please," "I would like the product replaced, please," or "I would like a replacement part, please.")
   e. *Include your name, address, and telephone number.*
   f. *Send your letter to the consumer service department of the company.* Send a copy of your letter to the Better Business Bureau and the State Consumer Protection Department.
4. Decide on a sample problem and have students write a complaint letter. Students may suggest different problems for practice letters.
5. Have students read and compare finished letters. Did all letters follow the rules? Modify those letters that do not follow the rules.

Writing Complaints

1. Although you sent a money order six weeks ago to a craft kit supplier, you haven't even received an acknowledgment.
2. A small piece of your hair dryer broke off; it can't be glued back on, but there is a repair station listed in the buyer's instruction booklet.
3. A letter to the editor of the newspaper in your town complained that most of the kids in your school were loud and poorly behaved at sports events. How would you respond?
4. The salespeople at the main store in town seem to hassle teenagers or treat them like second-class citizens.
5. You didn't save the sales slip on the item you bought yesterday. You've just discovered it's defective and you have to return it; but the sign at the customer service desk says, "You must have the sales slip for an exchange or refund." The item still has the store's price tag attached.
6. As a Christmas gift for you, your parents ordered a book that you really wanted. It was charged to their credit card. It's been more than two months since the order, and the purchase has appeared on their credit card statement. Dad suggested that it would be a good exercise for you to track it down.
7. Last year some rowdy kids in seventh grade got your whole school barred from the skating rink for the Spring Vacation Skating Party.
8. You know of six kids who have been short-changed by a guy selling hot dogs at the snack bar in one of the county parks.
9. Some people in your town have asked the city council to set a 11PM curfew on week nights for kids your age.
10. You just found out that there's going to be a big final test in school at the same time you promised to appear in court for a traffic violation.

It's My Opinion!

Objective	To write a letter to an editor of a newspaper.
Materials	Sample letters taken from "letters to editor" section of the local newspaper and magazines.
Procedure	1. Have students collect letters to the editor from newspapers and magazines for at least a week. Make a bulletin board display of these letters. Review collected letters with students and answer the following questions. (You may want to put selected letters on a ditto.)

- What kinds of letters are written to editors?
  (letters expressing pro or con opinions on different problems, letters expressing appreciation for certain articles, letters pointing out a problem in the community, letters complaining about editorial position on a problem, letters responding to another letter to editor)
- What kinds of wording choices were made?
  (emotionally charged words? angry words?)
- What approaches were used?
  (humorous? serious? hostile?)
- How many stated their main point in the first sentence?
- How many made a positive comment first, then stated their point of disagreement?
- What kinds of transition words or phrases were used between paragraphs?

2. Develop a set of guidelines with students for use in writing letters to an editor.
   Suggestions:

- Get to your point quickly.
- State the facts as you see them.
- Do not go into long drawn-out explanations or excuses.
- Avoid the use of emotionally charged words.
- State what kind of action, change, or response you would like to see.

3. Ask students to suggest a situation around the school or neighborhood that they have an opinion on and that they could use as a topic for a letter to the editor of the school or local newspaper.
   Examples:

- School lunch periods are too short.
- School starts too early in the morning.
- Too much (not enough) homework is given.
- Detention should be abolished.
- Grades should be abolished.

Extension 1	Have students choose a letter to the editor from the group on the bulletin board and rewrite it from the opposite point of view.
Extension 2	*Change the Audience* Have students write an opinion letter to a family member or friend. Remind them to use a friendly tone instead of the formal tone used in the letter to the editor. Discuss results by comparing the two types of letters.

Want Ads

Objective	To read and write ads of various kinds.
Materials	Classified ad section from local newspaper.

Procedure

1. Have students bring newspapers from home or contact a local newspaper office and try to get some complimentary copies for classroom use.
2. Have students look through the classified ad section and name the various kinds of ads that appear there. (Employment, automotive, used cars, real estate, rentals, service announcements.) Since papers handle ads differently, it may be useful to have classified sections from two or three papers.
3. Divide the class into small groups. Ask each group to find abbreviations and list all the abbreviations used in a particular section of the classified ads (e.g., employment, real estate, rentals, automotive). Ask students to list these abbreviations and their meanings on a ditto sheet or an overhead transparency. Duplicate the list of abbreviations for future activities in writing ads.
4. Compare ads in each newspaper with the same type of ads in other newspapers. Do all newspapers use abbreviations? Are the same abbreviations used?

Extension 1 *Car Sales*

1. Ask students to name the year and model of a car they would like to own. Have them read through the car sales section of the classified ads to see if they can find the car they have preselected.
2. Have students make a list of the kinds of descriptive information that owners or car dealers provide in their ads.
3. Review list of abbreviations used in car ads.
4. Then ask students to write an ad to sell a car (real or imaginary). Include appropriate descriptive detail.

Extension 2 *House/Apartment*

1. Have students look through real estate ads and locate an apartment or house that might be suitable for them after they leave high school.
2. Have students write an ad that describes their dream house.

Extension 3 *Garage Sale Ads*

Have students ask parents if they have some items in the house or garage that they would like to sell. (An old vacuum cleaner, an old lawn mower, a chest of drawers, a piano, an old swing set, a baby stroller, golf clubs, etc.)

Example: BEAT inflation. Shop for Christmas. Stereo set
with case. Sterling, silverplate flatware, baskets.
Christmas pinecone candleholders, leather books,
egg collection, prints. Much more! 854-6321
for appointment and information.

Extension 4 *Lost and Found Ads*

1. Have students write an ad for something they might have found (keys, puppy, bike, bookbag). Check the local newspaper to see how much it costs to run a "found" ad.
2. Have students write an ad for something they might have lost.

Teen Jobs Ads

Objective To write a job wanted ad for Teen Jobs Wanted section of classified ads.

Materials Sample teen job ads, ads from local newspaper (if available), classified ad cost schedule from local newspaper, sample blank ad form and ad rates (Figure 6-2).

1. Fill out form provided below.
2. Figure cost of ad using rate chart. (Minimum ad is 2 lines.)
3. Bring or mail ads to newspaper office. Be sure to include check or money order if you mail ad. Ads must be paid for in advance.

Name			
Address	Lines	# Of Weeks	Ad Cost
City, State, Zip	Exp. Date	Issue Date	By
Phone	Remarks Enclose Check Or Money Order With Ad		

AD RATES:

	1 Week	2 Weeks	3 Weeks	4 Weeks
2 lines	$1.30	$2.60	$ 3.90	$ 5.20
3 lines	$1.95	$3.90	$ 5.85	$ 7.80
4 lines	$2.60	$5.20	$ 7.80	$10.40
5 lines	$3.25	$6.50	$ 9.75	$13.00
6 lines	$3.90	$7.80	$11.70	$15.60

Figure 6-2
How to Place Your Classified Ad

Procedure 1. Read some of the following ads that were taken from a "Teen Jobs" column of a local newspaper. Compare them with teen jobs in your local newspaper. How are they the same? Different? What was mentioned first in these ads? Identify words that give you clues to the teenager's personality. Notice that the first word or two is all caps.

TEEN JOBS

HIGH SCHOOL student available for stable work, gardening, etc. $2.50 hour. 3 years experience. References. 354-7150 Jim.

EXPERIENCED IN hauling, painting, land clearing, field mowing, chainsaw work. Joe, 354-0307. Free estimates.

GOING AWAY this summer? College student will care for home and animals. References. Debbie 854-3416, eves.

WINDOW WASHING and odd jobs. Reliable and experienced. Call Ross, 854-7720.

MAGICIANS—Looking for a way to make your child's birthday party something special? Call the Wise Wizards. Magic for all occasions. Reasonable, experienced and references. Matt, 854-2425, Tom, 854-2298.

ODD JOBS: Teen-ager will do: minor repairs, pool service, deliveries, babysitting. Own transportation. Steve. 854-0915.

RESPONSIBLE 18 year old will clean house. References. Call Sarah at 851-7202.

ENTERTAINING? SISTERS (one college age, one high school age) will help prepare, serve and clean up. Call Anne or Suzy, 854-2806.

NEED A housesitter? Animal sitter? Garden sitter: I'm a very responsible, reliable, college bound student willing to take care of your home, garden & pets anytime throughout the summer. If interested, call Lisa, 854-1054.

HORSE CARE: College student will clean, feed, etc. Experienced and reliable. Liz, 854-0725.

RESPONSIBLE 17-year-old will feed and care for horses, dogs, cats, plants in Westridge area for $2.50 day. Excellent references available. Call Janice, 854-0162.

HIGH SCHOOL honor student will baby-sit and-or tutor child. Very experienced. References. Lael, 854-1848.

TWO experienced 18-year-olds avail. for odd jobs. Call Erik, 854-0693, Craig, 854-0655.

SOCCER lessons. 2 High School varsity players will teach your children the basic skills of soccer. For more information, call Tom, 851-8351, or Rich, 854-9045.

EXPERIENCED and responsible girl will clean, groom and do other barn work. Call Stephanie, 854-0993.

DIRTY stalls? Call Bryan at 854-4208. 8 years experience with horses, sheep, poultry. Responsible and fast.

2. Have students list some of the skills or jobs they have had or would like to have and plan an ad. Check with the local newspaper to figure costs for placing each ad. (Sometimes local newspapers run teen ads for free just before the summer season. Check to see whether your local paper does this.)

    Some rules to remember when writing a Teen Job Ad or other classified ad:

    a. *Get right to the point! Be specific!* Either state the job you want or who you are that qualifies you for a particular job.

    b. *Include all relevant information.* You may use standard abbreviations.
        First name
        Telephone number
        Your age or age range (e.g., teenager, high school student)
        Special facts: time available, own transportation, special tools owned (lawn mower, pick-up truck, etc.)
        Adjectives: *responsible, experienced, hard-working, fast, prompt service, reliable.*

    c. *Avoid excess words.*

3. Fill out blank ad form, then figure out the cost of the ad based on local rates or use rates given on ad worksheet.

Extension 1 Ask students to look for an ad that describes a job they could hold now. List features that job must have (e.g., part-time, requires no experience or specific

HELP WANTED

CASHIERS wanted, part and full time. No experience needed. Thrift Village, 875 Main St., 364-5545.

Childcare. Assist mother with infant & toddler. Afternoons. Refs. req. 326-4675 aft. 5

Housekpr. Cleaning, ironing, 1 day week or 2½ days. Recent refs. Own trans. English speaking. 325-2739.

RECEPTIONIST
NEEDED

Part-time person with excellent typing skills, cordial telephone manner. Small Office. Pleasant working conditions. 851-0730.

Salesperson-drug & variety store. Part and full time positions. 326-1930. Ask for Willis.

Sandwich shop help needed. Full or part time. Call after 2:00. Ask for Ida or Michelle. 323-4473

Service Stn. Attendant. Full & part time. AM & PM shifts avail. Up to $4hr. + comm. to start. Exper. or will train. Apply: Automotive Center btw. 9–4, Mon–Fri.

Service station attendant. Days. Gd. pay & benefits. 856-6388

SERVICE STA. ATTNDNT. The Bubble Machine, is now hiring P/&F time. Apply 1520 El Camino, R.C.

Service station, part time, 25 hrs/wk, day shift. Exp. pref. 948-0776.

TYPIST. Part time. Office in downtown. Flexible hours. EOE. 321-7911

Waiter/waitress, full or part time. Call Peggy, 948-1024

WAITRESS/WAITER
Now interviewing.
Family Restaurant
*No Experience Necessary
*Day & Night Shifts
W. El Camino, Mt. View, 2–4 p.m.

skills). Make a list of abbreviations found in employment ads. (See HELP WANTED ads.)

Extension 2 Ask students to write down the kind of job they would like to have in five or ten years. Next, have students read through the Classified Ads to find a job listing that comes closest to their desired job type.

Task Analysis

Objective To analyze the sequence of steps in a common task.

Materials Slips of paper with specific tasks written on them (e.g., "Make Scrambled Eggs").

Procedure
1. Ask students to help you analyze the steps in making scrambled eggs. Encourage students to suggest steps. Write these on the board as they are suggested. Do not attempt to rearrange steps as you go along.
2. Help students identify missing steps. (They generally say "put eggs in a bowl, beat them up, add milk, then cook them.") Add in missing steps (get eggs from refrigerator, crack egg shells against side of bowl, split egg shells apart, let eggs drop into bowl).
3. Ask students to identify the correct sequence of steps. Write these on another section of the board. Have one or more students pantomime the process of scrambling eggs.
4. Have students choose a slip of paper with another task listed on it. Ask them to analyze the task, listing as many steps as possible, then arrange the steps in appropriate sequence.

5. Ask some students to volunteer to read their directions aloud. Have several other students pantomime the actions. Caution students to do only what the directions say. Point out when they "fill in" steps for the writer.

Sample Tasks

tape a song from the radio
make a new data file disk for the computer
tape a movie using a VCR (video cassette recorder)
write one-page directions for using computer software
put up and trim a Christmas tree
make chocolate chip cookies
bake a cherry pie
wash the car
build a fire in the fireplace
change a flat tire
brush teeth
put on a belt
tie a tie
plant a bush
tie shoes
iron a shirt
prepare dinner
change sheets on a bed
make lemonade from frozen concentrate
make lemonade from lemons
polish a pair of shoes
make popcorn
make a cake
make a salad
make a bed
repot a plant
sew on a button
make a kite

Resources   *Carving: How to Carve Wood and Stone*
Harvey Weiss
Addison Wesley, 1976

Rube Goldberg: His Life and Work
Peter C. Marzio
Harper and Row, 1973

The Best of Rube Goldberg's Inventions
Charles Keller, editor
Prentice Hall, 1979

The Gadget Book
Harvey Weiss
Crowell, 1971

Time Machine: Past

Objective   To decribe an object, device, or mechanism.

Materials Pictures of means of transportation, household appliances, furniture, garden or yard machines.

Procedure 1. Tell students that they are going into a time machine that will take them to historical eras (e.g., prehistoric days, medieval times, colonial America). Choose one item and have students explain it in terms that would be understood (e.g., can opener, vacuum cleaner, automobile, motorcycle, stove).

2. Do a sample with the class. Follow the outline presented below. Go through whole process *orally* and make notes on the board.

    I. *Name of object, device, or mechanism*
       A. *Basic definition (description)*
       B. *Purpose/function*
       C. *How does it work?*
          1. *Parts and how related to whole*
          2. *How made*
          3. *How it operates*
          4. *Results*

3. Have students choose another object, device, or mechanism and complete the outline given above. You may want to have students work in pairs or small groups.

4. Have students write a short report on their object, device, or mechanism based on their outline.

5. Have students read their results to classmates.

6. Discuss the kinds of problems that students had when trying to explain object or device. (Frequently, many vocabulary words need to be explained.)

Extension 1 Tell students they are going into the future time machine. Ask them to design a mechanism to perform one of the following purposes: personal transportation, or public transportation.

Extension 2 Have students look in magazines for advertisements featuring historical figures using modern equipment (e.g., Benjamin Franklin using a Xerox machine). Put these advertisements on the bulletin board and use as examples for this activity.

Resources *The Time Machine, and Other Stories*
    H. G. Wells
    Scholastic Book Co.

    Tunnel Through Time
    Lester del Rey
    Scholastic Book Co., 1970

How Do I Get There?

Objective To write clear directions.

Materials Sample directions, Happy Valley map (Figure 6-3).

Procedure 1. Ask students what they do when they want to go to a new place that they don't know how to get to.

> *Suggestions:* look at a map
> call the place and ask directions
> ask parents for directions
> ask friends

2. Tell students that giving careful directions is very important. (They may remember a few occasions when they or their parents got lost because they did not have good directions or did not write the directions down.) Give students copies of the sample directions and ask them to decide which one is better and to explain what features make it better. (The first gives names of streets, exact numbers of blocks, landmarks, specific house numbers. Ask students to guess why the student who wrote the directions went that way. The second one is too vague.)

3. Ask students to write a different set of directions using the given map (Figure 6-3).

4. Ask students (in class) to write down directions to their house from school from memory. Allow five minutes or so to do this. Have them draw a sample map to go with the directions. Next, ask students to list the items they should have noted but could not remember (e.g., how many blocks from one place to another, what landmarks were along the way, names of all important streets).

5. For homework, ask students to write again directions from school to home. This time ask them to write directions down on the way home and include all specific information (street names, landmarks, number of miles or blocks, etc.).

Extension 1 Giving oral directions is also a very important skill. Have several volunteers slowly dictate their directions twice to the class while the class takes written notes. Have several writers read back the directions to see if all information was written down.

Point out that people frequently get lost because they think that they can remember directions and do not write them down, or they write down only parts of directions.

Extension 2 Locate a local map of your city (town, district) and put it on the bulletin board. Have students trade written directions to their home (the homework assignment), then read and track the directions on the map. Ask students to note where they had difficulty.

Extension 3 Using a road map or road atlas of the United States, plan a trip to a national park. Have students write sequence of directions that includes names of cities and states and specific highway numbers.

Sample Directions

1. From Brown Junior High School to 1039 Maple Street.
   Go out the main entrance of Brown Junior High School. Walk to the corner of Brown and Pine Streets. Turn left on Pine Street. Walk three blocks to Orange Street. A candy store will be on the corner. Turn right on Orange Street. Walk six blocks on Orange Street to Maple Street. A big church is on the corner. Turn left on Maple Street and walk to 1039 Maple. It is a big white house with green shutters. It is the fifth house from the corner on the left-hand side of the street.

2. From Brown Junior High School to 1039 Maple Street.
   Go down to the corner and turn left. Go a few blocks until you see the candy store. Then you have to go down that street for a ways. You'll see a big church. I live near the church.

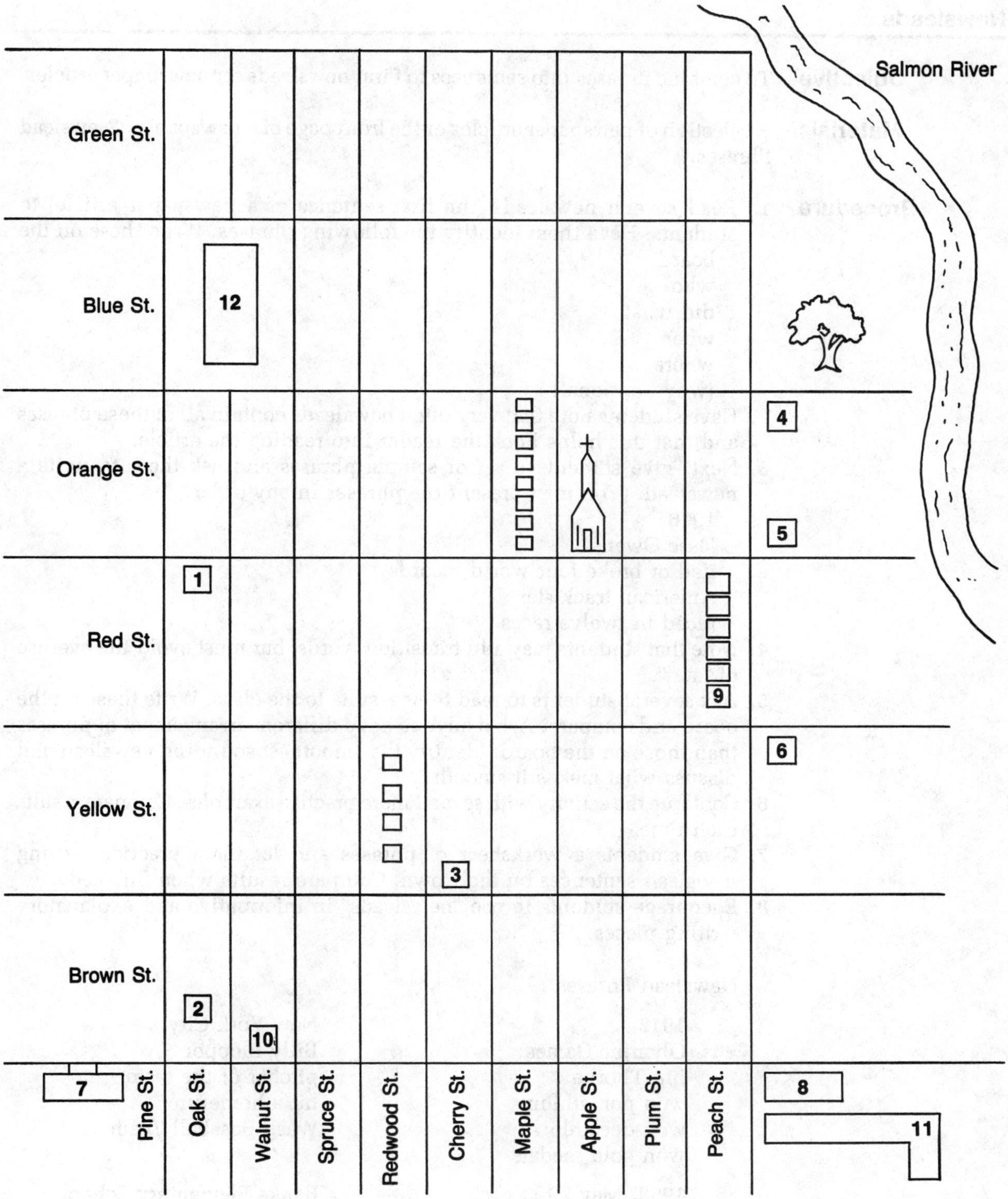

Salmon River

Green St.

Blue St. | 12 |

Orange St. | 4 |

| 5 |

Red St. | 1 |

| 9 |

Yellow St. | 6 |

| 3 |

Brown St.

| 2 |

| 10 |

| 7 | Pine St. | Oak St. | Walnut St. | Spruce St. | Redwood St. | Cherry St. | Maple St. | Apple St. | Plum St. | Peach St. | 8 |

| 11 |

Key:
1. Jelly Beans Candy Shoppe
2. Taco's Taco Shop
3. Happy Valley Municipal Pool
4. Green Acres Golf Course
5. Jolly Roger Miniature Golf
6. Park'n Fish Campground
7. Brown Junior High School
8. Happy Valley Senior High School
9. Pizza Heaven
10. McRonald's Hamburgers
11. Shopper's World
12. Happy Valley Hospital

Figure 6-3
Map

Newsleads

Objective To combine phrases into sentences to form newsleads for newspaper articles.

Materials A selection of newspaper articles or the front page of a newspaper, "Newslead Phrases."

Procedure 1. Read several newsleads (the first sentence of a newspaper article) to students. Have them identify the following phrases. Write these on the board.
>who
>did what
>when
>where
>(why—optional)

2. Have students note that very often newsleads contain all of these phrases and that this helps hook the reader into reading the article.

3. Next, give students a set of sample phrases and ask them to write a newslead. (You may present the phrases in any order.)
>1936
>Jesse Owens
>tied or broke four world records
>American track star
>raced in twelve races

4. Note that students may add transition words, but must avoid the overuse of "and".

5. Ask several students to read their results to the class. Write these on the board and compare. Ask if anyone has a different arrangement of phrases than those on the board. Identify the smoothest sounding newslead and discuss what makes it smooth.

6. Continue the activity with several more practice examples. Compare results each time.

7. Give students a worksheet of phrases and let them practice writing newslead sentences on their own. Compare results when finished.

8. Encourage students to use "newsleads" in informative and explanatory writing pieces.

Newslead Phrases

1912	New York City
Olympic Games	Billy Blepper
Jim Thorpe	pitcher of the team
won pentathlon	hit a homerun
won decathlon	Wasp Baseball Team
won gold medals	
1953, May 29	Banks Elementary School
Mount Everest	fifth grades
29,028 feet high	Friday, April 10
Edmund Hillary	sponsoring a fund-raiser
Tenzing Norgay	carnival
first people to reach peak	raise money for camping trip
Orville and Wilbur Wright	Thursday, March 15
December 17, 1903	downtown area of Homer,
flew more than 800 feet	Alaska

tested their flying machine	a bullmoose
were in the air a short time	walked through the streets
in early pioneering days	six inches of snow
explored Kentucky	April 1
settled in Kentucky	Soldotna, Alaska
estblished Fort Boonesborough	an early spring snowstorm
Daniel Boone	schools closed for the day

Eye Witness News

Objective   To write objective news reports.

Materials   Pictures that have characters and action (e.g., sports pictures, accident, fire, graduations, etc.) from newspapers or magazines.

Procedure
1. Choose one picture and have students identify, "who," "did what," "when," and "where" information. Write their comments on the board.
2. Encourage students to be very specific and objective in their comments. Remind them that news reporters cannot add their own emotional reactions and opinions in their reports.
3. Have the students choose a title for the picture and article. Then have them write an objective news report using the information provided on the board.
4. Let some students choose a different picture and do this assignment by themselves.
5. Have students read their news reports aloud. Have class members listen to see whether any statements that show emotional response or opinions were used.

Extension   Give some students interesting headlines from newspaper stories, and some a list of facts from the stories. Ask them to write news reports to go with the headlines. Then let them compare their report with the original report.

News News

Objective   To write sports news articles.

Materials   Sports pictures from newspapers or magazines.

Procedure
1. Collect interesting action pictures from the sports section of newspapers or magazines. Ask students to help you collect them.
2. Let students choose a picture and write an "on the spot" news report using an announcer point of view. (Read sample to class.)
3. Encourage students to use short sentences loaded with action verbs and exclamations of excitement.

4. Read results to class.
   Example: The score is ten to nine. First out. Second out. He's up at bat. Man on third. Strike. Holy Cow! What a hit! Looks like a home run! Oh, just missed first base. Man on third going home. He slides safe. What a game! Ten to ten.
5. Have each student rewrite their "on the spot" report as a report for the daily news. Remind students that newspaper reporting is more objective than "on the spot" type reporting and generally does not include the exclamations of excitement or statements of opinion. Remind them to include information on who, what, when, and where.
6. Read results to the class.

Extension 1   Present some articles or pictures without headlines. Let students write some catchy captions.

Extension 2   Present some catchy titles found in the sports section of the newspaper. Also present an outline of information that provides who, did what, when, and where. Let students write an article to match the title and information. Encourage them to describe an interesting scene in the game.

Extension 3   Have a student follow one team or sports hero through a period of time by collecting newspaper pictures and writing short reports on each picture. Bind all the articles and pictures in book format. Because newspaper pictures come out very well on a copying machine, many students can use the same pictures.

Extension 4   Have students listen to televised sports news programs. These programs generally use precise verbs in their descriptions of games. Ask students to jot down some of the descriptions and bring them into class.

Resources   See Chapter 4, "Use the Computer" for descriptions of *Super Scoop* (a software program that simulates a news story in the works) and *Newsroom* (a program that helps students create their own newspapers).

Targets

Objective   To make collages of products made for particular target groups.

Materials   Magazines, scissors, paste, poster paper.

Procedure
1. Have students go through different magazines and cut out advertisements. Try to have a wide variety of magazines available.
2. Have students sort the advertisements according to target groups; that is, which ads would appeal to new young mothers? to teen-agers? to young children? to homemakers? to men? to women? to retired people? etc.
3. Have individual students, or small groups of students, choose one target group and design a collage using ads that appeal to that particular target group.
4. Have students make a list of the products that are directed to their target group. Encourage them to think of others that might not be on their collage.

5. Have one group make a collage of products that might be used by anyone.
6. Display collages and lists of products in the classroom.

Extension 1   Make a collage of one kind of product: desserts, cleaning products, cosmetics, etc. Compare how different manufacturers advertise their products. Have students write a report on advertising techniques.

Extension 2   Have students make up a product and write an advertisement that describes the product and its benefits. This can be serious or humorous. Students may want to have a make-believe celebrity give an endorsement of the product.

Pro and Con

Objective   To identify pro and con arguments.

Materials   A controversial topic and a list of pro and con statements.

Procedure
1. Put topic and pro/con statements on ditto or overhead transparency. Have one student read the arguments.
2. Make a chart on the board—one side pro arguments, one side con arguments. Also decide whether arguments are fact or opinion. List facts at top and opinions at bottom.
3. Have students choose a side and write a paragraph giving the factual arguments. Next, have them rewrite the paragraph giving opinions. Encourage students to use lots of emotionally charged words when giving opinions.
4. Share both paragraphs with class members.

Extension   Have students write paragraphs from the opposite point of view that they chose in 3 above. Have them write both factual and opinion paragraphs.

Pro	Con
Facts	Facts
Opinions	Opinions

CHAPTER 7

Get It Organized!

Intermediate and secondary educational programs require that students have sufficient writing skills to answer test questions, write basic reports, and complete homework assignments. Poor writers have difficulty planning their writing. As a result, they do not always write clear topic sentences followed by appropriate, properly sequenced, supportive details, and relevant summaries or conclusions. Main ideas and details are improperly handled and are frequently unbalanced—either a generalization is given without supportive detail, or an overabundance of detail is provided with no generalization. Because poor writers lack planning skills, they have difficulty identifying a good starting point, keeping to their topic (they change line of thinking as new thoughts occur to them), and covering their topic completely.

Other students, who have mastered the basic paragraph structure (topic sentence, supportive details, conclusion), produce reports that are adequate but not interesting or well developed.

Poor writers need activities that focus on these problems. The emphasis of the activities in this section is on building organizational skills through thinking, listening, and reading activities before actual writing assignments are given.

Instructional objectives include the following:

1. *Identifying the topic.* Selecting the topic and narrowing it appropriately is an important skill. Students learn to use a Broad and Narrow Topics chart to help them develop this skill.

2. *Stating the main idea and making generalizations.* Writing topic sentences is a critical skill in expository writing. It involves the ability to make generalizations about a related group of facts or details. Students learn to restate questions in the form of topic sentences—a necessary skill for test taking.

3. *Eliminating hasty generalizations.* Students must learn to avoid making unsupported or emotionally based generalizations. Activities designed to help students identify and correct these unsupported generalizations are included in this chapter.

4. *Providing details, facts, examples, quotes.* In order for paragraphs to be well developed, sufficient appropriate details must be included. Students develop this skill by sorting and matching topic sentences and details and by selecting facts and details that *prove* basic generalizations.

Details can be arranged in a variety of ways in paragraphs. Practice in arranging details in different ways is also included in this chapter.

5. *Sequencing.* Sequencing in creative writing is relatively natural as students tell stories the way they happen. Expository writing, however, requires that students identify clear relationships (such as cause and effect, and comparison and contrast) and sequence them appropriately.

6. *Identifying comparisons and contrasts.* This skill is required in almost every school subject. Students must identify important similarities and differences in such areas as literature (e.g., the novel compared with a play, or one character compared with another); political science (e.g., communism compared with democracy); science (e.g., igneous rock formation compared with sedimentary and metamorphic). In everyday life, students must make comparisons and contrasts as they choose clothing, academic subjects, careers, and possibly colleges.

7. *Notetaking.* Students learn to take notes by listening to paragraphs that are read aloud and pinpointing the main ideas and details.

8. *Outlining.* Filling in a partially completed outline helps students understand broader and narrower relationships between topics and details. Partially completed outlines will be useful as guides in writing book reports or larger papers.

Broad and Narrow

Objective To narrow topics that are too broad.

Materials Sample topics, sample Broad and Narrow Topics chart (Figure 7-1).

Procedure 1. Explain that sometimes writers have difficulty with reports because the topics they choose are too broad. For most reports, it is best to choose a narrow topic because all relevant facts and/or generalizations can be easily covered.

2. To demonstrate the broadness of some topics, put an example on the board. Ask students to suggest as many possible subtopics as they can for the following example.
Example: Animals

Subtopic Suggestions
   How Animals Protect Themselves
   How Animals Find Food
   What Animals Eat
   Animal Homes
   Animal Habits
   Dangers That Animals Face
   Unusual-Looking Animals
   Farm Animals
   Wild Animals

3. Point out that even these subtopics are too broad. Ask students to suggest a narrower topic for each one. For example, choose specific animals to narrow the topic.

Too Broad	Still Broad	Narrow
Animals	Eating Habits of Animals	Eating Habits of Guinea Pigs _____ _____
Plants	Unusual Plants	The Strange World of Insect-Eating Plants _____ _____
Occupations	Careers in Communications Industry	Duties of a T.V. News Reporter _____ _____
Fishing	Fresh Water Fishing	Trout Fishing _____ _____
School	School Activities	Drama Club Activities _____ _____
The Universe	The Solar System	Jupiter _____ _____

Figure 7-1
Broad and Narrow Topics

Example:

How { Antelopes, Rabbits, Eagles } Hunt for Food, Protect Themselves, Make Their Homes

4. Ask students to choose one narrow topic and write a short report. Encourage them to use reference sources (encyclopedias) as well as nonfiction library materials.
5. Repeat the activity on another day using a different broad topic.

Extension   Give students a copy of the Broad and Narrow Topics chart. Ask them to fill in at least two additional narrow topics for each broad topic suggested.

Sentence Sort (Main Ideas and Details)

Objective   To group and sequence related ideas under topic heading (main ideas and details).

Materials   Strips of oaktag with sample sentences from "Sentence Sort".

Procedure   1. Choose two factual paragraphs on different topics. See "Sentence Sort" for example. Copy each sentence of each paragraph on a separate strip of paper. Or, write the sentences in mixed up order on a ditto and have students cut strips apart. Put titles on strips also.

SENTENCE SORT

Some snakes are very dangerous.
The giraffe is a strange-looking animal.
There are only seven bones in the giraffe's neck.
The largest and most dangerous is the diamondback rattlesnake.
It has the same number of bones that a mouse's neck has.
It can grow to be eight feet long.
This snake is easily identified.
The giraffe's thin legs are much stronger than they appear.
It can run at a speed of thirty miles an hour.
It has a rattle at the end of its tail.
Only the lion, the giraffe's only enemy, can run faster.
However, the giraffe can kill a lion with one kick from its hoof.
When people or animals approach the rattlesnake, it rattles its tail as a warning.
But the mouse's neck is much, much shorter.
Giraffes
Snakes

3. Give an envelope to each student. Have students first locate the two title cards and put them at the top of the desk. Next, have students sort sentences under the corresponding title, sequence the sentence strips in meaningful order, then copy one paragraph on a piece of paper and read it aloud to see whether it makes sense.

4. Have students reshuffle title and sentence strips and put them back in envelopes. Continue the activity on another day by giving students different envelopes with different paragraphs.

5. Control the level of difficulty by using appropriate reading vocabulary levels and a smaller number of sentence strips (two, three, or four at first). Or, just use one paragraph if students have difficulty sorting and sequencing the sentences.

What's the Big Idea?

Objective   To identify main idea, details, and conclusion in paragraphs.

Materials   "Main Ideas, Details, Conclusion Worksheet" or overhead transparency of worksheet. Copies of paragraph selections from materials suggested in Resources.

Procedure   1. Put copy of the "Main Ideas, Details, Conclusions Worksheet" on an overhead projector.

Main Ideas, Details, Conclusion Worksheet

Title: _____

Main Idea: _____

_____

_____

Detail 1 _____

_____

_____

Detail 2 _____

_____

_____

Detail 3 _____

_____

_____

Detail 4 _____

_____

_____

Conclusion _____

_____

_____

2. Point out that paragraphs or groups of related paragraphs generally have the same basic parts: an introduction or topic sentence that makes a general statement; details, facts, or examples providing proof for that statement; and a summary or conclusion that quickly reviews the topic sentences. Also point out that this type of arrangement helps the reader understand the content of the paragraph more easily.

3. Explain that you will read a selection and that the students must listen for main idea, details, and conclusion. Give students a copy of the paragraph so that they can follow along.

4. Read paragraphs to students.

5. Ask students to identify the title and main idea of the paragraphs. Write this information on the transparency.

6. Ask students to underline the details on their copy of the paragraph. List these under details.

7. Ask students to underline the conclusion. Write it on transparency.

8. Review the whole outline with students.

9. Repeat the procedure with several other paragraphs.

10. Save the outlines for several days, then ask students to write a paragraph using the outlines as a guide.

Extension 1   Continue this activity with several paragraphs for several days. Gradually ask students to complete worksheet on their own. Save completed worksheets for a week or so, then return them to students and ask them to write paragraphs from the outlines. The delay of a week after making the outline forces the students to rely on the outline, rather than on their memory for information. In addition, if any outlines are incomplete, students will have difficulty completing the paragraph. Frequently this forces them to pay closer attention to the actual outline making.

Extension 2   Assign a different paragraph to each student to outline. When outlines are complete, ask each student to trade outlines with another student. Ask the second student to write a paragraph using the first student's outline. Students very quickly realize the importance of making their outlines clear when someone else has to write a paragraph from them. Ask the students to comment on problems they had on this activity and to suggest ways to alleviate the problems.

Repeat this activity with multiple selections.

Resources   *Be A Better Reader Series*
Prentice Hall

New Practice Readers
Webster Division, McGraw Hill

Questions

Objective   To restate questions in the form of statements (topic sentences).

Materials   List of suggested questions.

Procedure   1. Write a question on the board. Ask students to rewrite the question as a statement using as many words from the question as possible.
   Question: What were the causes of the American Revolution?
   Restatement: There were several causes for the American Revolution.
   2. Have students compare and note the words from the question that were included in the restatement (causes for the American Revolution).
   3. Have students note the words that were added to the question (there were several).
   4. Ask students to identify the type of information that would be needed in a paragraph to answer the question.
   5. Point out that the restated question becomes the first sentence in a paragraph answer. The remainder of the paragraph provides additional information about the topic sentence.
   6. Continue changing questions to restatements and asking for the kind of information needed to answer the questions.
   7. Have students choose one restatement (topic sentence) and write a short paragraph that answers the question.

Examples

It is best to use questions directly related to the topics being studied in social studies, history, or science classes. The following questions are representatives of questions that could be asked in a history class.

What   What were the causes of the American Revolution?
   What did the first American flag look like?
   What did the stars and stripes of the flag represent?

Who	Who attended the first Constitutional Convention?
	Who was the first president of the United States?
	Who designed the first American flag?
Which	Which battles of the American Revolution did the British win?
	Which did the colonists win?
When	When was the American Revolution fought?
	When was the last battle of the American Revolution?
How	How were candles made in colonial America?
Why	Why was independence so important to the colonists? If you were a colonist, why would independence be important to you?
	Why did the colonists want to have a constitution?

Hasty Generalizations

Objective   To identify inaccurate generalizations.

Materials   Sample generalizations.

Procedure   1. Tell students that sometimes people make "hasty generalizations"—statements that are very broad and not always true. Give the example "Winters are always cold," and ask students to suggest times when this might not be true.
2. Ask students to identify the word that makes the statement untrue ("always"). Ask students to suggest places where it might be hot in winter.
3. Ask students to revise the statement to make it true. This can be done by adding the names of specific places where it is cold or by adding a qualifier to the sentence.
"Winters in the Arctic are cold." (specific place)
"Winters are cold in Alaska." (specific place)
"Winters are cold in *some* places." (qualifier)
4. Read other hasty generalizations to the class. Identify the words in each that make them untrue and put these words on a chart. Show parallel modifiers or specific details in chart.

General Words	Qualifiers
Always	Sometimes
Never	Occasionally
All	Usually
Everybody	Generally
Everyone	Some
Every	Most
	Many

5. Rewrite the hasty generalizations with the students, adding either a qualifier or a specific detail that modifies the sentence. Develop several modified versions of each hasty generalization.

Extension   Have students deliberately write some hasty generalizations, then switch papers with partners who read and add words to correct the statement. Read before-and-after results aloud to whole class. Have students try to think of exceptions to the modified generalizations.

Sample Generalizations

Generalizations	Exceptions
Everybody sleeps at night.	(Nightwatchmen usually don't.)
	(But even they sometimes fall asleep on job.)
All dogs are friendly.	(Dobermans are mean.)
	(Are *all* Dobermans mean?)
All apples taste delicious.	(Rotten apples taste awful.)
It never rains on Sunday.	(Sometimes it does.)
All Mexicans love hot food.	(Maybe some don't.)
Mexican food has chili peppers in it.	(Not all dishes.)
All students are lazy.	(Some are not.)

Listen for the Details

Objective To listen to a factual paragraph and recall details.

Materials Selections from student workbooks (see Resources).

Procedure
1. Ask students to listen for details in the selection that you read orally. (Adjust number according to ability of students. At first ask them to listen for two or three details. Gradually build up the number required.)
2. Read the paragraph to students twice.
3. Ask students to recall details. Write details on the board as students suggest them. If they omit some details, read selection again. Ask students to listen for omitted facts.
4. Ask students to write a summary of the paragraph, using the information on the board.
5. Have students read completed paragraphs aloud. Compare results.
6. Repeat this activity on another day with a different paragraph.

Extension This activity is especially useful in content subject areas such as social studies, science, and history. Read a factual paragraph from the class text and ask students to listen for and write down details.

Resources *New Practice Readers*
Webster Division, McGraw Hill

Reading for Concepts
Webster Division, McGraw Hill

Outline Match

Objective To make factual paragraphs with prepared outlines.

Materials Short detailed paragraphs, outlines of paragraphs, 3″ × 5″ index cards, envelopes.

Procedure   1. Select a number of factual paragraphs from student workbooks. Outline each paragraph. Cut out and tape each paragraph and outline on a separate 3″ × 5″ card.
2. Shuffle several paragraphs and outlines together and put them in an envelope.
3. Give an envelope to each individual or small group of students. Ask students to read the paragraphs and outlines and match them appropriately.
4. Check results.
5. Make this activity harder by preparing a set of paragraphs and *incomplete* outlines. Have students match paragraphs and outlines, then fill in the blanks on the outline.
6. Let students choose one paragraph outline several days later and have them write a paragraph. Then pass out the original paragraphs and have students compare their results with them.

Extension   Use multiparagraph articles with partially filled-in outlines. Ask students to match paragraphs and outlines, then complete the outlines. Save the outlines for several days. Return outlines to students and have them write a multiparagraph article using the outline as a guide. Have students compare their results with original paragraphs.

Compare and Contrast

Objective   To compare and contrast items in a similar category.

Materials   Chart paper and markers, or overhead transparency, "Compare and Contrast Chart"

Procedure   1. Choose a topic from the following suggestions and brainstorm all the comparisons that can be made. Consider physical characteristics (size, shape, color, weight, composition), purpose, function, and special features.
   Suggestions: two computer games   two friends
   two kinds of pets   two grocery stores
   two sports activities   two vegetables/fruits
2. Make a chart of these comparisons. Use the "Compare and Contrast Chart" format.
3. Next, brainstorm all the differences or contrasts that can be made about the topic. Note these on chart.
4. Have students do a fast write based on the information on the chart.
5. Next, have students read their papers to partners or small groups for peer suggestions and compliments.

Extension   Brainstorm unusual comparisons: for example, how are a computer and an elephant alike? (Students might respond "They both are powerful—a computer moves a lot of data and an elephant moves a lot of weight." Or, "They both have a lot of memory—elephants never forget.")
   Suggestions: a computer game and a pet
   a car and an alligator
   a bank and a battleship
   Have small groups work on the same topic and compare results.

Compare and Contrast Chart

	Object #1	Object #2
First Comparison		
Second Comparison		
Third Comparison		
First Contrast		
Second Contrast		
Third Contrast		

Spotting Details

Objective   To identify specific details in writing a description of an item.

Materials   Paper and pencil.

Procedure   1. Have each student choose an item in the classroom to describe. Have students write down as much descriptive information as possible. Encourage them to include information on color, size, shape, texture, movement, location, and, last, function. *Do not* name the item.
2. Have each student read his or her written descriptive information to the class without naming the item.
3. Ask class members to try to identify the item as the description is read.
4. Continue reading descriptions until all items are found.
5. Do this activity in a different setting, perhaps outside in the school yard (or in the library or the lunchroom) on another day.

Extension   Have students write descriptions of "things" not found in the schoolroom. Have students put *least* important clues first, and most important clues last. See how long it takes students to guess the answer.

Prove It!

Objective	To provide descriptive details that support a generalization.
Materials	List of generalizations.
Procedure	1. Write a generalized statement on the board. Ask students to suggest details that would prove the generalization. Write suggestions on the board.

Example: The man was very poor.

Proof: His clothes were faded and ragged.

He wasn't wearing a coat, even though it was very cold.

His shoes were very scuffed and had large holes.

2. Ask students to suggest behavioral clues that would suggest poverty.

Proof: He sat in the park every day.

He slept on a park bench every night.

He didn't have a job.

He asked people for money.

3. Have each student write a description of the man that shows he was poor.
4. Continue this activity on another day with another sample generalization.

Extension Other examples to use:

The weather has been horrible this week.

Mr. Jones was very angry.

The citizens of Brownsville were disturbed about the new taxes.

The boys got very dirty playing football yesterday.

Example: The weather has been horrible this week.

Proof: The temperature dropped to 20 degrees.

It has been foggy and damp every day.

Visibility has been very poor.

Winds reached 35 miles per hour.

The airport was closed because of fog and strong winds.

A lot of snow fell in the mountains, closing roads and causing accidents.

Jumbled Jokes

Objective	To sequence sentences in correct order.
Materials	Joke book.
Procedure	1. Select five or six jokes from the joke book. Choose shorter jokes (three or four sentences) at first, then gradually include longer jokes.

2. Copy each sentence of each joke on a separate strip of paper. Put strips of each joke in a separate envelope. Do not mix jokes together. Or, write sentences in mixed-up order on a ditto. Students can then cut ditto apart in strips.
3. Give one envelope (or ditto) to each student. Have each student read the mixed-up sentences and arrange them in logical order.
4. When finished, have students read jokes aloud to see whether they make sense.

5. Have each student mix up his or her own joke and return it to the envelope. Save jokes for another day and let students do this activity by themselves in their free time. This activity develops reading comprehension skills as well as sequencing skills.

JUMBLED JOKE

"He isn't hungry."
The rabbit ordered lettuce, carrots, and spinach.
The surprised waiter said, "What's the matter?"
The rabbit answered, "If he were hungry, I wouldn't be here."
The rabbit answered for the lion.
The waiter then asked the lion what he wanted to eat.
A rabbit and a lion were having lunch together.

Extension 1 Repeat this activity using other kinds of writing such as clearly sequenced songs, rhymes, jingles, or condensed fables. Try the jumbled fable that follows.

JUMBLED FABLES

She opened her mouth to sing.
Don't be fooled by flattery.
Then a clever fox came along.
A crow had stolen a piece of cheese.
He wanted the cheese for his supper.
"You look beautiful today. Your feathers are so shiny."
The crow was very flattered with his words.
The Fox and the Crow
She carried the cheese to a tree and sat on a branch.
"Good morning, Miss Crow," he said.
"I bet you sing beautiful songs too."
The cheese dropped out and the fox snatched it.

Extension 2 Ask the students to write their own version of any fable. The student versions can then be used for follow up activities for other students who might need extra practice.

Mixed-Up Stories

Objective To sequence a series of related paragraphs.

Materials A collection of articles cut from student workbooks (e.g., *New Practice Readers* or *Reading for Concepts*); index cards.

Procedure
1. Choose five or six multiparagraph selections from a student workbook. Cut selections into paragraphs. Put one paragraph on each index card. Then put each story in a separate envelope. Or copy selections on a ditto with paragraphs in mixed-up order. (Keep each selection on a separate ditto to avoid confusion.)
2. Give each student an envelope. Explain that there is a selection inside but that it is mixed up. Have the students take out the paragraphs, read them, and sequence them according to the context of the story.
3. To check, have each student read his or her selection out loud. Ask other students to listen for correct sequence.
4. Discuss the clues that students can use to help sequence the paragraphs (topic paragraph, key words, time).
5. When stories have been checked for accuracy, have students put cards back in envelope and pass to a person near them to repeat the activity.
6. Make a game out of this by dividing the class into groups. Give each group selections for each member in the group to sequence. The first group with stories in the correct sequence is the winner. Students may help each other.

Extension 1 Mix paragraph cards from three or four different stories together and put in one envelope. Have students sort paragraphs into appropriately related groups and then sequence the paragraphs into stories.

Extension 2 Try this activity another way. Dividing the class into groups, give each group three or four sets of related paragraphs all mixed up. Ask each group to sort out their paragraphs and to sequence them properly. The first group to sequence all paragraphs correctly wins.

Extension 3 Students may want to cut up some of their own stories for their classmates to read and sequence.

Resources *Be a Better Reader Series*
   Nila Banton Smith
   Prentice-Hall

   Multiple Skills Series
   Barnell-Loft

   New Practice Readers
   Reading for Concepts
   Webster Division
   McGraw Hill

Irrelevant Sentences

Objective To sequence relevant sentences in paragraph.

Materials Sample paragraphs: each sentence on a separate strip of oaktag.

Procedure
1. Choose a paragraph and write each sentence from paragraph on a separate strip of oaktag. Add one irrelevant sentence. Put all sentences in envelope in mixed up order.

Example: It is important to take good care of your teeth.
Be sure to brush them at least two times a day.
When you cannot brush them, rinse your mouth.
It is very cold in Alaska most of the year.
Use dental floss, too.
Visit your dentist twice a year.
Remember, too many sweets cause cavities.

2. Pass out one envelope to each student.
3. Ask students to read all the sentences, identify the irrelevant sentence, remove it, then sequence the sentences to rebuild the paragraph.
4. Check paragraphs for accuracy. If correct, have students mix up their paragraphs and irrelevant details, and return them to envelope.
5. Pass envelope to another person and repeat the activity.

Extension   Have students write paragraphs with one or two irrelevant details deliberately added. Have them copy each sentence of their paragraph on a separate strip of paper, put all the strips in an envelope in mixed-up order, then switch with another person in the room.

This activity helps students not only to identify irrelevant sentences (to alert them to identify irrelevant ideas in their own writing) but also to improve reading comprehension.

Sequence Words

Objective   To sequence stories using key words that represent time sequences.

Materials   Sentence strips that tell a short story, or ditto sheet with mixed-up story (see example, "First, Then, Finally").

Procedure   1. Use "First, Then, Finally" example. Write each sentence of the story on a ditto with each sentence on a separate line.
2. Explain to students that key words often help to sequence events in a story or paragraph. Ask students to suggest some "key words" that relate to time sequences. Give a few examples to get them started. Write suggestions on board.
Examples

first	morning	after
then	afternoon	afterward
finally	evening	immediately
next	last year	soon
last	next year	suddenly
second	now	previously
later	then	
earlier	before	

3. Give each student a copy of "First, Then, Finally". Have students read sentences, then arrange in correct order using key words as a guide.
4. Have students read stories aloud to check for accuracy.
5. Have students write a time sequence story using key words. Let them write their stories on strips of oaktag after the stories are checked, or write on a ditto in mixed-up order. Let classmates arrange sentences in correct order.

FIRST, THEN, FINALLY

Then he ran downstairs and ate a quick breakfast.
First he looked at the clock.
It said 8 a.m.
It was 8:30 a.m.
Finally, he looked at the school clock.
Phew!
Jim realized that his clock at home was wrong.
Jim woke up.
He got dressed in three minutes.
He was late for school.
He ran to school as fast as his legs could carry him.

Extension 1   Explain that another group of words can help to order sequence in writing: words that refer to arrangement of things in space. List a few key words and ask students to suggest additional words.

in, on, under
in front of, in back of, next to, behind
above, below, beyond, beside
next to, to the right of, to the left of
near, far

Have students write a description of the classroom. Next, ask a number of students to read their descriptions while class members listen for words that provide spatial clues.

Extension 2   Have students locate setting descriptions in their reading material, and list words that show spatial sequence. Read the selection from Chapter 10 of *Tuck Everlasting* by Natalie Babbitt (Farrar, Straus & Giroux, 1975) to students. This selection demonstrates the sequencing of spatial words in a description.

Grocery List

Objective   To categorize words and develop a simple outline.

Materials   None.

Procedure   1. Write a category name (e.g., Groceries) on the board and ask students to suggest as many items as possible that belong in the category (e.g., carrots, cheese, hamburger, milk, apples). Write words on the board or overhead transparency as students suggest them—do not attempt to organize the words as they are suggested.
2. Ask students to look over list to see whether any groups can be formed. Ask for group labels (e.g., fruit, vegetables, frozen foods, meat). Have students identify all foods that belong to each group.

3. Write suggested labels down in outline form. List all words that go with label.

I. Groceries
   A. Vegetables
      1. string beans
      2. lima beans
      3. peppers
      4. cauliflower
      5. broccoli
      6. onions
      7. carrots
      8. peas
      9. celery
      10. lettuce
      11. cabbage
      12. cucumbers
   B. Fruits
      1. apples
      2. bananas
      3. pears
      4. pineapple
      5. peaches
      6. plums
      7. oranges
      8. cherries
      9. grapes
      10. figs
      11. nectarines
      12. apricots
   C. Meats
      1. hamburger
      2. steak
      3. pork chops
      4. ham
      5. bacon
      6. hot dogs
      7. roast beef
   D. Poultry
      1. chicken
      2. duck
      3. pheasant
      4. cornish hen
      5. turkey
   E. Dairy Products
      1. milk
      2. cheese
      3. butter
      4. yogurt
      5. cottage cheese
      6. cream
      7. sour cream
      8. margarine
   F. Desserts
      1. cake
      2. cookies
      3. pie
      4. pudding
      5. ice cream
   G. Dry Foods
      1. macaroni
      2. spaghetti
      3. dried beans
      4. dried peas
   H. Snacks
      1. potato chips
      2. pretzels
      3. peanuts
      4. popcorn
   I. Herbs and Spices
      1. paprika
      2. chili powder
      3. garlic powder
      4. oregano
      5. bay leaves
      6. pepper
      7. salt

Is That So? (Fact or Opinion?)

Objective   To identify statements of fact and opinion.

Materials   List of statements: some factual, some opinion (see examples).

Procedure
1. Read a statement and have students decide whether it is a fact or an opinion. Does everyone agree with the statement? Can it be proved? If not, it must be an opinion.
   Examples   Ford Motor Company makes the best cars.
   Ford Motor Company makes Mustangs.
2. Make a chart on the chalkboard. List factual statements on one side and opinion statements on the other side. Notice how many opinions use "hasty generalizations." Notice the ways that opinions were modified. (Specific examples or details were added to make the statement true.)
3. Give students a factual statement and have them write an opinion statement on the same topic.
   Fact: "It is raining today."
   Opinion: "The weather today is great. I love rain."
4. Have students read their opinions aloud to the class. Ask other students to identify the words that changed the statement from fact to opinion.

Extension
Save all fact and opinion statements and copy them on a ditto or index cards in mixed-up order. Students can sort fact and opinion statements as an independent activity on another day.

Examples: Fact and Opinion
I waited exactly six minutes and thirty seconds to get my lunch.
We have to wait a long time to get our lunch. (How long is long?)
All cars need gasoline in order to run. (What about cars that use diesel fuel—Mercedes?)
My car, a 1977 Chevrolet, uses no-lead gas.
Pancakes make the best breakfast. (I like scrambled eggs.)
Pancakes are made out of flour, water, and eggs.
All students are lazy.
John did not do his science homework.
The temperature is 92 degrees today.
Phew, it's really hot today. (How hot is hot?)
That kid is really tall. (How tall? Taller than my father?)
That kid is 5 foot 10.
Our product, Fluffy Flour, is the best.
You use flour to make bread.
A new Cadillac is very expensive. (Even for a millionaire?)
That Cadillac cost $10,000.
Cadillacs cost more than Volkswagens.
Every family needs two cars. (My mother doesn't drive. The kids don't drive yet, either.)
That dress was very cheap. (How cheap? For me or the millionaire?)
That dress cost $249.50.
This book is too long to read. (What's too long? 100 pages? 800?)
This book has 545 pages in it.
We had a terrible lunch today.
The menu for today is hamburgers and french fries.

CHAPTER 8

Use the Right Word

The way that a writer selects and arranges vocabulary controls interest, meaning, and effectiveness of the written expression. Whereas experienced writers use a variety of word types, poor writers tend to overuse a limited number of commonly used words. As a result, their writing lacks clarity and precision and frequently fails to interest the reader.

The use of poor or inappropriate vocabulary in written expression has several causes. Some students simply do not have a good command of vocabulary in oral expression, while other students, who do have a broad speaking vocabulary, may use simpler words in writing because they are easier to spell. The first student needs more emphasis on building vocabulary comprehension and usage in *oral expression*, while the second needs more practice in *spelling the words he or she uses in oral expression*.

The activities in this vocabulary development chapter are based on the premise that students can broaden their command of vocabulary and spelling by working and playing with words in a variety of ways.

The following specific vocabulary skills are developed in this chapter.

1. *Using specific vocabulary.* Developing an awareness of alternative vocabulary choices to the most commonly used words is essential to increasing effectiveness in writing. Emphasis is placed on identifying specific nouns, verbs, synonyms, and antonyms to replace those overused, nonspecific words.
2. *Using descriptive words.* Examples of beautiful imagery in poetry, fiction, and nonfiction help students visualize images. These serve as a stimulus for students' own writing.
3. *Using abstract words.* Defining abstract words encourages students to provide specific facts, details, or examples.
4. *Playing with words.* Arranging words in interesting patterns according to sounds creates interesting poetic effects in writing. Activities that emphasize alliteration and onomatopoeia allow students to play with words.
5. *Making original comparisons.* Students frequently use stereotyped phrases in their writing without stopping to think of different ways that the same

idea could be expressed. Playing with these stereotypes and rephrasing them with precise vocabulary choices draw students' attention to the problem.

Use the Vocabulary Checklist (Table 2-5) with the students to identify strengths and weaknesses in vocabulary use.

Playing with Words

Objective   To substitute specific words for overused words.

Materials   Copies of "Feelings About Words" by Mary O'Neill, chart paper, marking pens.

Procedure   1. Give copies of the poem to class members and have them read it orally. Discuss any unfamiliar vocabulary.
2. Divide class into groups of five or six students. Give each group a large piece of chart paper and a marker. Have each group choose a recorder to write down ideas.
3. Pick out some of the overused words in the poem (e.g., *small, sad, slow, hot, fat, light*.) Have students try to identify how the author of this poem chose her words. (She used specific examples to represent the word.)
4. Next have students list as many words as they can that show what each word means. Reread the poem several times until the students understand the idea.
5. Have groups share their results with the whole class. Display charts around classroom.

*Feelings About Words**

Some words cling	Some words are hot:
as ice in drink.	Fire, flame and shot.
Some move with grace:	Some words are sharp,
A dance, a lace.	Sword, point and carp.
Some sound thin:	And some alert:
Wail, scream and pin.	Glint, glance and flirt.
Some words are squat:	Some words are lazy:
A mug, a pot,	Saunter, hazy.
And some are plump,	And some words preen:
Fat, round and dump.	Pride, pomp and queen.
Some words are light:	Some words are quick,
drift, lift and bright.	A jerk, a flick.
A few are small:	Some words are slow:
A, is and all.	Lag, stop and grow,
And some are thick,	While others poke
Glue, paste and brick.	As ox with yoke.
Some words are sad:	Some words can fly—
"I never had . . ."	There's wind, there's high:
And others gay:	And some words cry:
Joy, spin and play.	"Goodbye . . . Goodbye . . ."
Some words are sick:	
Stab, scratch and nick.	

Vocabulary Brainstorming

Objective   To identify alternatives to common, overused vocabulary.

Materials   Copies of most frequently used vocabulary (Tables 8-1, 8-2, and 8-3), chart paper, magic markers.

Procedure
1. Decide on one category of words, for example, verbs. Give copies of "Most Frequently Used Verbs in Children's Writing" to students.
2. Divide class into groups. Have each group choose one word from the verb list and brainstorm all the specific words that could be used in its place. Allow students to use dictionaries and thesauri.
3. Have students write their common verb and their specific verbs on a large chart. They may add illustrations if they wish.
4. Have students identify the most specific word on their list.
5. Have groups share their word charts with other class members. Display final charts in the classroom or hallway.
6. Repeat this activity with other verbs or choose words from Tables 8-2 and 8-3.
7. Encourage students to refer to the class charts when working on writing assignments.

TABLE 8-1
Most frequently used nouns in children's writing

anything	everyone	lady	room
baby	everything	life	school
ball	everywhere	light	ship
baseball	eye	love	sister
bed	face	lunch	snow
bird	family	man	someone
boat	father	men	something
book	feet	minute	story
box	fire	Mom	summer
boy	floor	money	stuff
brother	flowers	moon	space
candy	food	morning	spring
cat	fun	mother	teacher
car	game	mouse	television
Christmas	girl	name	thing
city	hair	night	things
clothes	happiness	nothing	time
color	head	parents	today
Dad	home	part	town
day	horse	party	tree
dinner	hour	paper	trouble
dog	house	people	vacation
dollar	ice	person	way
door	idea	place	week
dream	island	police	winter
earth	job	rain	wish
Easter	kids	ride	world
everybody	king	rocket	

Adapted from R.L. Hillerich, *A Writing Vocabulary of Elementary Children.* Springfield, IL: Charles C Thomas, 1978. Used with permission of author and publisher.

TABLE 8-2
Most frequently used verbs in children's writing

ask	(asks, asked, asking)
be	(is, am, are, was, were)
come	(comes, coming, came)
call*	(calls, called, calling)
can*	(could)
do	(does, doing, done, don't didn't)
eat	(eats, eating, ate)
get	(gets, getting)
go	(goes, going, gone)
have	(has, having, had)
know	(knows, knowing, knew)
like	(likes, liked, liking)
live	(lived, lives, living)
look	(looked, looking, looks)
make	(makes, making, made)
name*	(names naming)
play*	(plays, played, playing)
put	(puts, putting)
run	(runs, running, ran)
say	(says, saying, said)
see	(sees, seeing, saw)
start	(starts, started, starting)
tell	(tells, telling, told)
think	(thinks, thinking, thought)
try	(tries, tried, trying)
walk*	(walks, walked, walking)
want	(wants, wanted, wanting)
will*	(would)
work*	(works, worked, working)

*Indicates that word may be a different part of speech depending on context in which it is used. Word frequency lists do not distinguish between parts of speech.
Adapted from Hillerich, R. L. A Writing Vocabulary of Elementary Children. Springfield, IL: Charles C Thomas Publisher, 1978. Used with permission of the author and publisher.

Ten-Dollar Words

Objective   To listen for and identify specific words from student writing.

Materials   Student compositions.

Procedure   1. Have students listen for specific words as their peers read their own writing samples to the class or small groups. As words are identified, discuss their meaning and how the specific word added to the piece of writing.
2. Have students assign monetary value to words; for example, *is, was, were,* would be one-cent words; *building* might be a two-dollar word, but *The Empire State Building* might be a five-dollar word because it is so specific. *Beautiful* might be a one-dollar word, whereas *elegant* might be a ten-dollar word. *Said* might be a one-cent word, whereas *chattered* might be an eight-dollar word.
3. Have students count up the dollar value of each other's writing samples. Have the most highly valued ones read to the class and posted on the bulletin board.

TABLE 8-3
Most frequently used adjectives and adverbs in children's writing

adjectives		adverbs	
afraid	last	almost	where
all	little	always	which
another	long	any	while
bad	lucky	both	
beautiful	mad	early	
best	many	enough*	
better	more	finally	
black	most	first	
blue	new	here	
brown	next*	how	
cold	nice	just	
cute	old	later	
dark	orange	never	
different	other	next*	
enough*	pink	now	
every	pretty	often	
famous	purple	only	
fast	quick	probably	
favorite	real	quite	
few	red	quickly	
fine	sad	really	
first*	short	so	
funny	slow	some*	
great	small	soon	
green	some*	suddenly	
good	terrible	then	
happy	unhappy	there	
hard	white	too	
hot	yellow	very	
kind		when	

*Starred words can be both adjective or adverb depending on use in sentence.
Adapted from R.L. Hillerich, *A Writing Vocabulary of Elementary Children*. Springfield, IL: Charles C. Thomas, 1978. Used with permission of author and editor.

4. Make charts of ten-dollar words and their meanings to hang around the room. Point out when students use the words on the chart.

Using Specific Nouns

Objective   To list specific nouns in different categories.

Materials   Chart paper and magic markers.

Procedure   1. Choose a category word and ask class members to suggest specific nouns that would fit this category. Write suggestions on the board (e.g., *dogs*: Great Dane, beagle, poodle, cocker spaniel, Irish setter, elk hound, terrier, sheep dog).

2. Explain the reason for this activity: Very often we use common nouns in our writing when we really could use very specific nouns. This activity will alert students to other possible word choices.
3. Divide the class into small groups and let each group choose a category. Ask them to list specific nouns in their category on the chart. Dictionaries or other reference materials may be used.

   Suggested categories: states, countries, cars, trees, flowers, desserts, vegetables, fruits, zoo animals, birds, occupations, sports, tools, meats, toys, and games.
4. Have each group write five sentences using specific nouns from their categories, then read sentences to the class. Ask class to identify the specific nouns used and name the category.
5. Put finished charts with specific nouns and sample sentences on bulletin board as a reminder to students to use specific nouns in writing whenever possible.

Extension 1   Let students choose a category and illustrate specific nouns from that group.

Extension 2   *Categories*

Have students make a grid on their paper, then list some category words along the side of the grid and their name across the top of the grid. (See Figure 8-1.) The students must fill in each box with a word from the category that begins with the specific letter at the top of the column. Students may use a dictionary to help find appropriate words.

You can use scoring procedures with this activity. Give five points for each block that is filled in. The student with the highest score wins. Use the same word across the top of the grid when using scoring procedures because some names have more difficult letters. An open time allowance will allow slower students to compete with faster students. To shorten the time necessary to complete this activity, pair students of different ability levels. The better student can help the poorer student.

	N	A	N	C	Y
animals	newt				
food	noodles				
clothes	necktie				
countries	New Zealand				
states	New York				

Extension 3   See "Grocery List" Activity in Chapter 7.

Count the Izzes and Wazzes

Objective   To identify and eliminate overused and passive verbs in a writing selection.

Materials   Chart of most commonly used (and thus overused) verbs, sample compositions, student compositions.

Procedure   1. Put a sample composition on an overhead transparency, ditto, or chalkboard. Ask one student to read the composition aloud while class listens for the error pattern.
2. If students have difficulty identifying the problem, ask them to suggest ways to improve the composition.
3. Have students circle all verbs (if using a ditto) or have one student circle all the verbs with class help.
4. Count the number of different verbs and how often each appears in the sample. Point out that overused verbs are "lazy verbs."
5. Next, go through the composition line by line, asking students to substitute stronger verbs for the overused verbs.
6. Now have students look over one of their own compositions and circle all the verbs. Ask how many identified at least one verb that was overused.
7. Make a chart of lazy verbs and place it on the bulletin board. Remind students to avoid lazy verbs.

Sample Compositions

There are two men on a yellow raft. They are in a fast river and they are going fast through the rapids. The rapids are dangerous but the men are brave. They are excited. One man is shouting. The other one is rowing the big oar. All of a sudden the raft tips. One man is in the water now but the other man is still in the raft. They are both scared. The man in the water is very cold and he is screaming for help. The other man throws a rope and pulls him in. He is safe.

It was the last inning of the baseball game and the last batter of the Phillies team was at bat. The score was 9 to 8 and the Phillies were losing. The crowd was screaming. A fast pitch was thrown by the pitcher to the nervous batter. The ball was nipped by the batter. A second pitch was thrown. Whack! The ball was hit out towards center field. The crowd was screaming again. Would this be the home run that was needed to bring that runner on first base in and win the game? The screaming was suddenly changed to loud moans. The high fly ball was caught by a rookie outfielder. "Three outs" called the umpire. The game was over.

Substitution

Objective   To substitute specific words for general words.

Materials   Sample sentences.

Procedure   1. Write a sample sentence on the board or overhead transparency.
2. Underline one word at a time and ask students to suggest a *more specific word* that would make sense in the sentence (the words do not have to be synonyms). Rewrite the sentence with the new word.

The <u>old</u> man walked slowly.
The <u>comical man</u> walked slowly.
The comical clown <u>walked</u> slowly.
The comical clown tumbled awkwardly.

3. Read completed sentences. Compare first sentences with the last sentence. What happened?
4. Continue this activity by using a new sample sentence. Some students may wish to continue the activity on their own, while others may need more practice with the group.

Examples
1. The little girl played a game.
2. My puppy chewed something.
3. David quickly climbed the tree.
4. The thing was big and black.
5. The football player threw the football.
6. That big elephant ate the grass.
7. Several children played a game.
8. A little old lady sang a song.

Extension 1   1. Use only *synonyms* in the new sentences: The elderly gentleman ambled awkwardly.
2. Use only *antonyms* in the new sentences: The teenage football player dashed briskly.

Extension 2   *Unusual Opposites*

Get the book *Opposites* by Richard Wilbur (Harcourt Brace Jovanovich). You may find it in the children's section of your school or local library. Read several of the questions found in the book to your students (e.g., "What is the opposite of a prince?"). Let students give their suggestions before you read the rest of the selection. Write student suggestions on the board; then read Wilbur's answer. Your students may be surprised by the answers! Continue by trying out other selections from the book. Next, let students choose some words and write some of their own "unusual opposites."

What Is the Opposite of a Prince?

What is the opposite of a prince?
A frog must be the answer, since,
As all good fairy stories tell,
When some witch says a magic spell,
Causing the prince to be disguised
So that he won't be recognized,
He always ends up green and sad
And sitting on a lily pad.

From OPPOSITES, copyright © 1973 by Richard Wilbur.
Reprinted by permission of Harcourt Brace Jovanovich, Inc.

Repetitive Words

Objective To substitute specific words for repetitive words.

Materials Sample paragraphs with repetitive words (following).

Procedure
1. Read a sample paragraph to the students and ask them to identify the problem (in this case the repeated use of the word *nice*). Emphasize the repeated word as you read.
   Example: "nice"

   It was a *nice* warm day in April. I was wearing my *nice* new clothes that I had just bought at the *nice* store. A *nice* breeze was blowing *nice* leaves across the *nice* street. There were *nice* children playing in the *nice* yard with their *nice* dog. I could hear the *nice* chirping of the birds who were perched on the *nice* branches of the *nice* oak tree. It was really a *nice* day.

2. Give students a copy of the paragraph and let them suggest alternatives for the repeated word. Read the corrected paragraph to the class.
3. Give students another paragraph to do on their own. Encourage them to use a thesaurus to find alternatives to the repeated word.
4. Have individual students read their original paragraph, then their corrected paragraph to the class. Make a list of different words used by the students.
5. Place corrected paragraphs on the bulletin board.

Repetitive Word Stories

"said"

   "I want to go to the park," *said* the little girl.
   "Not now," *said* her mother. "I'm getting dinner ready."
   "Please take me to the park. I want to see my friends," *said* the girl.
   "I told you I am busy," *said* the mother.
   "If you don't take me to the park, I won't eat dinner," *said* the girl.
   "Well, if you don't stop complaining, you'll go to your room without any dinner," *said* the mother.
   "O.K.," *said* the girl.

"good"

   Yesterday was a *good* day for a picnic. Early in the morning I telephoned my *good* friend Larry and asked him whether he wanted to join me. He said a picnic was a *good* idea. We decided that a *good* time to meet would be twelve o'clock in front of the park entrance. I brought some *good* roast beef sandwiches and a jar of *good* potato salad. Larry brought some *good* lemonade, which he carried in his father's *good* thermos. He also brought along some *good* homemade chocolate cake. When we found a *good* spot to eat near a stream, we spread out my *good* picnic blanket and unpacked the *good* food. After having a *good* feast we went on a *good* long walk. Larry and I left the *good* park at four o'clock. We both felt *good*.

Mary Had a Little Lamb

Objective To rewrite nursery rhymes using *specific* nouns, verbs, and adjectives.

Materials Several nursery rhymes that have nouns, verbs, and adjectives omitted.

Procedure
1. Choose a nursery rhyme and write it on an overhead transparency, leaving blanks for all nouns, verbs, and adjectives (see sample following).
2. Tell students that they are going to help write a nursery rhyme by suggesting *specific* words for categories that you call out. Encourage the use of proper nouns in order to get extremely specific responses. *Do not give students a copy of the ditto sheet yet.*
3. Read the first category and ask for suggestions for the blank (e.g., "girl's name"). Encourage students to think of uncommon responses (e.g., Melody instead of Mary). Write the response in the blank on the transparency. Do not put transparency on the overhead projector until it is completely filled in.
4. Put completed transparency on overhead projector and have a student read the final version.
5. Ask students to guess the name of the original nursery rhyme.
6. Have students write additional original nursery rhymes by using the word substitution method.

SAMPLE NURSERY RHYME
(Mary Had a Little Lamb)

_____ had a _____ _____	
(girl's name) (size—adj.) (noun—animal name)	
Its _____ was _____ as _____	
(noun—body part) (color) (noun—weather word)	
Everywhere that _____ the _____	
(repeat girl's name) (repeat animal name)	
was sure to _____.	
(verb—action word)	
It followed her to _____ _____	
(noun—place) (when phrase)	
to _____ _____	
(repeat place) (repeat when phrase)	
to _____ _____	
(repeat place) (repeat when phrase)	
It made the _____ _____ and _____	
(collective noun) (verb—action word) (verb—action word)	
To see a _____ at _____.	
(repeat animal name) (repeat place)	

Descriptive Words

Objective   To pick out descriptive phrases in reading material.

Materials   Several books that have good descriptive selections, drawing materials.

Procedure
1. Read to students several pages from a book that contains vivid descriptions. Ask students to listen for descriptive phrases and sentences that help them form a specific visual picture in their mind.
2. Write phrases on the board as students recall them. Talk about different ideas that students had as they heard the descriptive words.
3. Ask students to identify the way the author helped them to imagine the scenes or picture (e.g., specific words, colorful words, concrete images, comparisons). Write these ideas on the board.
4. Read several more pages and continue to identify and talk about the descriptive phrases.
5. Ask students to select one descriptive phrase or sentence from the reading selection to illustrate. Have them write the phrase under the illustration.

Extension   Have students look for interesting descriptive phrases as they read on their own. Keep an ongoing bulletin board for these phrases. Have students illustrate the phrases and add them to the bulletin board. Share new phrases during group discussions.

Resources   *Have You Seen Trees?*
  Joanne Oppenheim
  Addison-Wesley, 1967
Specific details and varied vocabulary are used to describe trees.

The Clean Brook
  Margaret Bartlett
  Crowell, 1960
The author uses specific details when describing objects and settings.

The Brook
  Carol and Donald Carrick
  Macmillan, 1967
Many beautiful watercolor illustrations along with beautiful usage of words help form visual images.

Poems Make Pictures, Pictures Make Poems
  Giose Rimovelli and Paul Pimsleur
  Pantheon, 1972
Each poem in this collection makes a picture. The book will give students all kinds of ideas about the many different forms that poems can take. Some of the poems form the shape of a shoe, a boat, or a building.

First Voices, Vol. 1 and Vol. 2
  Geoffrey Summerfield
  Random House (Singer School Division), 1971
This four-volume anthology presents an *outstanding* collection of original and traditional rhymes and poems by poets from around the world. Some of the material included is written by children. Photographs and illustrations provide added interest.

There Is No Rhyme for Silver
  Eve Merriam
  Atheneum, 1962
This collection includes invented words.

Ounce, Dice, Trice
  Alistair Reid
  Little, Brown, 1958
Like to make up new words and definitions? You will enjoy some of the invented vocabulary and definitions in this book. Kids will really get the idea of "playing with words" after hearing some samples from this book.

Silly Songs and Sad
  Ellen Raskin
  Crowell, 1967
Here is another good collection of poems. Ellen Raskin's poems are delightfully written and give students some excellent samples of ways to "play with words."

I'm Nobody! Who Are You?
The Poems of Emily Dickinson for Children
  Stemmer House Publishers, Inc., 1978
This edition of Emily Dickinson's poems features illustrations of the costumes and settings of nineteenth-century New England and contains such familiar poems as "Hope is the Thing with Feathers," and "There is no Frigate Like a Book."

I See the Winds
  Kazue Mizumura
  Crowell, 1966
Kazue Mizumura captures the many forms of wind through the seasons in free verse and beautiful illustrations.

Wind, Sand, and Sky
  Rebecca Caudill
  Dutton, 1976
Caudill uses beautiful phrases of imagery in her writing, and gives us a romantic view of the desert. The illustrations by Donald Carrick add tone and depth to this beautiful book. Many beautiful comparisons are made.

Make It Real

Objective To list concrete details for abstract words.

Materials Paper and pencil.

Procedure 1. Tell the class that specific details often make abstract words seem very real to the reader. List some abstract words on the board. Have students suggest others.

fear	loneliness	bravery	love
sadness	happiness	solitude	friendship
hate	anger	beauty	contentment

2. Have each student write a phrase or sentence about "happiness" on a piece of paper. Collect the papers and read the phrases. Write them on the board in the form of a poem.

Happiness is . . .
getting a new little kitten for a birthday
sharing an ice cream cone with a friend
playing jump rope with friends
playing baseball after school

3. Choose another abstract word and have students think of concrete experiences to represent the word. Students may want to write a poem completely on their own.

Extension Collect the abstract "poems" and put them in a notebook. Let students add to them as they come across new abstract words.

The Sun Is a Golden Earring

Objective To recognize and write original comparisons (metaphors).

Materials Library books: *The Beautiful Things, The Sun Is a Golden Earring.*

Procedure 1. Read either of the suggested books to the students and ask them to listen for descriptive comparisons.
2. Ask students to list some of the comparisons that were just read. Write these comparisons on the board. Read the comparison from the book again if students cannot remember the whole sentence. Here are a few examples:

"The tree is a cloud of leaves anchored to the earth by its roots." *(The Beautiful Things)*
"The moon is a white cat that hunts the gray mice of the night." *(The Sun Is a Golden Earring)*

3. Write one phrase (e.g., *The Wind is . . .*) on the board and have each student finish the comparison on a slip of paper. Collect slips of paper and read comparisons anonymously. Write them on the board with the other comparisons.
4. Continue the activity by writing more phrases on the board and having students write more comparisons.

Extension Illustrate the metaphors and put them on the bulletin board. Keep a chart of interesting comparisons that students find in their reading.

Resources *The Sun Is a Golden Earring*
N. Belting
Holt Rinehart, and Winston, 1962

The Beautiful Things
T. McGrath
Vanguard Press, 1960

Orange Is a Color: A Book About Colors
Sharon Lerner
Lerner Publications, 1970

Words, Words, Words
Mary O'Neill
Doubleday, 1966

Hailstones and Halibut Bones
Mary O'Neill
Doubleday, 1961

Have You Seen Roads?
Joanne Oppenheim
Addison-Wesley, 1969

What Is That Sound!
Mary O'Neill
Atheneum, 1968

Strange as It Seems

Objective   To illustrate literal interpretations of common clichés.

Materials   List of clichés, drawing paper, crayons or magic markers.

Procedure   1. List several clichés on the board and discuss their meaning. Have students give examples of how each cliché is commonly used.
2. Ask students to suggest other clichés that they have heard or used. List these on the board and discuss their common meaning.
3. Have each student choose one or several clichés to illustrate. Ask them to draw the *literal* interpretation of the words. (For example: "It's raining cats and dogs" might show dark rain clouds overhead and cats and dogs falling from the clouds to the ground.)
4. Ask students to make up a story that explains the way their unusual events (e.g., cats and dogs falling from the rain clouds) occurred. Encourage them to use their wildest imaginations.
5. Share stories and illustrations by reading aloud. Bind the stories in a booklet entitled *Strange as It Seems* or *Believe It or Not*.

Extension   Remind students to avoid clichés in their own writing.
    Have students look for other clichés to add to the list and to the *Believe It or Not* books.

Sample Clichés

a finger in every pie	barking up the wrong tree
a little bird told me	beating around the bush
a wolf in sheep's clothing	be at loose ends
alive and kicking	bite your tongue
all thumbs	blind leading the blind
apple of my eye	blow off steam
apple pie order	blue blood
as the crow flies	born with a silver spoon in one's
at the end of the rope	mouth
at wit's end	building castles in the air
ax to grind	bull-headed

bury the hatchet
button your mouth
by hook or by crook
by the skin of his teeth
can't carry a tune in a bucket
can't get over it
caught red-handed
chip off the old block
chip on his shoulder
cook one's goose
cost a pretty penny
crocodile tears
cut a long story short
cut corners
cut it out
done to a turn
down in the dumps
drive a hard bargain
drop a line
eat your heart out
eat your words
egg one on
elbow grease
face the music
fall head over heels in love
feather in your cap
fit as a fiddle
flying high
food for thought
frog in your throat
full of baloney
full of hot air
get it straight from the horse's
  mouth
give a hand
go fly a kite
gone to the dogs
grease my palm
handle with kid gloves
have a green thumb
heart of stone
he's a fence sitter
he's a fish out of water
he's a square peg in a round
  hole

he's a walking encyclopedia
in a nutshell
in hot water
in the bag
in the nick of time
kick the bucket
learn by heart
like two peas in a pod
long arm of the law
my hair is standing on end
not my cup of tea
once in a blue moon
on cloud nine
on edge
on pins and needles
on the up and up
on the wagon
one foot in the grave
out of the woods
over the hill
pain in the neck
pass the buck
pie in the sky
pin a rap on
pipe down
play second fiddle
pound the pavement
pull a fast one
pull strings
pulling up stakes.
pulling your leg
put wool over his eyes
rack one's brains
raining cats and dogs
read between the lines
scratch the surface
seal your lips
second thoughts
see eye to eye
shell out (money)
skeleton in the closet
spill the beans
take place
teach an old dog new tricks

Happy as a Lark

Objective   To write original comparisons.

Materials   List of worn-out comparisons (clichés).

Procedure 1. Ask students whether they have heard phrases like:

happy as a lark	cross as a bear
quick as a wink	quiet as a mouse
brave as a lion	stubborn as a mule
funny as a monkey	lazy as a dog
nervous as a cat	cute as a button
cold as ice	

2. Ask students to add more to the list if they can.

3. Explain to class that these are worn-out phrases or clichés that are frequently used in speech or writing. Choose one phrase and ask the students to suggest some original comparisons. Try to get four or five different examples from the students.

"nervous as a cat" can become
"nervous as a mexican jumping bean in a hot hand"
"nervous as a bird being stalked by a hungry cat"

4. Choose another example and try to think of additional examples.

"as quiet as a mouse" can become
"as quiet as a leaf falling from a tree"
"as quiet as a cloud floating in the sky"

Point out that a specific action added to the comparison helps the reader visualize more clearly.

5. Read the poem "It Doesn't Always Have to Rhyme" by Eve Merriam. Put a copy on the bulletin board.

6. Have students write some original comparisons on their own to share with the class. Students may want to illustrate them and put them on the bulletin board.

7. Point out that original comparisons make writing much more interesting.

Extension 1. Have students watch for original comparisons in their reading. Have them copy the comparisons on an index card and put them on the bulletin board.

2. Have students collect clichés from their reading and make a class chart labeled "Avoid These Clichés."

black as ink	high as an elephant's eye
black as night	hungry as a bear
blind as a bat	large as life
busy as a bee/beaver	mad as a hatter
clean as a whistle	nutty as a fruitcake
clever as a fox	old as the hills
cool as a cucumber	pale as a ghost
cold as ice	plain as the nose on your face
cute as a button	poor as a churchmouse
dead as a doornail	pretty as a picture
deep as the ocean	proud as a peacock
dry as a bone	quick as a flash
fit as a fiddle	quick as a wink
flat as a pancake	red as a beet
free as a bird	scarce as hen's teeth
fresh as a daisy	sharp as a tack
green as grass	sick as a dog
happy as a clam	slippery as an eel

slow as molasses
snug as a bug in a rug
soft as butter
sour as a pickle
strong as an ox

sweet as sugar
thin as a rail
tough as nails
warm as toast
white as a sheet

It Doesn't Always Have to Rhyme
   Eve Merriam
"A Cliché"
A cliché
is what we all say
when we're too lazy
to find another way

and so we say
warm as toast
quiet as a mouse
slow as molasses
quick as a wink.

Think!
Is toast the warmest thing you know?
Think again, it might not be so,
Think again: it might even be snow!
Soft as lamb's wool, fleecy snow.

Listen to that mouse go
scuttling and clawing,
nibbling and pawing.
A mouse can speak
if only a squeak.
Is a mouse the quietest thing you know?
Think again, it might not be so.
Think again: it might be a shadow.
Quiet as a shadow,
quiet as growing grass,
quiet as a pillow,
or a looking glass.

Slow as molasses,
quick as a wink,
Before you say so,
take time to think.

Sound Poems

Objective   To write a "sound poem."

Materials   Sample "sound poem."

Procedure   1. Write a "sound poem" on the board and have students read it aloud together (e.g., "Thunder").
2. Ask students to comment on the way the poem was written. (It's a list of words that tell about the title.)
3. Write a different sound word on the board (e.g., *rain*) and ask *each* student to write down three words that tell what sounds or actions the word uses. Have students read these words aloud when everyone is finished. Write words on the boad in a list. Read the new "sound poem" in unison. Ask students whether they would like to rearrange any words to make the poem sound smoother.
4. Repeat this activity with another word.
5. Put a list of suggested words on the board and let each student choose a title word for a "sound poem." Students may want to suggest additional words for this list.

rain	wind	motorcycles	quiet
snow	breeze	cars	loud
lightning	ocean waves	machines	noise
laughter	trucks	planes	

6. Have students write their own "sound poem" and then read their results to the group.
7. Have students copy and illustrate their "sound poems" on another day. Bind poems and their illustrations in a "Sound Book."

Extension   Make a book of sounds. Have each student draw a picture of something that makes a sound and then write the sound somewhere on the picture. Show Peter Spier's book *Crash! Bang! Boom!* as an example.

Example: Sound Poem

> *THUNDER*
>
> rumbles,
> tumbles,
> rolls,
> bangs,
> booms,
> bumps,
> bounces,
> cracks,
> snaps,
> crackles,
> echoes.
> LOUD NOISE!!!

Resources   *Crash! Bang! Boom!*
    Peter Spier
    Doubleday, 1970

Street Poems
    Robert Froman
    McCall Publishing Co., 1971

Something Special
    Beatrice S. DeRegniers and Irene Haas
    Harcourt Brace Jovanovich, 1958

Klippity Klop
Ed Emberley
Little, Brown, 1974

Alphabet Antics

Objective   To write sentences using alliteration.

Materials   Book: *A Twister of Twists, A Tangler of Tongues*; dictionaries.

Procedure
1. Read the following tongue twister to students and ask what they notice about it.

   "A pale pink proud peacock pompously preened its pretty plumage." (p. 26, *A Twister of Twists*)

2. Explain to students that use of the same letter or letters at the beginning of each word in a group of words is called "alliteration." Ask students whether they know any other tongue twisters that use alliteration. List student suggestions on the board.
3. Have each student choose a letter of the alphabet. (They may want to use the first letter of their names.) Have them write down words that begin with their chosen letter. Encourage them to use a dictionary to find additional words.
4. Ask students to create a sentence using only words on their list. They may add articles and conjunctions.
5. Have them read their finished sentences to classmates. They may illustrate their sentences if they choose.

Extension   Read "Shrewd Simon Short" (p. 50, *A Twister of Twists*). Every word in this three-page story begins with "s." Ask students to write longer pieces using only one letter. Share results with the class. (See *The Knight, the Knave, and the Knapsack* for another example.)

The Knight, the Knave, and the Knapsack

The knight left his knapsack of knives on the knotty tree on the knoll. A knave wearing knitted knickers noticed the knapsack and knelt on his knees on the knoll. He tried his knack at unknotting the knot on the knapsack. As he did, he cut his knuckle on a knife in the knapsack. The knight-errant soon returned and knocked the knife-stealing knave down on the knoll. The knave had learned some new knowledge: never kneel on a knoll and try to take knives from the knight's knapsack!

List all *kn* words, then put them in alphabetical order.

kna	kne	kni	kno	knu
_____	_____	_____	_____	_____
_____	_____	_____	_____	
_____	_____	_____	_____	
		_____	_____	

Resources   *My Tang's Tungled and Other Ridiculous Situations*
Sara and John Brewton and G. Meredith Blackburn III
Crowell, 1973

Tongue Tanglers; More Tongue Tanglers and a Rigamorole
Charles Francis Potter
World Publishing Co., 1962 and 1964

A Beastly Collection
Jonathan Coudrille
Frederick Warne Co., 1975

A Beastly Circus
Peggy Parish
Simon and Schuster, 1969

CHAPTER 9

Build Sentence Sense

To be effective, written expression needs a variety of sentence patterns. The inexperienced writer, however, tends to rely heavily on simple sentence structure and on the most common vocabulary. Awkward constructions appear in the work of those writers who *do* attempt to vary sentence structure. Omission of words and phrases, inappropriate wording (verb tense, pronoun agreement), and missing or inaccurate punctuation cause some of this awkwardness. The writer's original ideas are thus lost in this inability to communicate clearly through accurate and interesting sentences.

Good ideas are the starting point for written expression. Beyond that, a well-developed "sentence sense" that leads the student to use a variety of sentence patterns is essential. The activities in this chapter provide opportunities for students to experiment with techniques for building different kinds of sentences. Students who have poor sentence sense will need to start at the beginning of the sequence and work carefully through the activities over a period of time. Others who have some degree of sentence sense can move more quickly through the sequence and focus on sentence combining and reducing activities.

Several principles form the basis for this sequence of activities.

1. *Sentences have two basic parts; the naming part and the action part.* It is *not* necessary for students to remember the terms *subject* and *predicate* as long as they can understand the purpose for each part of the sentence: the subject *names* the participant(s), while the predicate provides the *action*. At first, focus strictly on physical action verbs (e.g., *jumping, running*), then move on to "brain work" verbs (e.g., *thinking, knowing*) to linking verbs (e.g., *is, are*).
2. *Sentences can be expanded by:*

   * adding descriptive detail, and
   * adding *when, where, how,* and *why* phrases.

3. *Sentence arrangement can be varied by:*

   • changing sequence of *who/what, when, where, how,* and *why* **phrases**.

4. *Sentences can be combined to:*

   • eliminate excess words;
   • replace short, choppy sentences; and
   • develop longer, more interesting sentences.

5. *Sentences can be reduced to two basic parts by:*

   • deleting descriptive detail; and
   • deleting *when, where, how,* and *why* phrases.

TABLE 9-1

Command/Request Sentences	Eat! Run! Help! Stop! Fire!
Kernel Sentences contain subject and verb	Dogs eat. Fish swim. Bears growl.
Simple Sentences contain subject (noun or pronoun), verb, and object or adjective and may use a form of the verb "to be"	The dogs eat <u>bones.</u> It <u>is</u> a boat. They <u>are</u> hungry.
Expanded Sentences are really simple sentences with additional descriptive details or phrases*	
1. descriptive words	(Large, slender, rusty-colored) Irish Setters munch (crispy, crunchy) dog bones.
2. when, where, how phrases	An enormous bear chased me (in the woods) (yesterday afternoon).
3. compound subject	A mother bear and chased me. her baby bear

4. compound predicate	An enormous bear growled at me
	                   and
	                 chased me.

Compound Sentences contain two independent clauses** joined by and, but, or, nor, for	(The students go outside for recess) (but) (the teachers go to the library.)
Complex Sentences contain one independent clause and one dependent clause*** joined by a subordinating conjunction	(The students go out for recess) (*when* the weather is good.)
Compound-Complex Sentences contain two or more independent clauses and at least one dependent clause	(The students go outside for recess) (when the weather is good) (but) (the teachers go to the library.)

*A *phrase* is a group of related words that does not contain a subject or verb. Generally a phrase adds when and where information.

**An *independent clause* contains a subject and predicate and can stand alone as a complete sentence.

***A *dependent clause* is *not* a complete sentence but depends on an independent clause to complete its meaning, even though it does have a subject and predicate. It is joined with an independent clause by a subordinating conjunction (if, when, since, that, who, where, etc.)

By building and expanding kernel sentences, by constructing compound and complex sentences, and by combining sentences, students gain familiarity with constructions they would not ordinarily use. Reducing sentences of all types to their basic components will help students to eliminate fragments, run-on sentences, and awkwardness in longer sentences.

Although this chapter emphasizes building and writing longer sentences, *the ultimate goal is to have students use a variety of sentence types and lengths in their writing.* Keep in mind that writing skills are developmental. Do not rush students into writing highly complex sentences before they have mastered the simpler types, and do not expect a student to go from writing basic simple sentences to writing complex sentences in a short time. "Sentence sense" develops gradually, over a period of time, as students have experience writing sentences. See Table 9-1 for a summary of sentence types.

Kernel Sentences

Objective   To develop a list of kernel sentences for use in subsequent activities.

Materials   Kernel Sentences, Set 1, paper, and pencils.

Procedure   *Part One*

1. *Write the following words (from Set 1, Kernel Sentences) on the board in a column:*

    <u>Dogs</u>   <u>Cats</u>   <u>Bears</u>   <u>Birds</u>

2. *Ask students to identify the way all these words are alike.*

    - all words name *living and moving things*
    - all begin with capital letters
    - all have an "s" to indicate more than one.

    (It is *not* necessary to identify these as *nouns*, although you may if you wish.)

3. Ask students to name other words that would fit into this category. Write suggestions on the board.

    giraffes, snakes, witches, boys, teachers

4. Have students fold their paper in half and number side 1 and side 2.

    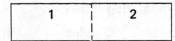

5. Have students write five words in column 1 that would fit in the category. Encourage students to think of other words that are not listed on the board if they can. Do not say words aloud. Fold papers so that words cannot be seen.

Part Two

6. Write the following words on the board and ask students to identify how they are alike.

     eat.   run.   climb.   sing.

 • all *action* words (you may also identify them as *verbs*)
 • all followed by a period

7. Ask students to suggest other words that would fit in this category. Write suggestions on the board.

     whistle, giggle, dance, climb, wiggle

8. Have students pass their folded papers to another student so that the first group of words cannot be seen. Ask the second student to write five words that would fit in category 2 in column 2 on their papers.

9. Have students open papers and read the resulting kernel sentences. List student kernel sentences on the board.

IMPORTANT:

10. *Review* with students that kernel sentences have *two basic parts*—a naming word and an *action word*. Check to see whether all sentences had a naming word and an action word.

11. Ask students to write more kernel sentences as a follow-up exercise.

12. *Save all kernel sentences for future activities.*

Extension   Repeat this activity using other kernel sentences from Set 2.

Kernel Sentences

Set 1 (present tense—living and moving things)

Dogs	eat.	Soldiers	march.
Cats	run.	Dentists	drill.
Bears	climb.	Horses	gallop.
Birds	sing.	Customers	buy.
Whales	swim.	Umpires	shout.
Babies	cry.	Teachers	teach.
Boys	read.	Parents	work.
Girls	play.	Students	study.
Horses	eat.	Secretaries	type.
Lions	roar.	Detectives	investigate.
Owls	hoot.	Astronauts	explore.
Tigers	run.	Voters	vote.
Kids	play.	Carpenters	build.
Fathers	work.	Termites	chew.
Snakes	wiggle.	Leaves	flutter.
Flowers	grow.	Parrots	talk.
Kings	rule.		

Set 2 (present tense—nonliving things)

Boats	sail.	Candles	flicker.
Trucks	rumble.	Snowflakes	fall.
Clocks	tick.	Bombs	explode.
Saws	cut.	Whistles	blow.
Planes	fly.	Rivers	flow.
Rockets	blast.	Winds	blow.

Rocks	fall.	Raindrops	fall.
Balls	roll.	Spaceships	explore.
Stars	shine.	Nutcrackers	crack.
Seeds	slide.	Waves	splash.
Guns	shoot.	Marbles	roll.
		Mirrors	reflect.

Building Simple Sentences

Objective   To build simple sentences.

Materials   Two sets colored cards: set 1 (green), noun phrases; set 2 (red), verb phrases. Keep verb tense consistent within each set. (See sample Noun Phrases and Verb Phrases.)

Procedure
1. Pass out *noun phrases* to students and have them read cards aloud to class. List phrases on the board as students read them. Ask, "How are these cards alike?"

   That boy scout
   A girl scout
   A working mother
   A busy father

   (They are all naming phrases.) Ask students to suggest other phrases that would fit in this group. Add these to the list on the board.
2. Pass out verb phrases and ask, "How are these phrases alike?"

   chopped some wood.
   fixed some dinner.
   basked some bread.
   washed the dishes.

   (They are all action phrases.)
3. Remind students that a simple sentence is composed of two parts: a *naming phrase* and an *action phrase*. Have students note the difference between kernel sentences and simple sentences. (Kernel sentences have two words: a naming word and an action word. Simple sentences have additional words, articles, adjectives, noun objects.)
4. Ask students to build several sentences with the cards they have on their desk. Ask individual students to read their completed sentences to the class.
5. After each sentence is read, ask, "Does that sentence have a naming phrase? What is it? Does it have an action phrase? What is it?"
6. Collect cards. Shuffle each deck. Let students build and read additional sentences.

Noun Phrases	*Verb Phrases*
The United States president	prepared a speech.
Our school librarian	read an encyclopedia.
The apartment house owner	painted the building.
A police sergeant	arrested a robber.
The radio engineer	watched television.

Noun Phrases	*Verb Phrases*
The television news broadcaster	announced the news.
A famous astronaut	photographed the moon.
The telephone repairman	climbed the telephone pole.
A meterologist	prepared a weather report.
The bank teller	cashed a check.
A busy electrician	fixed the toaster.
The professional basketball player	scored two points.
An architect	designed a mansion.
The neighborhood pharmacist	sold some medicine.
The forest ranger	noticed a fire.
A supermarket cashier	checked the price.
A furniture maker	hammered on a table.
An oil well driller	discovered some oil.
A private investigator	followed the spy.
An insurance salesman	visited the neighbors.
The riverboat captain	maneuvered the boat.
The school custodian	raked the leaves.
A meter maid	ticketed a car.

Extension *Use the Computer*

Have one group of students make up sentence fragments using only a noun phrase. Have another group of students make up sentence fragments using only verb phrases. Save these on the computer with a word processing program. Next, have groups switch; then load the verb fragment file for the first group to complete. Load the noun fragment file for the second group to complete. Have students print out their completed sentences for checking. (This could be done by individuals, but students enjoy working together on this type of computer activity.)

Sentence Collage

Objective To make "sentence" and "fragment" collages.

Materials Magazines, scissors, paste, poster paper.

Procedure
1. Review the meaning of *sentence* and *fragment* by reading samples to the class. Remind students that a complete sentence must have a naming phrase and an action phrase and may have *when* and *where* phrases added.
2. Have students cut out whole sentences and sentence fragments from brightly colored pages in magazines.
3. Ask students to separate the sentences and fragments, then to paste them on posters labeled *sentences* and *fragments*.
4. Encourage students to form a message, letter, or short poem with the phrases and sentences found.
5. Display complete posters around the classroom or hallways.

Dogs Eat (Descriptive Detail)

Objective	To add descriptive detail to kernel sentences.
Materials	List of kernel sentences from kernel sentences activity.
Procedure	1. Write a kernel sentence on the chalkboard or transparency (e.g., *Dogs eat.*).

2. Ask students to suggest size words that might describe a dog. If students suggest common words, e.g., *big*, encourage them to think of more specific synonyms. Continue the activity by asking for color words, then personality words (*friendly, mischievous*).

Encourage students to use very specific words. When someone suggests "big" say, "What's another word for big?" When someone suggests a common color, such as brown, ask "How brown?" Chocolate brown? Cocoa brown? Continue to ask "What's another word for _____?" for any common words that are suggested. Write all suggestions on the board.

3. Put the following sentence pattern on the board and have students suggest sample sentences incorporating some of the words previously suggested.

_____, _____, _____ dogs eat.

4. Have students write some descriptive sentences on their own using the above pattern. Remind them that commas are needed when words are listed in a series.

5. Have students read results to the class. Have classmates listen for interesting vocabulary.

Extension 1   Continue this activity for several weeks, using one or two kernel sentences a day, brainstorming details, and writing expanded sentences. *Save the descriptive sentences for the following activities.*

Extension 2   Use the expanded sentences and substitute more specific nouns and verbs:

Large, slender, rusty-colored *Irish setters* eat.
Large, slender, rusty-colored Irish setters *munch*.

Extension 3   Use expanded sentences and add objects. Add descriptive detail to the object.

Large, slender, rusty-colored Irish setters munch *bones*.
Large, slender, rusty-colored Irish setters munch *crispy, crunchy* dog bones.

Extension 4   Use expanded sentences and add adverbs:

Large, slender, rusty-colored Irish setters *quickly* munch crispy, crunchy dog bones.

Extension 5   When students become familiar with this expansion process, they quickly learn to add descriptive detail to subject and object, and to add adverbs all in one step.

Use this pattern sentence:

_____, _____, _____ dogs eat _____,

_____, _____, bones _____.
(how)

Extension 6 To vary the activity on different days, choose sample kernel sentences from different sets provided. All sentences are divided into *sets* to control for verb consistency within a lesson. All sets are divided into *levels* to accommodate different reading levels of students. Choose the level most appropriate to the needs of your students.

What's Going On?

Objective To listen for *who*, *did what*, *when*, and *where* phrases in expanded sentences.

Materials Four index cards for each student, labeled <u>who</u> <u>did what</u> | when | where; sample sentences.

Procedure 1. Give each student a set of *who*, *did what*, *when*, *where* cards.
  3. Read a sentence, one phrase at a time, to the students.

>   Yesterday morning   the starving puppies
>   gobbled up their food   from their dish in the kitchen.

  3. Ask students to listen to the phrase and hold up the category card that identifies the phrase. Check student responses and discuss any differences.
  4. Continue in this manner until five or six sentences have been read. Repeat the activity on different days as it reinforces reading skills.
  5. Change the activity to a reading task when students gain proficiency at the listening level. Make a ditto sentence with phrases widely spaced. Have students mark the phrases in the following manner.

> <u>who</u>   <u>did what</u> | when | where
>
> | Last night | some quiet campers   <u>heard a strange noise</u>
>
> <u>near their campsite.</u>

  6. Gradually reduce the spacing between phrases. Students must then determine the phrasing on their own.

Extension 1 Put phrases from sample sentences on index cards. Have students read and sort cards into piles according to category. Have students build new sentences by choosing a phrase from each category.

Extension 2 Have students write sentences with *when* and *where* phrases. Prepare for this activity by writing kernel sentences on index cards or on a worksheet. Have each student choose four or five kernel sentences and write appropriate *when* or *where* phrases.
  Have students read their completed expanded sentences to the class. Ask students to rearrange phrases in sentences.

<u>WHO</u> <u>DID WHAT</u> | WHEN | <u>WHERE</u> SENTENCES

Set 1

  1. Last night   some quiet campers
      heard a strange noise   near their campsite.

  2. Last week   the black widow spider
     spun a huge web   in the dark, dusty attic.
  3. The ambitious student   wrote a book report
     in the library   two weeks ago.
  4. An old army sergeant   marched back and forth
     on the train platform   just before the parade.
  5. Yesterday morning   the starving puppies
     gobbled up the food   from their dish in the kitchen.
  6. Last month   John and Jerry
     climbed the old oak tree   in the back yard.
  7. Many foreigners   travel freely
     in the United States   every year.
  8. At three a.m. this morning a mysterious stranger
     knocked noisily   on my door.

Set 2

  1. An angry bee   buzzed noisily
     around the picnic table   at lunch time.
  2. After the game   the injured football player
     moaned quietly   in the hospital emergency room.
  3. The magnificent magician   pulled a rabbit
     from a black, satin hat   during intermission.
  4. Before presidential elections   American citizens
     must register to vote   at city hall.
  5. The mournful guitar player sang a sorrowful song
     after work   at the corner of Maple Street.
  6. After the game   the angry crowd
     threw rotten tomatoes   at the umpire.
  7. Last week   in Hawaii
     the ancient volcano   erupted violently.
  8. Two jazzy sports cars   crashed suddenly
     during the race   at Indianapolis Speedway.
  9. Out in the garage   two mischievous boys
     let the air out of some tires   near midnight.
 10. The grumpy waitress   carelessly spilled coffee
     on the customer   during the noon rush hour.
 11. At the air show   a group of skydivers
     opened their chutes   after their free fall.
 12. Before the final attack   the brave astronauts
     watched the enemy   from inside their spaceship.

Zany Sentences

Objective   To build expanded sentences using *who, did what, when, where,* and *why* phrases.

Materials   Five sets of colored cards, one set for each category; (e.g., *who* phrases on red cards; *did what* on green cards, etc.); *who, did what, when, where, why* phrases.

Procedure

1. Divide the class in small groups and give each group five sets of cards with phrases. Do not mix the piles. If you do not have colored cards, put phrases on a ditto and mark each phrase in a different manner; e.g., draw a line under the *who* phrase, a double line under the *did what* phrase, a rectangle around the *when* phrase, and a wiggly line under the *where* phrase. Have students cut phrases apart and separate into appropriate piles.
2. Ask students to rearrange the phrases within the sentence and read to the group again and decide whether the sentence sounds right. Encourage students to try additional phrase arrangements.
3. Continue the activity by having students choose new phrase cards.
4. To make this task more difficult, put all phrases on white cards or on a ditto without special markings. The students must then read and sort phrases into categories before building sentences.

Extension   *Zany Sentence Card Game*

Shuffle *all* cards together. Deal out five cards per person. Students must try to build a five-phrase sentence. Cards are placed face up on the table until a complete five-phrase sentence is made. Two additional cards may be drawn on each turn. *Winner:* the person with the most complete sentences.

WHO   DID WHAT | WHEN | WHERE   SENTENCES

Who

a reckless robber	the broken-hearted broadcaster
a trembling trapeze artist	this tight-fisted tourist
a phony fisherman	that sober sailor
a methodical meteorologist	an ingenious inventor
your calculating cashier	that pale, puny poltergeist
my diabolical dentist	our proud, praiseworthy president
a soft-spoken spook	that discourteous disc jockey
this pious pioneer	that science fiction writer
the grandma goblin	the patriotic parachuter
a devoted daydreamer	the wicked wishy-washy witch
your bungling bungler	an absent-minded ad writer
a jazzy gentleman	her terribly timid teacher
this wandering minstrel	Sam's sullen servant
that jealous judge	the impatient patient
my bargaining barber	the single scientist
a scheming scholar	the gargantuan gourmet

Did What

sauntered slowly	drooped drearily
clawed clumsily	plunged pleasantly
bragged bravely	promised profoundly
yelled yearly	insulted insistently
cruised craftily	studied sufficiently
hurried hungrily	graduated gratefully
knocked knowingly	recruited recently
poisoned politely	vaccinated valiantly
cried hysterically	announced acrimoniously
defended defiantly	balanced believably
complained constantly	haunted haphazardly
haggled hopefully	invited enthusiastically

jumped jubiliantly

gambled gallantly

called cautiously

polished politely

rehearsed relentlessly

tripped triumphantly

dawdled deliberately

triggered tragedy

When

during dinner

in early evening

while waiting

as time ran out

later and later

ahead of schedule

before breakfast

many minutes ago

at break of day

before sunrise

while whistling whimsical tunes

at 10:20 p.m.

after *Sesame Street*

at approximately 8:08

in the Middle Ages

as cymbals sounded

ages and ages ago

before sailing south

at the last moment

during the dance

at breakfast time

during dawn's early light

in prehistoric times

while Christmas caroling

during the last speech

as the ticker ticked away

at the stroke of midnight

while riding in a rickshaw

as the last bell rang

before being elected

yesterday morning

as the sun sank slowly in the west

Where

in a terrible tenement

at a patriotic party

on a funny farm

in a deep, dark dungeon

across the continent

beneath the bristling bear

in the flaming forest

around the reading room

among primitive people

at a raging rebellion

under an amber umbrella

around arguing diplomats

between the fighting fans

on a foreign freighter

in a cluttered classroom

in the dry, deserted desert

on a capsizing catamaran

on a purple picket fence

near the threatening throng

in a tiny telephone booth

at the Singing Society Sale

behind the battered battleships

around a round, rotating room

among the amiable amateurs

below billions of bubbles

in a hospitable hospital

on the second secret safari

beneath the border bridge

beside broken-hearted bystanders

between belligerent believers

in a dilapidated apartment

above a balanced barricade

Why

because the apple had worms

because the knife slipped

since the payment was late

since it was so easy to do

since you've gone away

since the homework was done

because mother was angry

because she/he was brainwashed

since it was so late

because bugles were blowing

because the ship sailed for Singapore

so the diamonds could be delivered

so the news could spread

because the natives were restless

so the bills could be paid

because his/her brain wasn't
functioning

because he/she had a vivid
imagination

in order to earn some money

unless he/she got his/her own way

unless her/his shoes were shined

so the boss wouldn't fire him/her

since money was hard to get

because she/he wanted to be alone

so he/she wouldn't be alone

in order to maintain her/his way of life

because the teacher was on a tirade

because everyone was so bored

since the stagecoach had already left

if conditions weren't exactly right

if not allowed to do what he/she wanted

so that the noise would stop

because the room was empty

Pass It On

Objective To write expanded sentences using *who, did what, when, where,* and *why* phrases.

Materials Pencil and paper.

Procedure
1. Divide the class into groups of five.
2. Have students fold their paper down like an accordion five times and number each section.

3. Have the first person in each group write a *who* phrase on the paper, fold the paper over, and pass it to the next student without exposing the phrase.
4. The second student writes a *did what* phrase without looking at the *who* phrase. The paper is passed to the third student. Students continue in order, writing *when, where,* and *why* phrases.
5. Have the student open the paper and read all five phrases to the class. Ask students to rearrange phrases within the sentence.
6. Continue the activity by changing the starting place in the group. Have the second student start the second set and write a *who* phrase. Continue the activity until everyone in the group has had a chance to start a new sentence.
7. Continue the activity by changing the sequence of phrases; e.g., *when, where, who, did what, why;* or *where, who, did what, when, why.*

Extension *Whisper*

Divide the class into groups of five. Have one student whisper a *who* phrase to the second student. The second student must repeat the *who* phrase and add a *did what* phrase to the third student, and so on. The last student must repeat the entire sentence aloud, or write it down and read it.

Example:

1	A wicked witch
2	caught a rabbit
3	in an elevator
4	as the sun went down
5	because she couldn't sleep.

Reducing Expanded Sentences

Objective   To reduce expanded sentence to kernel elements (subject and verb).

Materials   Sample expanded sentences. (Use sentences developed by students from kernel sentence activity or sample sentences following.)

Procedure
1. Tell students that you want them to reduce expanded sentences to two words. (*Note:* At first, limit the sentence reduction activity to expanded sentences. Compound and complex sentences should be avoided until after completion of the following activities.)
2. Write one expanded sentence on the chalkboard and ask students to identify all descriptive words. Circle descriptive words as students identify them. See example in 4, below.
3. Ask students to identify all *where, when, how,* and *why* words and phrases. Circle them as they are identified.
4. Ask students to identify the kernel sentence elements. (There may be a few words remaining; i.,e., objects of verb, determiners.) Draw a line under the subject and a double line under the verb.
   Example: When it is dinner time, that large, slender, rusty-colored <u>Irish setter</u> noisly and swiftly <u>gobbles</u> crispy, crunchy dog bones in the kitchen.

   Write the remaining subject and verb on the board.

   <u>Irish setter</u> <u>gobbles</u>.

   Point out that this is a kernel sentence and that all sentences, no matter how long, can be broken down into kernel sentences.
5. Repeat this activity with the student, using another expanded sentence before asking students to do some on their own.

Sample Expanded Sentences
1. On his way home from work on Thursday, the lazy, science-fiction writer loudly sang numerous, cheerful, patriotic melodies to his giant, black labrador retriever who was sound asleep on the black, leather car seat.
2. The young, impatient research scientist unfortunately forgot to put the bubbling chemicals in the tall, shiny flask for the most important experiment of the year.

3. At midnight, in the light of the full moon, the wicked, wishy-washy witch merrily danced the tango to the jazzy sounds of the Mexican dance band.

4. The courageous, African safari leader carefully searched through dense brush, tangled vines, and tall, dry, meadow grasses for the elusive, ferocious, overweight male lions.

5. Just before Easter, on a warm, humid, Friday afternoon, the absent-minded ad-writer carefully typed a full page advertisement for the gigantic, downtown, department store Christmas extravaganza sale.

6. Early on Christmas eve, during a blowing snowstorm, a jolly, rolly-polly, red-suited Santa cheerfully arrived in a shiny, red sleigh piled high with elaborately wrapped presents of all sizes.

7. After the last, jangling bell at the end of the school day, the tired, over-worked, grumbling students quickly and eagerly climbed on the muddy, yellow school buses for the long, bumpy ride out to the wooded countryside.

8. After the last football game of the season, the excited Senior cheerleaders tearfully sang the school song to the amazed football heroes.

Building Compound Sentences

Objective   To form compound sentences by combining related sentence pairs.

Materials   List sentence pairs.

Procedure   1. Write two sample sentences on the board and ask a student to read them aloud.
   Example: Betty washed the dishes.
                   Ann dried them.

2. Point out that two short sentences can be combined into one longer one by adding a joining word called a conjunction. The most commonly used conjunctions are:

and	for	so
but	or	yet

   (Write these on the board.)

3. Ask students to form a new sentence by joining the two sample sentences with the conjunction *and*.
   Example: Betty washed the dishes, | and |
                   Ann dried them.
   Note: A comma usually follows the first clause in a compound sentence. It can be omitted if the first clause is very short.

4. Draw a square around the conjunction for emphasis.

5. Continue with other sample sentences pairs that require the use of other conjunctions.
   Examples: We lost our money.   (so)
                     We went home.

                     It rained hard.   (but)
                     We stayed dry in the tent.

John will do his homework.   (or)
He will stay after school.

Sally ate four candy bars.   (yet)
She was still hungry.

He did not pay for the coat.   (for)
He did not have his money.

6. Draw a square around each conjunction for emphasis.

Extension Have students form compound sentences with the following sentence pairs and the joining word (conjunction) that makes the most sense.

and	for	so
but	or	yet

Sentence Pairs

1. The circus came to town. All the children wanted to go.
2. The bus came on time. I wasn't ready.
3. The landlord will lower the rent. We will move anyway.
4. It had been a hard day. Benjamin was tired.
5. There was a terrible blizzard yesterday. School was cancelled.
6. The students planted the seeds. They didn't grow.
7. John will get his way. He will cry.
8. You can buy new dungarees. You can patch your old dungarees.
9. The teacher gave the assignment. The students did it.
10. Charlotte wanted to go. Her mother wanted her to stay home.
11. Vic likes ice cream. Jan likes cookies.
12. At the basketball game, John scored ten points. Bill scored two.
13. I have a long fur coat. I never wear it.
14. The weather might change. It might stay nice and sunny.
15. The toast is in the toaster. The butter is on the table.
16. Ten fire engines came to the fire. The building burned down anyway.
17. Everyone was going to the football game. I had to stay home.
18. Turn the radio off. Turn the TV off.

Sentence Combining

Objective To combine related sentences and eliminate excess words.

Materials Pairs of related sentences.

Procedure 1. Write a sample sentence pair on the chalkboard or overhead transparency. Ask the students to combine them in one short sentence. (Some students try to combine the sentence simply by adding *and*. Remind them to make the sentences *shorter* than the two previous sentences combined.)

The baby was happy. He was laughing.
The happy baby was laughing.

2. Write the revised sentence on the board. Ask students to identify the changes that were made. Illustrate by drawing arrows to indicate a change

in a word's position and circling unnecessary words.

The baby was happy. (He was) laughing.

3. Continue the activity by using four or five additional sentence pairs. Then have students combine the remaining sample sentence pairs independently. Read results to the class. Write the combined sentences on the board, noting how each sentence was changed.

- words rearranged
- extra words eliminated
- sentence reduced in length

4. Remind students that the overall goal in sentence development is to write efficient sentences that vary in length. (This activity helps to eliminate the use of short, choppy sentences and excess words.)

Sentence Combining: examples of simple sentence pairs

1. The boys are angry. The boys are fighting.
   (The angry boys are fighting.)
2. The newspaper boy is cheerful. He is earning some money.
   (The cheerful newspaper boy is earning some money.)
3. The child is frightened. He hears a strange noise.
   (The frightened child hears a strange noise.)
4. The boys are hungry. They want to eat their sandwiches.
   (The hungry boys want to eat their sandwiches.)
5. The student is forgetful. He didn't do his homework again.
   (The forgetful student didn't do his homework again.)
6. That bear is angry. She can't find her cubs.
   (That angry bear can't find her cubs.)
7. The cows were hungry. They began to moo.
   (The hungry cows began to moo.)
8. The pig is dirty. He is wallowing in the mud.
   (The dirty pig is wallowing in the mud.)
9. That businessman is jubilant. He just received a raise.
   (That jubilant businessman just received a raise.)

Extension 1   *Simple sentences changed to descriptive detail*

1. James got a new bike.
   It is a shiny, red bike.
   It is a ten-speed bike.
   He got it for his twelfth birthday.
   (James got a new, shiny, red, ten-speed bike for his twelfth birthday.)
2. Mr. Brown bought a new Cadillac.
   The Cadillac was huge.
   The Cadillac was shiny.
   The Cadillac was green.
   He bought it for his wife.
   (Mr. Brown bought a new, huge, shiny, green Cadillac for his wife.)
3. Mrs. Jones bought a new dress.
   She is going to wear it to a party.
   It is a beautiful dress.
   It is a green dress.
   It is a long dress.

(Mrs. Jones bought a beautiful, new, green, long dress to wear to the party.)

4. The boys are going to camp.
   It is a small camp.
   It is a boy scout camp.
   The camp is in the mountains.
   The boys are young.
   (The young boys are going to a small boy scout camp in the mountains.)
5. We have a new teacher.
   The new teacher has beautiful hair.
   It is very long.
   It is very shiny.
   It is dark brown.
   It is curly.
   (Our new teacher has beautiful, long, shiny, dark brown, curly hair.)
6. My grandfather owns a Model T Ford.
   It is a very rare model.
   It is shiny black.
   It is an antique.
   (My grandfather owns a very rare, shiny black, antique Model T Ford.)
7. The kitten chased the pretty butterfly.
   He chased the busy bee.
   He chased the bouncing ball.
   He chased the piece of string.
   He is a silly kitten.
   (The silly kitten chased the pretty butterfly, the busy bee, the bouncing ball, and the piece of string.)
8. I like to grow things in my garden.
   I like to grow tomatoes.
   I like the tomatoes to be juicy.
   I like to grow peppers.
   I like the peppers to be hot.
   I like to grow onions.
   I like the onions to be fat.
   (I like to grow juicy tomatoes, hot peppers, and fat onions in my garden.)

Extension 2   *Simple sentences changed to when, where, and why phrases*

1. It is dawn.
   Many ducks are quacking.
   They are looking for food.
   They are near the pond.
   (Many quacking ducks are looking for food near the pond at dawn.)
2. The soldier is tired.
   He is on guard duty.
   He is working near the campground entrance.
   He will work until midnight.
   (The tired soldier will be on guard near the campground entrance until midnight.)
3. It was the first game of the season.
   The Red Sox played the Cardinals.
   The Red Sox won the game.
   The game was played in Fenway Park.
   Fenway Stadium is in Boston.

(The Red Sox beat the Cardinals at the first game of the season in Fenway Park in Boston.)

4. That old man is tired.
   He sits on a bench.
   The bench is in the park.
   He sits there every afternoon.
   (The tired old man sits on a bench in the park every afternoon.)

5. The boys are going fishing.
   They are boy scouts.
   They are going to the Snake River.
   They are going tomorrow.
   (Tomorrow, the boy scouts are going fishing on the Snake River.)

6. The dogs barked.
   They barked loudly.
   They barked at the neighborhood cat.
   They were German shepherds.
   (The full-grown German shepherds barked loudly at the neighborhood cat.)

7. The football players were tired.
   They lost the game.
   It was the championship game.
   It was Saturday, October 4th.
   (On Saturday, October 4th, the tired football players lost the championship game.)

8. It was a dark, Halloween night.
   A big, black cat sat on the fence.
   It screeched loudly.
   It screeched at the moon.
   It was a Tom cat.
   (On a dark, Halloween night, a big black cat sat on the fence and screeched loudly at the moon.)

Resources   *Sentence Combining*
   Milliken
   Available for Apple II computers
   Designed for grades 4 to 9
This program shows students how to get rid of short, choppy sentences by rearranging and combining words and phrases. Students combine sentences using coordinating and subordinating conjunctions, prepositional phrases, restrictive and non-restrictive clauses, appositives, gerund phrases, and infinitive phrases. Students work through guided practice examples, then move on to test examples. If students give incorrect answers, the program provides assistance.

Write Channel
   Mississippi Authority for Educational Television
   Fifteen 15-minute programs, videocasette, designed for grades 3, 4.
Mr. R. B. Bugg, an animated character and young television reporter, learns good writing techniques from Red Green, news director. R. B. consistently writes short, choppy sentences, and Red teaches him to use sentence-combining techniques to make his writing more interesting. Red also provides review on punctuation and capitalization skills.

The following sentence-combining techniques and editing skills are demonstrated in *Write Channel* tapes.

1. And, Capital Letters
2. Adjective Modifications, Periods
3. And, But; Commas
4. Base Sentence Additions; Date, Punctuation and Capitals
5. Who, That; Question Mark and Exclamation Point
6. With
7. Preposition Phrases; City and State Capitals
8. Review
9. When, After, and Before
10. Because, Although, If
11. Infinitives and Participal Phrases
12. Appositives
13. Commas
14. "That" in Noun Clause; Book Titles
15. Series Review of Sentence Combining

Make It Parallel

Objective   To write sentences using parallel structure.

Materials   Sample sentence patterns.

Procedure   1. Put a sample sentence pattern on the chalkboard or overhead transparency. Ask students to identify the pattern.

The woman sings, dances, skips, shouts, whistles, hums, and claps.

Point out that all the verbs are present tense and end with s.
2. Ask students to repeat the pattern with the following phrase

The man _____, _____, _____,

_____, _____, and _____.

3. Put a second sample sentence on the chalkboard or transparency. Ask students to identify the pattern.

The women are singing, dancing, skipping, shouting, whistling, humming, and clapping.

Point out that all verbs are present tense and have an ing ending.
4. Ask students to repeat the pattern with the following phrase:

The boys are _____, _____, _____,

_____, _____, and _____.

5. Point out that it is important to keep verb tense consistent within sentences.
6. Write another sample sentence on the board in the following pattern. (This time phrases are used.)
Dogs can eat a bone,
   chase a cat,
   chew a slipper,

chase a car,
bite a child, and
kill a rat.

7. Ask students to repeat the pattern using the following sentence.
Boys can climb a tree,

_____,

_____,

_____,

_____, and

_____,

Extension   *Use the Computer*

This activity is easily done on a computer word processing program. Have each student type in the parallel phrases and print them out. Put them on the bulletin board to share and compare.

Help

Objective   To deliberately write excessively worded sentences.

Materials   Sample sentence, kernel sentences.

Procedure   1. Write the sample word sentence on the board or on an overhead transparency.

> "I am in desperate need of assistance because cold water is rushing very rapidly into my lungs and it is difficult for me to breathe so please send the required assistance as soon as poss . . . BLUB . . . blub . . . blub . . ."

2. Ask the students to translate the message to one word.
(Help!)
3. Emphasize to students the need to have a *variety* of sentence lengths in their writing and to avoid writing excessively long sentences that could be more effective if shortened.
4. Put a word on the board and ask students to elaborate on it and deliberately build an excessively long sentence.
"Danger!"
Have students read their long sentences to classmates.
5. Ask students to develop another excessively long sentence on their own. Have them read their sentences to the class and let class guess what the single word should be. "Stop!" "Run!" "Fire!" "Go!" "Eat!" "Wait!" "Danger!" "Stop, Look, Listen!"
6. Share the following excessively worded sentences with students and repeat the activity.

Excessively Worded Sentences

Billows of dense smoke and brilliant, flickering flames are leaping through the room and burning the wooden beams and window frames, as well as the curtains, carpets, and upholstery, so it would be best if you would evacuate the building as quickly and quietly as possible, using the nearest available exit.
(FIRE!)

It is important that you bring your vehicle to a complete halt and that you rotate your head from side to side while your eyes check for the proximity of a large, heavy iron vehicle, commonly known as a train, which travels at great speed on these parallel steel rails. Also be sure to make your ears function in the manner in which they were designed to function in order to distinguish the warning signal of the great iron vehicle.
(STOP, LOOK, and LISTEN!)

═══ CHAPTER 10 ═══

Tackle the Troublespots

Several persistent errors, or troublespots, are found in the written expression of poor writers. Run-on sentences, incomplete sentences, incorrect punctuation, incorrect subject–verb agreement, and confusing noun–pronoun usage are among the most troublesome. Errors are made by four basic groups of students:

1. Students who think faster than they write and do not proofread;
2. Students who proofread, but just do not know what to look for (these students read the passage as it was intended rather than as it was actually written);
3. Students who have weak basic writing skills because of a lack of training and/or motivation; and
4. Students who write only one draft.

The previous chapter presented activities for building up completely new sentences by combining words and phrases; this chapter builds sentence skills through analyzing sentences or stories that are already written and that isolate one type of error. These activities generally focus on mechanical problems and attempt to develop proofreading and editing skills. Responsibility for identifying and correcting errors is placed on the student, although the number of errors in an assignment may be given as a clue. Important points in this process are as follows:

1. *Focus on specific problems in students' writing as the need arises* rather than on teaching the rules of grammar in a predetermined sequence. *Avoid isolated exercises (workbook type)* that bear no relationship to the students' immediate problems.

2. *Identify and remediate errors in order of importance.* A student who is writing run-on or incomplete sentences does not need to work on parallel structure or complex sentences.

3. *Isolate one persistent type of error at a time.* Require students to proofread for, and correct, only this one kind of error. If a student has a great deal

of difficulty proofreading her or his own paper, present some of the activities in this chapter that isolate one type of problem. Students must be able to recognize the problem before they can correct it in their own work. Provide oral practice so that students can "hear" their own errors.

4. *Recognize that as students master simpler forms and attempt higher levels of written expression, they will make different kinds of errors.* The student has to feel free to experiment with more difficult forms before being able to master them. (The student who is using a variety of sentence structures in his or her writing, but who is making a few errors on compound or complex sentences, is developing more skill than a student who consistently uses *only* simple sentences.) Again, isolate the error category and use specific teaching strategies to help the student recognize, identify, and correct these errors.

Instructional objectives for this chapter include the following:

1. To review rules for capitalization;
2. To identify missing capitalization and punctuation;
3. To identify and correct run-on sentences;
4. To review punctuation rules;
5. To use consistent verb tense; and
6. To use correct non/pronoun referents.

Capital Contest

Objective   To review rules of capitalization.

Materials   Sample paragraph, overhead projector, acetate sheet, marking pen, atlas, maps of the United States and the world, copies of Table 10-1.

Procedure
1. Review rules of capitalization with the students by having them suggest when capital letters are needed. Make a chart as they make suggestions. Post chart in the classroom. Compare with copies of Table 10-1.
2. Announce that you are going to have a "Capital Contest." Show sample story (below) on overhead projector. Have students note where capital letters should be and let them write them in on the transparency.
3. Ask students to write a short story using as many capital letters as possible. Remind them to use as many of the rules from the chart as they can. Ask for suggestions of the kinds of stories that could be written.
    Possible Suggestions: Travel Story
                    Sports Stories with names of teams, players, and cities visited
                    Leisure Time Activities (movies, TV programs, books, magazines)
    Students may use reference sources to get correct spelling (atlases, maps, encyclopedias, etc.).
4. Have students share their stories when finished. Count the number of capitals in each story. Give the person with the highest number a rousing cheer and a funny prize.

Extension   Save completed capital stories for review practice on another day. Let each student carefully copy her or his story on a transparency or a ditto, omitting the correct capital letters. Let the student lead a discussion on where capital letters should go.

TABLE 10-1
Capitalization Rules

Capitalize . . . . .

first word in sentences	Zebras have stripes.
names of people, nicknames	Susan, Tom, Mike, Mr. Jones, Mrs. Hall
the pronoun I	I
days, months, holidays	Sunday, July 24th, Christmas, New Year's Day
streets, roads	Woodside Road
cities, states, countries	San Francisco, California
	United States of America
other *specific* places	Grand Canyon, Rocky Mountains
(names of schools, parks, oceans)	Lincoln School, Fenway Stadium, Atlantic Ocean
first word in quoted speech	John exclaimed, "Wait, I want to go."
the title of books, plays, poems, magazine articles,	*The Black Stallion*
student papers	*The Mixed-up Files of Mrs. Basil E. Frankweiler*
(Not: *a, an, the; and, but, or;* or prepositions)	
abbreviations	Mr., Mrs., Dr.
titles of persons and organizations	Queen Elizabeth, President Carter
	United States Marines, Peace Corps
races, nationalities	Caucasian, Negro
	French, Mexican, Spanish
religions	Protestant, Catholic, Jewish
words pertaining to deity,	God, the Father, the Creator
sacred writings	Bible, Torah, Koran
saints	Saint Peter
historical periods	Middle Ages, Renaissance
events	World War II, Battle of the Bulge
documents	The Constitution, Magna Carta

Capital Contest Checkup

the rotary club was organizing a three-week trip to europe for its club members during september. mr. and mrs. harry jones were extremely excited about the trip and were among the first to sign up to go. mr. jones had always dreamed of going to paris, france, so he started to practice his french lessons right away. he had a special interest in french history and was eager to visit the sites of world war II battles. he was also interested in visiting the french museums, especially the louvre, and seeing some of the work of the famous artists: renoir, monet, cezanne, and toulouse-lautrec.

mrs. jones shared her husband's enthusiasm for the trip. she went to the boston public library and got the following books to read:

the sun king   by nancy mitford,

the french revolution   by douglas johnson,

art centers of the world—paris   by alexander watt.

soon august 5th arrived and mr. and mrs. jones went to logan international airport in boston to meet their group. They boarded trans world airlines flight #65 to england. they discovered that another group, the massachusetts teachers association, had also chartered space on the same flight. everyone had high expectations for an interesting and exciting trip.

Hidden Sentences

Objective	To locate and punctuate hidden sentences.
Materials	A series of words that contains a hidden sentence.
Procedure	1. Write a series of words that contains a hidden sentence on the board. "ring circus the lion tamer jumped into the lion's cage whip zoo"
	2. Have students read the sample and locate the sentence that is hidden. Next have them underline it, then point out the type and location of capitalization and punctuation needed.
	3. Pass out a worksheet that contains some hidden sentences. Have students locate and underline the hidden sentences.
	4. Have student copy the "found" sentences with correct capitalization and punctuation.
Extension 1	Ask each student to write some "hidden sentences" for a classmate. Switch papers when completed and have the second student locate and correct the hidden sentences. Save the papers for review practice on other days.
Extension 2	*Use the Computer*
	Put these sentences on the computer using a word processing program and save on a file disk. Next, have students work in pairs and load the file and edit the sentences by deleting the extra words.

Set 1

1. song please turn off the record player noise music record now
2. that painter dropped his paint bucket on the floor sloppy mess
3. husky happy most people enjoy football and basketball gym yell
4. workman that workman fell in a huge manhole street working water
5. once upon a door dogs that zoo keeper wanted to eat his lunch
6. trip suitcase train that tourist packed his clothes and left
7. red warm woolen mittens are used on cold days winter blizzard
8. little pictures have big chief has small muscles indian teepee
9. holiday joyful a plump turkey was sizzling in the oven roast
10. noisy jets fly above the clouds airport weather is leave

Set 2

1. crowds of people were at the train station ticket money good-bye
2. tinsel packages pretty lights christmas is not coming this year
3. a painful toothache my dentist will remove the decayed tooth
4. black furry gorillas weigh four hundred pounds dangerous cage
5. growl angry a gorilla had a thorn in his foot painful aspirin
6. hunters trap young gorillas are caught and tamed for the zoo
7. when you go on vacation in the summer you can swim fish and play
8. look at the bright side of things be happy smile more often more
9. watch out the sky is falling said chicken little its time to go
10. hurry up and finish your work so we can go outside to play soon

Set 3

1. terrific smile sour a smile will brighten your entire face happy
2. television commercials are too long interrupt good programs and

   3. sneakers baseball hockey soccer and tennis are exciting games
   4. fire call the fire department throw on some water it's out now
   5. many many years ago yesterday history teaches us many lessons
   6. water swimming pool help I can't swim sink butterfly stroke
   7. science social students match homework is your homework done
   8. impending disaster tornadoes hurricanes the weather is nice
   9. magazines newspapers and television provide up to date news
   10. furniture carpenters appliances salesman we need a new T.V.

Run-on Sentences

Objective   To identify and correct "run-on" sentences.

Materials   Several paragraphs with punctuation replaced with *and, and then,* or *so.*

Procedure   1. Reading a paragraph, emphasize the repeated word or words. Ask students to identify the repeated word.
2. Put a written copy of the paragraph on an overhead transparency. Have students locate the repeated words and draw a box around each one, then draw a big X through the box.
3. Have the students put a period in the sentence before the box and a capital letter on the first word after the box.
4. Read the corrected story aloud.
5. Put another run-on story on a ditto and give out to students. Let them find the "run-ons" by themselves, putting boxes around the repeated words, and inserting correct capitalization and punctuation. Ask them to copy the paragraph correctly if it is not too long.

Extension   Have students write run-on paragraphs deliberately, then switch papers with another student. The second student must then locate all the run-ons, eliminate them, and correct capitalization and punctuation. The first writer checks the work for accuracy.

Examples: "Run-On" Stories

The Strange Event

The little girl heard a big noise and she went up on the roof to see what happened and she saw something and it looked like a fireball and then she went to bed and when she got up the next morning she listened to the news on the radio and then she heard that the big noise was really a rocket taking off.

The Turtle Race

The turtle race is held every year at the pool and everyone is invited to bring a fast turtle and each person holds his turtle at the starting line and somebody yells, "Let them go!" and everybody lets go and some turtles start walking very fast and some turtles start going off in the wrong direction and everyone starts yelling and finally one turtle crosses the finish line and everybody cheers some more and they give a prize to the owner of the winning turtle.

Making Cookies

Geraldine wanted to make some cookies and so she went into the kitchen to get everything ready and she read the cookie recipe and it told her she needed eggs, flour, milk, and sugar and then she began to mix the flour with the milk and then she added some nuts and then she finished mixing the other stuff in the bowl and then she put the cookies on the cookie sheet and then she put the cookies in the oven to bake and then when the cookies were done she gave them to her friends.

Punctuation Dictation

Objective To identify required punctuation in an unpunctuated paragraph by listening to vocal intonation.

Materials Unpunctuated paragraphs (at first, eliminate only capital letters and periods from paragraphs; gradually exclude other types of punctuation).

Procedure 1. Give each student a copy of the unpunctuated paragraph. Tell them that you will read the paragraph through once at a normal rate and then you will repeat it at a slower rate.
2. Point out the type of punctuation omitted from the paragraph. Or ask students to identify the type of punctuation missing. At first, use paragraphs from which you have omitted only periods and capital letters; later, use paragraphs without quotation marks, commas, and question marks.
3. Have students write a goal at the top of the paper.
   Example: Find missing capital letters and periods.
4. Read paragraph to students twice.
5. Put unpunctuated copy of paragraph on overhead projector. Ask students to identify where omissions are. Have students check their papers against the corrected copy on the overhead projector.

Ask or Tell

Objective To distinguish between questions and statements.

Materials List of questions and statements; two cards for each statement, labeled ask? tell.

Procedure 1. Review the difference between a statement and a question with the class: that is, a statement tells something, and a question asks something. Remind them that a question always need a response.

2. Read a few samples and ask students to note changes in voice patterns.
3. Read a sentence to the class. If it *asks* something, tell the students to hold up the ask? card. If the sentence *tells* something, have the students hold up the tell. card.
4. Have students give an appropriate answer to the questions that you use.

Examples: Statements and Questions

1. Is your class going on a picnic?
2. The students were playing different games on the playground.
3. What is your favorite game?
4. Did you see the boy fall down the stairs?
5. Jane always complains that her work is too hard.
6. Would you like to go to the movies with me?
7. Giraffes have long necks so they can reach the high leaves.
8. Why does a monkey climb a tree?
9. A monkey climbs a tree to keep away from other animals.
10. Did you finish your homework?
11. Yesterday, Ann had two ice cream cones after school.
12. Everyone in my family likes music.
13. What would you like to do on your vacation?
14. The vendor on the corner was selling hot pretzels.
15. The principal of our school came into our class today.
16. Was Pam invited to the party?
17. What do you want for Christmas?
18. What do you want for your birthday?
19. How many people are in your family?
20. Five people are in my family.

Extension Put these *ask/tell* sentences on strips of paper and keep in an envelope. Have individual students sort them into two groups during independent activity time.

Ask, Tell, Exclaim!

Objective To identify statements, questions, and exclamations.

Materials List of statements, questions, and exclamations; three small cards per student, labeled ask? tell. exclaim! .

Procedure
1. Give each student a set of three labeled cards.
2. Review the difference between asking and telling sentences by giving students some samples and having them hold up the card that corresponds.
3. Give students the exclaim! card if students are accurate with ask? and tell. cards.
4. Explain that an exclamation shows excitement or emphasis. Give several examples.
   Wait!   Stop thief!   Fire!

5. Continue by reading a variety of sentences. Ask students to hold up the appropriate response card. Discuss any differences of opinion. Be sure to read exclamations with extra emphasis.
6. Ask students to suggest other sentences that would be exclamations.

Extension   Put these ask, tell, and exclaim sentences on strips of paper and put them in an envelope so that students can sort them during free periods.

Examples: Statements, Questions, Exclamations

Sample Exclamations: an exclamatory sentence shows excitement!

1. Fire!
2. Help!
3. Watch out!
4. Don't do that!

Statements, Questions, and Exclamations

1. The snow kept falling all through the night.
2. Do you know what tomorrow's weather will be like?
3. Wow! What a hit!
4. Watch out! That's hot!
5. The first game of the baseball season will be on Thursday.
6. Can we go to the first baseball game?
7. Don't run in the halls! Take your time!
8. He hit a home run.
9. The long freight train pulled into the station.
10. Did you do your homework last night?
11. Do you have any money?
12. "That's a poison snake!" he yelled.
13. The newspaper boy threw the paper on the porch.
14. Did you ever catch a fly ball at a baseball game?
15. The Red Sox won! What a game!

Foolish Questions

Objective   To use question marks at the end of questions.

Materials   Sample questions.

Procedure   1. Write several "foolish questions" on the board.
   Examples: Is a 50-pound canary heavy?
   Do hyenas laugh?
   Do bears live in the woods?
   Do giraffes have long necks?
2. Ask students to suggest other "foolish questions." Write suggestions on the board. Emphasize the use of the question mark at the end of the question.
3. Ask students to write five or ten foolish questions on a piece of paper.
4. Have student volunteers read the questions to the class. Have the class decide on the most foolish question.
5. Ask students to think of original answers to some of the foolish questions.

Extension   *The Question Game*

Have each student choose a partner. Explain the rules of the game: one person must ask a question; the second person must answer the first question by asking another question; the first person must answer the second question by asking a third question, and so on. (Have students write their conversations down. Remind them to use question marks and quotation marks.)

Example:

First student:	"Want some lunch?"
Second student:	"Do you have any tuna fish?"
First student:	"Would you like mayonnaise on it?"
Second student:	"Do you have to put mayonnaise on it?"
First student:	"Would you like something else instead?"
Second student:	"Do you have any peanut butter?"
First student:	"Do you want a peanut butter sandwich?"
Second student:	"Do you have any milk to go with it?"
First student:	"Want some chocolate milk?"
Second student:	"Is it fresh?"
	etc., etc., etc.

Which students created the longest conversation that stays on the topic?

Resources   *Rube Goldberg: His Life and Work*
   Peter C. Marzio
   Harper & Row, 1973
"Foolish Questions" was a popular Goldberg cartoon series. In this series Goldberg made fun of some of the questions that people ask in obvious situations. Foolish Question No. 40,976 shows a father who asks, "Son, are you smoking that pipe again?" The son, who *is* smoking a pipe responds, "No, Dad, this is a portable kitchenette and I'm frying a smelt for dinner."

Conversations

Objective   To write dialogue with quotation marks.

Materials   Two different-colored felt tip pens, list of topics.

Procedure   1. Ask students to work in pairs and to choose a topic from the topic list or to think of another topic to write a dialogue about.
   2. Tell each student in the pair to use a different-colored pen. Write one person's conversation in one color and the responses in another color. Skip lines between each person's speech, and put quotation marks before and after each statement.
   3. Read the conversations to the class.
   4. Add names of characters and response words. Try to avoid the repetitive use of *said* by making a list of alternatives with the class. Remind students to use commas after the character introduction (e.g., *Amelia yelled,*).
   5. Try to vary the placement of the tag by placing it at the beginning, end, or middle of the sentence. Show students samples, or put samples on the bulletin board for reminders.

Examples: *Topic List*

One teacher discussing a hard day with another teacher.
Two invaders from space on their first visit to earth.
The newspaper boy talking to an angry customer.
Two boys arguing over a baseball.
Two mischievous boys planning a camping trip.
Two girls going to a gymnastics meet.
Two housewives complaining about the price of groceries.
A news reporter and the fire chief at the scene of a fire.
A student and a parent talking about a good/bad report card.
Two old-timers chatting about the weather.
A mechanic and an owner of an old broken-down car.
A police officer and a motorist stopped for speeding.
A sales representative trying to sell a vacuum cleaner to a home owner.
A farmer talking to his cow.
Two girls planning a shopping trip.

Extension   *Use the Computer*

This activity works well with a computer. Ask two students working together on a word processing program to carry on a conversation about one of the suggested topics. Encourage them to use speaker tags (e.g. *Harry answered, George questioned*) and other words besides *said* and *asked*.

Add the Ending (Verb Tense)

Objective   To identify and add omitted endings on verbs.

Materials   Incomplete stories with endings omitted on verbs. (See examples below.)

Procedure   1. Read one incomplete story to the class. Tell them that something is wrong and ask them to listen to see whether they can identify the error. (Consonants have been doubled or final "e" vowel dropped when necessary to avoid confusing the lesson by introducing additional rules.)
2. Have students state the error. (The endings are missing from the action words.)
3. Give students a copy of the story and have them state the goal of the activity on the "Goal line."
    Goal: Put endings on action words.
4. Have students read and correct incomplete story, then add an ending to the story.
5. Have students share their different endings by reading them aloud to their classmates.

Extension   After students have done several of these, have them write stories with endings omitted deliberately. Put these stories on dittos and give out to the rest of the class for correction. Let the person who wrote the story be the corrector.

Example 1

Boston Bruins versus _____

"The last period of the Bruins versus the _____

hockey game is about to begin! What an excit_____

game this is. The score is 2 to 2. The fans are

scream_____ in the stands. In just a few minutes, we

will know who the championship playoff winners will be.

There they go. Both teams are skat_____ back on

the ice after the quarter break. Wow, look at that! Phil Esposito is

break_____ away and is skat_____ down the

ice like mad. _____ is chas_____ him. Oops,

now _____ is knock_____ him with his stick.

Phil is fall_____ down.

Wait! Bobby Orr is skat_____ up on the side.

Look at that! He's sav_____ the puck and now he's

shoot_____ right for the net. Fantastic! It's

go_____ right in. Listen to the fans. They are really

scream_____ now. The score is 3 to 2.

The _____ are really feel_____ the

pressure now. Only sixty seconds to go. Wait! _____ is

break_____ away. He's _____

_____

_____

_____

Example 2

The Gymnastics Meet

Yesterday, Geraldine, Kelly, and Wendy went to the gym-

nastics meet. They perform_____ many difficult acts for

the audience. Wendy tumbl_____ on the mats and did

somersaults on the trampoline. Geraldine perform_____

on the parallel bars. Kelly walk_____,

jump_____, and roll_____ on the high

balance beam. The audience clapp_____ and

yell_____ after every act. The girls were very proud of

their performance.

Then everyone turn_____ their attention to the ropes. Kelly climb_____ to the very top of the ropes and start_____ to do fancy movements with her hands and feet. Suddenly her right hand slipp_____ and

_____

_____

_____

_____

_____

_____

Example 3

The Undersea World

Yesterday, Cindy and her two friends want_____ to go scuba diving. They need_____ rubber suits, goggles, and air tanks. They collect_____ all their equipment together, then check_____ the air tanks to make sure they were fill_____ with air. They load_____ their equipment in the car and start_____ off.

At the beach, they unload_____ the car and pil_____ the equipment on their blanket. Then, they dress_____ in their rubber suits, hook_____ up their oxygen tanks, and climb_____ on the boat.

A mile out in the ocean, the boat stopp_____. The girls jump_____ off into the water and explore_____ the undersea reef. Cindy was near a large jagged rock, when suddenly her air hose caught on the rock and it was cut open. She _____

_____

_____

_____

_____

Sports News (Verb Tense)

Objective   To write sports news articles using present and past tenses.

Materials   Sports pictures from newspaper or magazines.

Procedure   1. Collect interesting action pictures from the sports section of newspapers or magazines. Ask students to help you collect them.
2. Let students choose a picture and write an "on the spot" news report from an announcer's point of view. Read sample to class. This activity encourages the use of present tense verbs.
3. Encourage students to use short sentences loaded with action verbs and exclamations of excitement.
4. Read results to class.
5. On another day, have each student rewrite the "on the spot" report as a report for the daily news. Remind students that newspaper reporting is more objective than "on the spot" type reporting and generally does not include the exclamations of excitement or statements of opinion. This time the story will be written in past tense.
6. Read results to the class. Compare the difference in style between the "on the spot" report and the follow-up newspaper report.

Extension 1   Have students listen to televised sports news programs. These programs generally use precise verbs in their descriptions of games. Ask students to jot down some of the descriptions and bring them into class.

Extension 2   Have a student follow one team or sports hero through a period of time by collecting pictures from the newspaper and writing short reports on each picture. Bind all of the articles and pictures in book format. Because newspaper pictures come out very well in a copier, many students can use the same pictures.

Extension 3   Present some catchy titles found in the sports section of the newspaper. Also present an outline of information telling who, did what, when, and where. Let students write an article to match the title and information. Encourage them to describe an interesting scene in the game.

Mixed-Up People

Objective   To detect pronoun inconsistency.

Materials   Short story with pronouns used incorrectly; ditto copy of story.

Procedure   1. Give students a ditto copy of "The Picnic."
2. Tell the students that something is wrong with the story. Ask them to try and identify the problem as you read it and they follow along on the ditto.
3. Read "The Picnic." Emphasize the pronouns as you read.

4. Ask the students to state the problem. (It is not necessary for them to say that the "pronouns" are incorrect. They may say that the *he's*, *she's*, *they's*, etc., are all mixed up.)
5. Give students a copy of the story with pronouns omitted. Have them fill in the correct pronouns.
6. Have one student read the corrected story to the class.
7. Continue this activity on another day with another "mixed-up" story. Or have students write some mixed-up stories for the class to correct.

Example 1

THE PICNIC

Yesterday, Joe, Robert, Susan, and Ruth went on a picnic.
He met at the entrance to the town park.
Susan told the others that he knew the perfect spot near a lovely little pond.
She all agreed that would be a terrific place for the picnic.
When he all reached the pond, he spread the blanket, unpacked the food, and ate lunch.
After lunch, he suggested that everyone go for a walk.
It started to walk around the pond.
While taking the walk, she tripped over a twig and he landed in the pond.
What a sight they was!
The others started to laugh and so did he.
He were sure that she would always remember his first picnic.
She was a perfect day and everyone had a wonderful time.

Example 2

THE PICNIC

Yesterday, Joe, Robert, Susan, and Ruth went on a picnic.
_____ met at the entrance to the town park.
Susan told the others that _____ knew the perfect spot near a lovely little pond.
_____ all agreed that would be a terrific place for the picnic.
When _____ all reached the pond, _____ spread the blanket, unpacked the food, and ate lunch.
After lunch, _____ suggested that everyone go for a walk.
_____ started to walk around the pond.
While taking the walk, _____ tripped over a twig and _____ landed in the pond.
What a sight _____ was!
The others started to laugh and so did _____.
_____ were sure that _____ would always remember _____ first picnic.
_____ was a perfect day and everyone had a wonderful time.

═══ **CHAPTER 11** ═══

Check Their Spelling

Spelling instruction should be integrated into the language arts curriculum, emphasizing spelling accuracy in students' everyday written work. Spelling errors should not be ignored; specific time needs to be set aside for proofreading, identifying errors, and correcting them. In addition, students need direct spelling instruction on a daily basis if they are to write with a measure of skill; however, a number of research conclusions must be considered when designing or adopting a spelling program.

A recent survey of spelling research (Fitzsimmons, 1980) points out the following important guidelines.

1. The spelling pretest, along with teacher-supervised self-correction, is the single most important factor contributing to achievement in spelling.

2. Students learn words best in list format.

3. Formalized spelling lessons should include a number of the following word types each week:

       a. high-frequency words representing a mix of patterned and non-conforming words;
       b. other forms of words on the list (i.e., prefixes and suffixes added);
       c. challenge words for proficient spellers; and
       d. content words from grade-level subject areas.

4. Twelve to fifteen minutes a day is adequate for spelling instruction (for a total of sixty to seventy-five minutes per week).

On the other hand, some definite conclusions were listed regarding what does *not* contribute to spelling success.

1. Copying words multiple times does not improve spelling skill; instead, after looking carefully at a word, students should try to write it from memory, then check it and try again if it was misspelled.

2. Teaching phonetic generalizations seems questionable because a substantial number of the most frequently used words in writing do not conform to any generalizations.

3. Presenting words in syllabified form presents no advantage; instead words should be taught as whole units.

4. Pointing out hard spots in spelling words has little value.

One major conclusion of research is that words put immediately into writing production are most easily learned. The spelling approach presented in this book emphasizes improving spelling through greater writing productivity. Remember that communicating ideas is the first focus of the writing program and that students should be encouraged to write freely without worrying about perfect spelling on first drafts. Once ideas are down on paper and reviewed, then spelling errors can be corrected.

Specific strategies to assist students with spelling can be initiated at three different points in the writing process: prewriting, writing, and postwriting.

Prewriting

1. Write key words and phrases on the board as students discuss topic.
2. Have students suggest any additional words they might need to complete their writing assignment. Write these on the board. Students can refer to them as needed during the writing session.

During Writing

1. Encourage students to sound out as much as possible of the unknown word and to draw a line to indicate that they need help (e,g., ani _____). This keeps the students writing and prevents them from getting bogged down while waiting for spelling help.
2. Write the needed words on a piece of paper for the student. Or ask a second student to write out the words.
3. Give positive reinforcement for every word attempted.

Proofreading, Editing, Revising

1. Do not circle errors in red!
2. Have students proofread their papers and circle all words that they think might be wrong. (They may *not* find all errors—that's O.K.) This method reduces teacher judgment of spelling errors and gives the students more responsibility for finding their own errors. If students cannot find all their misspelled words, write the misspelled words correctly on a separate piece of paper. Ask students to go back over the writing and find the misspelled words, then substitute the correctly spelled words.
3. Ask students to proofread each other's papers and identify spelling errors. Students may colloborate to find correct spelling.
4. Have students keep a personalized notebook or file of special interest words and also their own commonly misspelled words.

Publishing

Identify class spelling experts and have them proofread final drafts for errors.

Evaluating

Use the Spelling Checklist, Table 2-7, to determine level of performance in spelling. Use a diagnostic spelling test to determine grade level of student spelling ability.

Spelling Interviews

Objective   To develop lists of difficult words.

Materials   Pencil and paper.

Procedure   1. Ask the students to name the words that they have difficulty spelling. Put these on a chart.
2. Next, have different class members interview students in other classrooms and find out which words they have difficulty spelling. Add these words to the chart.
3. Tally the number of times each word was mentioned. Keep the chart posted in the classroom.
4. Sponsor a "Spelling Mastery Contest" based on the list of words collected in the interviews.

Extension   Point out that teachers have some spelling troublespots, too. Have students interview other teachers to make a list of words that they have trouble spelling. Add these to the "Spelling Mastery Contest" and see whether everyone can learn all of the troublespots.

Visual Dictation

Objective   To develop visual memory of spelling words.

Materials   Sentences or short paragraphs slightly above the students' level of spelling ability.

Procedure   1. Write a sentence or short paragraph on the board or overhead projector. At first use only one sentence, but gradually build up to short paragraphs. (This activity works best with small groups of students.)
2. Ask the students to read the sample aloud several times. Ask them to pick out the words that they think might be hard to spell. Spell these aloud as a group, then write them down on a scrap piece of paper.
3. Read the sample one more time; then ask the students to take one last careful look before you cover it up.
4. Dictate the sample slowly in short phrases and have students write down what you say. Repeat several times or until all students are finished.
5. Have students proofread their papers and underline any word they had trouble with or they think they have misspelled.

6. Exposing the sample again, ask students to compare their version with the original. Focus specific attention on any words that were misspelled. Have students spell them aloud and write them down (one at a time).
7. Repeat using the same paragraph. Compare results.
8. Repeat this activity frequently for students who are making errors on basic sight words.

Extension   For added interest, have students make up short stories using weekly spelling word lists, then use these for visual dictation.

Resources   *Crossword Magic*
   Mindscape, Inc.
   Available for Apple II, IBM, Commodore computers
   Designed for teachers and students grades 2 to 12
This program helps you create crossword puzzles on any subject you choose. You select the words and clues, and the program arranges the words in the puzzle format.

Master Spell
   MECC
   Available for Apple II computer
   Designed for all grades
Master Spell features a set of teacher utility programs designed to create student diskettes with up to eighteen spelling lists. The program records all misspelled words and automatically provides review lessons until the words are mastered. *Master Spell* also enables the teacher to determine the style of word presentation (in lists or in sentences), type of feedback (smiley face, right/wrong, correct/incorrect), and type of remediation (repeat word, compare misspelling with correct spelling, word blanks). Because word lists are created by the teacher, this program could be used at any grade level.

The Spelling System
   Milliken
   Available for Apple II computers
   Designed for grades 3 to 10
Each of the four drill and practice disks in this program features the Milliken Management System, which allows the teacher to give specific class or individual assignments and keeps records of student progress. The program features over 1400 words at several levels of difficulty. For example, first level words might be *bath, jelly, hammer, under;* while the highest level of words might be *acceptable, adolescent, exaggerate,* and *courageous.* You may also enter a selection of your class-specific words. Each program disk can store records of one hundred students. Practically speaking, the disk must remain in the computer as each student goes through the assigned lesson, so multiple copies would be necessary in a lab setting. Levels could be divided between classrooms if computers are based in classrooms.

   Words are presented and practiced in context and in a variety of motivating ways: flash spelling, cloze techniques, scrambled letters, missing vowels codes, alphabetical sequence, and others. The graphics (pictures) are motivational and hold student attention.

Puzzles and Posters
   MECC
   Available for Apple II computers
   Designed for teachers and students

This software package contains four utility programs useful for both teachers and students.

Word Search lets the user create and print out hidden word puzzles.

Crossword Puzzle enables the user to make a crossword puzzle using any word list.

A-Maze-Ment prints mazes in a variety of sizes.

Posters and Banners prints banners, signs, bulletins, headlines, announcements, posters, and bulletin board labels.

Word Wizards
  MECC
  Available for Apple II computers
  Designed for grades 1 to 6

This drill and practice program features four spelling options using a fantasy theme and provides timed, visual memory practice on spelling words designated by the teacher. Program management options enable the teacher to create a spelling data disk based on the classroom spelling text.

Working Words in Spelling
  Curriculum Associates
  Available for Apple II computers
  Designed for grades 1 to 8.

Students can study their spelling words by using "Flash Review" or "Scramble Review". The "Spelling Manager" keeps track of student progress and provides reports for the student and/or teacher. Reports list difficult words and mastered words.

The Bare Bear

Objective To illustrate and write sentences with homophones.

Materials Drawing paper, crayons, colored pencils, or magic markers.

Procedure
1. Explain the meaning of *homophone* to the students (i.e., words that sound the same, but have different spellings and different meanings). *Note:* The term homo<u>nym</u> is frequently substituted for homo<u>phone</u>. Homonyms are words that sound the same and have the same spelling but different meanings. Sometimes homonyms are called homo<u>graphs</u> because they are written with the same spelling.
2. Write several pairs on the board for examples.
      nose-knows   pair-pear   plane-plain   beat-beet
3. Ask students to suggest other pairs. Add them to the chart as they are suggested. Give students clues if they have trouble thinking of words.
      "The post office delivers the _____."
4. Read aloud to the class one of the suggested resources that use homophones. Have students listen for homophones to add to the list.
5. Ask students to choose some pairs of homonyms to use in sentences and to illustrate.

6. Ask individual students to read their sentences to the class. Have class members decide on the correct spelling to fit the sentence meaning.
7. Put illustrated homonyms and sentences on bulletin board.

Extension 1   Encourage students to add homonym pairs to the charts and sentences and illustrations to the bulletin board.

Extension 2   Have students check the library for books that use homonyms. (See Resources.)

Extension 3   Play Homophone Concentration. Put homophones on separate cards (see suggested sets). The sets increase in difficulty. Two or more students can play at one time.

Resources   *How a Horse Grew Hoarse on the Site Where He Sighted a Bare Bear*
Emily Hanlon
Delacorte Press, 1976
The tale of an odd assortment of characters and their sail on the high seas, all based on the use of homonyms.

Your Art is a Which: Fun with Homophones
Bernice Kohn Hunt
Harcourt Brace Jovanovich, 1976
Presents homophones in rhyme.

*Homonyms: Hair and Hare and Other Words That Sound the Same
but Look As Different As Bear and Bare.*
Joan Hanson
Lerner Publications Co., 1972
A delightfully illustrated book on "hair and hare and other words that sound the same but look as different as bear and bare." Students could make a similar collection of illustrated homonyms.

CHAPTER 12

Improve Handwriting

Cursive writing is most commonly taught using commercially available writing programs. While there is general agreement on a number of areas in these programs (e.g., the need for legibility, the need for purposeful practice), there are surprising differences in letter formation, letter sequencing, and teaching practices among the programs (Otto, McMenemy, and Smith, 1973). The biggest drawback in the commercial programs is that letters are introduced very quickly and without sufficient practice allowed for mastery before new letters are introduced. Some students may be able to handle this; but others, especially those with fine motor problems, need much more practice before attaining mastery. Ideally, the teacher should provide additional practice both before and after the exercises are completed in the workbook.

By third or fourth grade, most students begin to make the transition from manuscript to cursive writing. The average student makes the transition with little difficulty when practice and teacher supervision are part of the program. Other students, who have immature fine motor coordination, may need program adjustments. Suggested adjustments follow.

Introducing Letters

1. *Establish realistic expectations.* Recognize that cursive writing instruction is time-consuming but that eventually the results will justify the effort. Slow the pace and provide additional monitored practice for those students who are having difficulty. Do not expect students to make the transition from manuscript to cursive writing quickly. Requiring the use of cursive writing before all letters are known may result in the formation of poor writing habits.

2. *Emphasize the importance of posture, paper placement, and pencil grasp.* These factors can affect the consistency, slant, and legibility of writing.

Generally, for right-handed cursive writers, the paper should be slanted slightly toward the left so that the lower *left* corner points toward the belt buckle. For left-handers, the paper should be slanted to the right so that the lower *right* corner points to the belt buckle. This arrangement of paper allows left-handers to keep their hand below the line of writing instead of above and hooked around as is frequently seen. If this hooked position has developed, it is inadvisable to attempt to change it (Wiederholt, Hammill, and Brown, 1978).

Be sure that the student has the appropriate size chair and desk while completing writing tasks.

3. *Teach letters with common formations.* The letters with the simplest formations should be taught first. (See Table 2-8 for letter groupings.) In addition, all vowels, except "y," should be taught quickly since these letters form the basic shape of the more difficult letters. Once the basic forms are taught, the more difficult letters with their "families" can be taught. As these patterns become automatic, speed will increase. Verbalize the movements as they are made. Ask a student who has mastered the letter formation in question to demonstrate and verbalize the sequence of movements to the rest of the group or class.

4. *Practice letters in isolation until they are mastered.* When the letter has been mastered, it can be integrated and used with previously learned letters through writing short words, phrases, sentences, and paragraphs.

5. *Provide practice at the chalkboard.* It is easier to monitor four or five students who are working at the chalkboard than it is to monitor them while they write at their desks. Using black magic markers, draw parallel lines about two inches apart on one chalkboard. These lines last quite a long time and are helpful to students as they practice their letter formations.

Practicing Letters, Words, Sentences

1. *Give frequent, short, guided cursive writing practice sessions.* It is essential that the teacher provide specific handwriting lessons that emphasize correct letter formation and correct spacing. This is particularly important during the transitional stages of changing from manuscript writing to cursive writing. Without careful instruction and supervision, students may learn to form letters incorrectly and, through repeated practice of the incorrect formation, establish a pattern difficult to break. A minimum of ten minutes a day should be spent in guided handwriting practice.

2. *Allow the student to write in a comfortable style during creative and other writing sessions.* This will prevent overloading (requiring the use of too many new skills at one time). It might mean a return to the manuscript style for the first draft of a story or report. As students become more comfortable with cursive writing, they will be able to use it more effectively and effortlessly.

Evaluating Handwriting

1. *Use evaluation procedures outlined in Chapter 2.* If students have been using cursive writing, check different writing samples to identify specific problems in letter formation, size, or slant. Ask the student to identify the letters that are most difficult to write. Use Handwriting Checklist (Table 2-8).

2. *Encourage students to evaluate their own letter formations.* Have students make quality comparisons of their work. Provide copies of the Handwriting Checklist and evaluation scales from commercial programs so that students may compare their own writing. When all letter formations are known, have student copy one of the following sentences in order to make a weekly or biweekly comparison.

1. The quick brown fox jumps over the lazy brown dog.
2. Pack my box with five dozen jugs of liquid.
3. The five boxing wizards jump quickly.

At the bottom of the paper put these sentences:

I have trouble with the following letters: _____

I write these letters the best: _____

Sample words for cursive writing practice
Cursive lower case-basic groups

1. *i* u *t* *w*   "swing up, then trace back down"
      it   wit   ti
                    tut
                    tutti
                    tutu

2. *l* e   "swing up, then loop back down"
words using *l* and e and previous letters

l	e	i	t	w
let	eel	ill	tee	we
lie	ell	it'll	tell	well
lit	elite		tie	welt
little			tile	wet
lull			till	will
lute			tilt	wilt
			title	wit

phrases emphasizing *i, u, t, w, l* and e

let it wilt	we will tile it
it will tell	we will title it
will it tilt?	little wet eel
it will tilt	little ill eel
tie it well	little lie
it will wilt	we will wet it
we will tell	we will let it wilt
we will tie it	well, will it wilt?
title it	it'll wilt

3. n m   "forward and over the hill(s)"
words with n and m as first letter

n	m		
net	me	millet	mull
nettle	meet	mine	mullet
new	melt	mini	mute
newt	men	mint	mutt
nil	menu	minuet	
nit	met	minute	
nitwit	mettle	mite	
null	mew	mitt	
nut	mile	mitten	
	mill	mule	

words with n and m in random positions

n		m
in	tent	elm
inn	tin	emit
lent	tint	lime
lentil	tune	mime
line	until	time
lint	went	mum
nine	win	
nineteen	wine	
nun		
ten		

phrases emphasizing n and m

nine men will tell	we went in
time will tell	nine ill men
it will melt	ten well men
we met in line	we will win
until we meet	let me win
we met ten little men	let me wet it
let me meet ten tin men	let me melt it
we met nineteen men	let me win it
until we win	in a minute
will nineteen men tell?	we went in tent

4. c o a   "swing up, go back down and around"
words with c, o, or a as first letter

c	o	a
cell	oil	ace
cent	omelet	aim
cite	omit	all
clue	on	alone
cue	once	allowance
cull	one	am

c	o	a
cut	out	an
cute	outline	animal
	owl	ate
	own	

words with c, o, and a in random positions

c	o	a
accent	locomotion	catamaran
account	lotto	mallet
calculate	moon	mammal
cancel	motion	mama
catcall	motto	manual
coconut	mountain	nation
cocoon	ocelot	tattle
collect	onion	tattoo
comic	total	wallet
mecca	women	wallow

sentences emphasing c, o, and a

1. Ten clean comical clowns eat coconut at a cinema.
2. An ocelot ate an onion omelet at noontime.
3. At noontime, nine mice ate a coconut.
4. A comical clown will call a collie to eat.
5. Ten women want to come out on a little tan catamaran.
6. A nice niece will not tell a tattletale.
7. A nice tattoo on a clown will be cute.
8. A cow on a moon at noontime will eat a cocoon.
9. Ten women want to nominate one woman in an election.
10. A location on a tall mountain will be nice.

Cursive lower case-families

5. *i* family   i   u   t   w   j   p   s   r
   words with j, p, s, and r as first letter

j	p	s	r
jail	palace	sails	raccoon
jean	panic	scales	ration
jell	papoose	scouts	rattle
jest	peace	sense	react
jet	pest	sentences	reclaim
jewel	piece	smells	relation
join	place	smiles	remote
joint	plant	snails	roasts
jolt	plate	snowmen	roosts
jowl	plea	solution	route

words with *j, p, s,* and *r* in random positions

j	*p*	*s*	*r*
ajar	apple	distress	erase
adjective	appear	missiles	error
adjust	apply	possess	mirror
eject	ripple	scissors	scrape
enjoy	supper	seasons	scream
rejoin	suppose	session	screen
rejoice	support	sisters	terrace
juju	snapper	somersault	terrier
jujitsu	supermarket	stainless	terror
pajamas	reappear	suspense	warrior

sentences emphasizing *j, p, s,* and *r*

1. Put peas on a nice new plate please.
2. A snowman loses a smile as a sun appears.
3. A terrier smells a raccoon near a tree.
4. We want to somersault at a palace supper.
5. Use scissors to cut out a paper snowman.
6. A scout roasts a nice raccoon to eat at suppertime.
7. An error on a paper is not nice at all.
8. A roast for supper is at a supermarket.
9. A jetsetter is on a jet to a mountain.
10. One sister is in a missile on a trip to a moon.

6. *l* family: *b f h k*
words with *b, f, h,* and *k* as first letter

b	*f*	*h*	*k*
balance	fable	habit	kennel
batter	false	hammer	kerchief
better	famous	hamster	kettle
blister	fashion	harbor	kimono
bluff	feature	harmonica	kitchen
brilliant	flask	hollow	kitten
bullet	fleet	horse	knee
bumper	follow	hospital	knife
burrow	forest	human	knot
burst	fourth	humble	know

words with *b, f, h,* and *k* in random positions

b	*f*	*h*	*k*
babble	baffle	champ	knock
barbell	cliff	phantom	knuckles
barber	coffee	phone	khaki
blubber	cuff	shallow	knapsack
bomb	fluff	shelter	knack
rabbit	raffle	shoe	knickknack

b	f	h	k
remember	ruffle	shuffle	knickers
robber	staff	while	nickel
terrible	stiff	whiskers	polka
	waffle	witch	rocket

sentences emphasizing b, f, h, and k

1. The barber babbles while he swallows waffles.
2. The robber has a khaki knapsack full of knickers.
3. A champ horse swallows a shoe while in the shelter.
4. A wise human whistles while he shaves whiskers in the shower.
5. The batter must balance the bat and hit the ball better.
6. A hamster with a harmonica follows a human into a hospital.
7. That famous phantom phones for a fellow freak to join him.
8. A fashion show will feature a famous fearful foursome.
9. A rocket will blast off for the trip to another planet.
10. A white rabbit will remember to look for a new hutch.

7. c family: d g q
   words with d, g, and q as first letter

d	g	q
dabble	gallon	quack
daffodil	gallop	quail
dancer	gamble	quake
dawn	garden	quarrel
dentist	glimmer	quarter
different	gobble	queen
difficult	goblet	question
dinosaur	grade	quick
dipper	graduation	quiet
dribble	grammar	quill

words with d, g, and q in random positions

d	g	q
adder	dagger	acquaint
fiddled	gaggle	acquire
griddled	garage	conquer
haddock	giggled	conquest
handicap	goggle	consequence
handled	gorgeous	equal
huddled	grudge	frequent
riddle	jiggled	jonquil
saddled	juggled	kumquat
salamander	suggest	sequel

sentences emphasizing d, g, and q

1. A gaggle of gorgeous geese gobbled grits and grain.
2. A dangerous gambled drew good cards with quick and quiet skill.

3. A juggler jiggled and juggled a group of bats and balls.
4. The queen quarrels with her subjects about equal rights.
5. The dentist's daughter has a difficult riddle.
6. The consequence of the conqueror's conquest is a quarrel.
7. A saddled salamander huddled against a difficult dinosaur.
8. The giant judge giggled when he saw the dangerous robber gagged.
9. A gallant knight galloped to the queen's castle on a dinosaur.
10. At graduation, we had a quarrel about a juggling contest.

8. family: v x y z
   words with v, x, y, or z as the first letter

v	x	y	z
vacation	xebec	yacht	zany
valentine	xenon	yardstick	zebra
vampire	xeric	yawn	zero
vegetable	xylem	yellow	zigzag
velvet	xylophone	yesterday	zillion
victory		yodel	zinc
violence		yogurt	zinnia
vision		yonder	zodiac
vocabulary		young	zoo
volunteer		youngster	zoom

words with v, x, y, or z in random positions

v	x	y	z
believe	ax	biology	blaze
cover	axle	berry	dazzle
develop	complex	dillydally	enzyme
evolution	exact	family	fizzle
government	exchange	gabby	freeze
gravity	exciting	geography	graze
gravy	exhaust	happy	jazz
heaven	exit	kayak	lazy
native	explode	pygmy	puzzle
valve	oxen	pyramid	quartz

sentences emphasizing v, x, y, and z

1. At valentine vacation, a velvet vampire volunteered to yodel.
2. Many good, green vegetables grow in the garden in spring.
3. Yonder by the river grows a happy, gabby pygmy family.
4. A zillion lazy zebras zigzag through the jungles.
5. Yesterday a dazzling blaze developed near the zoo.
6. Youngsters enjoy freezing as they build jazzy snowmen.
7. My family likes to dillydally around kayaks or yachts.
8. My geography homework is to find some zinc and quartz.
9. A xylophone player is happy when he can play some jazz.
10. The zoo exit is next to the zebra's jazzy new cage.

Cursive upper case

Use names and addresses of students in the classroom for practice on cursive upper case letters. Gradually, introduce additional upper case letters based on similarities in their formation. See the Handwriting Checklist (Table 2-8) for groupings of upper case letters.

Bibliography

Alaska Department of Education. *Hand in Hand: The Writing Process and the Micro-computer: Two Revolutions in the Teaching of Writing.* Juneau: Alaska Department of Education, 1985.

Anastasiow, N. "The Picture Story Language Test." In O.K. Buros, ed., *The Seventh Mental Measurements Yearbook.* Highland Park, NJ: Gryphon Press, 1972.

Anderson, Velma R., and Thompson, Sheryl K. *Test of Written English (TWE).* Novato, CA: Academic Therapy Publications, 1979.

Arena, J. (ed.). *Building Spelling Skills in Dyslexic Children.* San Rafael, CA: Academic Therapy Publications, 1968.

Bateman, Donald, and Zidonis, Frank. *The Effect of a Study of Transformational Grammar on the Writing of Ninth and Tenth Graders.* Champaign, IL: National Council of Teachers of English, 1966.

Bates, Jefferson D. *Writing with Precision.* Washington, DC: Acropolis Books, 1978.

Beach, R., and Bridwell, L.S. (eds.). *New Directions in Composition Research.* New York: Guilford Press, 1983.

Beaven, M.H. "Individualized Goal Setting, Self-Evaluation, and Peer Evaluation." In C. Cooper and L. Odell, eds., *Evaluating Writing: Describing, Measuring, Judging.* Urbana, IL: National Council of Teachers of English, 1977.

Bernstein, Ruby S., and Tanner, Bernard R. *The California High School Proficiency Examination: Evaluating the Writing Samples.* Berkeley, CA: Bay Area Writing Project, 1977.

Bloom, B. *Handbook of Formative and Summative Evaluation.* New York: McGraw-Hill, 1971.

Bloomington Public Schools. *Bloomington Writing Assessment 1977; Student Exercises, Teacher Directions, Scoring.* St. Paul: Minnesota State Department of Education, 1977. (ED 155 692)

Bloomington Public Schools. *Bloomington Writing Assessment 1977: A Report to Students, Public and Teaching Staff.* St. Paul: Minnesota State Department of Education, 1977.

Boder E. "Developmental Dyslexia: Prevailing Diagnostic Concepts and a New Diagnostic Approach." In H. Myklebust, ed., *Progress in Learning Disabilities.* New York: Grune and Stratton, 1971.

Braddock, R., Lloyd-Jones, R., and Schoer, L. *Research in Written Composition.* Urbana, IL: National Council of Teachers of English, 1963.

Britton, J., Burgess, T., Martin, N., McLeod, A., and Rosen, H. *The Development of Writing Abilities (11–18).* London: Macmillan Education, 1975.

Bruce, B., et al. *A Cognitive Science Approach to Writing. Technical Report No. 89.* Washington, DC: National Institute of Education (DHEW), 1978. (ED 157 039)

Burgess, Carol, et al. *Understanding Children Writing.* Harmondsworth, Middlesex, England: Penguin Books, 1973.

Buros, O.K. *The Seventh Mental Measurements Yearbook.* Highland Park, NJ: Gryphon Press, 1972.

Burrows, Alvina T., ed., *Children's Writing: Research in Composition and Related Skills.* Champaign, IL: National Council of Teachers of English, 1961. (ED 090 546)

Burrows, Alvina T. "Composition: Prospect and Retrospect". In H. Robinson, ed., *Reading and Writing Instruction in the United States: Historical Trends.* Newark, DE: International Reading Association, 1977.

Burrows, Alvina T., Jackson, D.C., and Saunders, D.O. *They All Want to Write: Written English in the Elementary School.* Rev. ed. Englewood Cliffs, NJ: Prentice-Hall, 1964.

Burrows, Alvina T. *What Research Says to the Teacher.* Washington, DC: National Education Association, 1966. (ED 017 482)

California State Department of Education. *Handbook for Planning an Effective Writing Program.* Sacramento: California State Department of Education, 1982.

California State Department of Education. *Technology in the Curriculum, Language Arts Resource Guide, K–12: A Guide to the Use of Computers and Instructional Television in Language Arts.* Sacramento: California State Department of Education, 1986.

Caplan, R., and Keech, C. *Showing Writing: A Training Program to Help Students Be Specific.* Berkeley, CA: Bay Area Writing Project, 1980.

Carlson, R.K. *Sparkling Words: Two Hundred Practical and Creative Writing Ideas.* Rev. ed. Berkeley, CA: Wagner Printing Company, 1973.

Center School's Eighth Graders and Marashio, N. *Writing: A Window to Our Minds.* Berkeley, CA: National Writing Project, 1982.

Clegg, A.B. *The Excitement of Writing.* London Chatto and Windus, 1964.

Cohen, C., and Abrams, R. *Spellmaster. Spelling: Teaching and Learning, Book One.* Exeter, NH: Learnco Incorporated, 1976.

Cohen, C., and Abrams, R. *Spellmaster. Spelling: Teaching and Learning, Book Two.* Exeter, NH: Learnco Incorporated, 1976.

Collins, J.L., and Sommers, E.A. *Writing On-Line: Using Computers in the Teaching of Writing.* Montclair, NJ: Noybton/Cook, 1987.

Committee on Writing Standards. "Standards for Basic Skills Writing Programs." Urbana, IL: National Council of Teachers of English, March 1979.

Cooper, Charles R., and Odell, Lee, eds. *Evaluating Writing.* Urbana, IL: National Council of Teachers of English, 1977.

Cooper, Charles R., and Odell, Lee. *Research on Composing, Points of Departure.* Urbana, IL: National Council of Teachers of English, 1978.

Dellinger, D.G. *Out of the Heart: How to Design Writing Assignments for High School Courses.* Berkeley, CA: National Writing Project, 1982.

Diederich, Paul B. *Measuring Growth in English.* Urbana, IL: National Council of Teachers of English, 1974.

Dolch, Edward W. *A Manual for Remedial Reading.* Champaign, IL: Garrard Press, 1939.

Dubrow, H.C. *Learning to Write.* Cambridge, MA: Educators Publishing Service, 1968.

Duvall-Flynn, J. *Writing for Reading: Will Resistant Readers Teach Each Other?* Berkeley, CA: National Writing Project, 1983.

Elbow, Peter. *Writing with Power.* New York: Oxford University Press, 1980.

Eldridge, Cornelia C. "A Study of the Relationships Between the Oral and Written Composition of Third Grade Children." In English Curriculum Study Center, *Research in Cognate Aspects of Written Composition.* Athens: University of Georgia, 1968. (ED 026 368)

English Curriculum Study Center. *A Curriculum in Written Composition, 4–6: A Guide for Teachers.* Athens: University of Georgia, 1968. (ED 026 364)

English Curriculum Study Center. *Research in Cognate Aspects of Written Composition.* Athens: University of Georgia, 1968. (ED 026 368)

English Curriculum Study Center. *Use of Literary Models in Teaching Written Composition, K–6.* Athens: University of Georgia, 1968. (ED 026 365)

Evertts, Eldonna L. *Explorations in Children's Writing.* Urbana, IL: National Council of Teachers of English, 1970.

Ewing, June B. "A Study of the Influence of Various Stimuli on the Written Composition of Selected Third Grade Children." In English Curriculum Study Center, *Research in Cognate Aspects of Written Composition.* Athens: University of Georgia, 1968. (ED 026 368)

Fader, D. *The New Hooked on Books.* Berkeley, CA: Berkeley Medallion Books, 1976.

Fadiman, C., and Howard, J. *Empty Pages: A Search for Writing Competency in School and Society.* Belmont, CA: Fearon-Pitman Publishers, 1979.

Finn, Patrick, J. "Computer Aided Description of Mature Word Choice in Writing." In C.R. Cooper and Lee Odell, eds., *Evaluating Writing.* Urbana, IL: National Council of Teachers of English, 1977.

Fitzsimmons, Robert J., and Loomer M., *Spelling: The Research Basis.* Iowa City: University of Iowa, 1980.

Flesch, R. *The Art of Readable Writing.* New York: Macmillan, 1949.

Foley, J. "Evaluation of Learning in Writing." In B. Bloom, T. Hastings, and G. Madaus, eds., *Handbook on Formative and Summative Evaluation of Student Learning.* New York: McGraw-Hill, 1971.

Gessell, A., and Ilg, F. *The Child from Five to Ten.* New York: Harper & Bros., 1946.

Geuder, P., Harvey, L., Wages, J., and Lloyd, D. *They Really Taught Us How to Write.* Urbana, IL: National Council of Teachers of English, 1974.

Golub, L. "Stimulating and Receiving Children's Writing: Implications for an Elementary Writing Curriculum." In R. Larson, ed., *Children and Writing in the Elementary School.* New York: Oxford University Press, 1975.

Golub, L. "Syntactical and Lexical Deviations in Children's Written Sentences." Unpublished paper, 1972. (ED 073 475)

Golub, L. "Written Language Development and Instruction of Elementary School Children." Paper presented to the National Conference on Research in English, 1973. (ED 073 474)

Good, Phillip I. *Choosing A Word Processor.* Reston, VA: Reston Publishing Company, 1982.

Graves, D. "Andrea Learns to Make Writing Hard." *Language Arts,* 1979, 56, (5): 569–576.

Graves, D. "A Six Year-Old's Writing Process: The First Half of First Grade." *Language Arts,* 1979, 56, (7): 829–835.

Graves, D. "What Children Show Us About Revision." *Language Arts,* 1979, 56, (3): 312–319.

Graves, Donald. *Writing: Teachers and Children at Work.* Portsmouth, NH: Heinemann Educational Books, 1983.

Gray, S., and Keech, C. *Writing from Given Information.* Berkeley, CA: Bay Area Writing Project, 1980.

Green H., and Petty, W. *Developing Language Skills in the Classroom.* 5th ed. Boston: Allyn and Bacon, 1975.

Greene, Amsel. *Pullet Surprises.* Fullerton, CA: Sultana Press, 1969.

Grose, L.M., Metler, D., and Steinberg, E. *Suggestions for Evaluating Junior High School Writing.* Pittsburgh, PA: Association of English Teachers of Western Pennsylvania.

Hailey, J. *Teaching Writing K–8.* Berkeley, CA: Instructional Laboratory, University of California, 1978.

Hall, Janice. *Evaluating and Improving Written Expression: A Practical Guide for Teachers.* Boston: Allyn and Bacon, 1981.

Hammill, D.D., and Bartel, N.R. *Teaching Children with Learning and Behavior Problems.* Boston: Allyn and Bacon, 1978.

Hammill, D.D., and Larsen, S.C. *Test of Written Language* (TOWL). Austin, TX: Pro-Ed, 1983.

Hanna, P.R., and Hanna, J.S. "Applications of Linguistics and Psychological Cues to the Spelling Course of Study." In T.D. Horn, ed., *Research on Handwriting and Spelling*. Champaign, IL: National Council of Teachers of English, 1966.

Harris, A.J., and Jacobson, M.D. *Basic Elementary Reading Vocabularies*. New York: Macmillan, 1972.

Hill, A., and Boone, B. *If Maslow Taught Writing*. Berkeley, CA: National Writing Project, 1982.

Hill, Edwin C., and Hill, Margaret K. *Written Language Development of Intermediate Grade Children*. Pittsburgh, PA: University of Pittsburgh, School of Education, 1966. (ED 010 059)

Hillerich, R. *A Writing Vocabulary of Elementary School Children*. Springfield, IL: Charles C. Thomas, 1978.

Hillerich, R. "Developing Written Expression: How To Raise—Not Raze—Writers." *Language Arts*, 1979, 56: 769–777.

Hillerich, R.L. *Teaching Children to Write, K–8: A Complete Guide to Developing Writing Skills*. Englewood Cliffs, NJ: Prentice-Hall, 1985.

Hodges, R.E. "The Psychological Bases of Spelling." In T.D. Horn, *Research on Handwriting and Spelling*. Champaign, IL: National Council of Teachers of English, 1966.

Horn, Ernest. *A Basic Writing Vocabulary*. University of Iowa Monographs in Education, First Series, No. 4, 1926.

Horn, T.D. *Research on Handwriting and Spelling*. Champaign, IL: National Council of Teachers of English, 1966.

Horne, Rose N. "A Study of the Use of Figurative Language by Sixth Grade Children." In English Curriculum Study Center, *Research in Cognate Aspects of Written Composition*. Athens: University of Georgia, 1968. (ED 026 368)

Howgate, L. *Building Self-Esteem Through the Writing Process*. Berkeley, CA: National Writing Project, 1982.

Hunt, K. *Grammatical Structures Written at Three Grade Levels*. Urbana, IL: National Council of Teachers of English, 1965.

Huntington Beach Union High School District. *The Test of Everyday Skills*. Monterey, CA: CTB/McGraw-Hill, 1978.

Jastak, J.F., and Jastak, S. *The Wide Range Achievement Test*. Wilmington, DE: Guidance Associates of Delaware, 1965.

Judine, Sister M., ed. *A Guide for Evaluating Student Composition*. Urbana, IL: National Council of Teachers of English, 1965.

Kaufman, H.S., and Biren, P.L., "Cursive Writing: An Aid to Reading and Spelling." *Academic Therapy*, 1979, 15 (2): 209–219.

Kincaid, Gerald L. "Some Factors Affecting Variations in Quality of Students' Writing." In R. Braddock, R. Lloyd-Jones, and L. Schoer, eds., *Research in Written Composition*. Urbana, IL: National Council of Teachers of English, 1963.

Kinneavy, J.L. *A Theory of Discourse*. Englewood Cliffs, NJ: Prentice-Hall, 1971.

Knapp, Linda Roehrig. *The Word Processor and the Writing Teacher*. Englewood Cliffs, NJ: Prentice-Hall, 1986.

Larsen, R., and Hammill, D. *Test of Written Spelling* (TWS). San Rafael, CA: Academic Therapy Publications, 1976.

Larsen, Richard L. *Children and Writing in the Elementary School, Theories and Techniques*. New York: Oxford University Press, 1975.

Loban, W.D. *The Language of Elementary School Children*. Champaign, IL: National Council of Teachers, 1963.

Lundsteen, S. *Children Learn to Communicate: Language Arts Through Creative Problem Solving*. Englewood Cliffs, NJ: Prentice-Hall, 1976a.

Lundsteen, S., ed. *Help for the Teacher of Written Composition: New Directions in Research*. Urbana, IL: National Conference on Research in English, 1976b.

Macrorie, K. *Writing to Be Read*. Rev. 2nd ed. Rochelle Park, NJ: Hayden Book Co., 1968.

Mann, P., Suiter, P., and McClung, R. *Handbook in Diagnostic Prescriptive Teaching*. 2nd ed. Boston: Allyn and Bacon, 1979.

Marzano, R., and DiStefano, P. *DiComp: A Diagnostic System for Teaching Composition.* Indian Rocks Beach, FL: Relevant Productions, 1977.

Mellon, John C. *National Assessment and the Teaching of English.* Urbana, IL: National Council of Teachers of English, 1969.

Mellon, John C. *Transformational Sentence-Combining.* Urbana, IL: National Council of Teachers of English, 1969.

Moberg, Goran George. *Writing on Computers in English Composition.* New York: The Writing Consultant, 1986.

Moffett, J., and Wagner, B. *Student-Centered Language Arts and Reading, K–13.* 2nd ed. Boston: Houghton Mifflin Company, 1976.

Moffett, James. *Teaching the Universe of Discourse.* Boston: Houghton Mifflin Company, 1968.

Mosenthal, P., Ramor, L., and Walmsley, S. *Research on Writing: Principles and Methods.* New York: Longman, 1983.

Murray, D. *A Writer Teaches Writing: A Practical Method of Teaching Composition.* Boston: Houghton Mifflin Company, 1968.

Myklebust, Helmer R. *Development and Disorders of Written Language, Volume One, Picture Story Language Test.* New York: Grune and Stratton, 1965.

Myklebust, Helmer R. *Development and Disorders of Written Language, Volume Two, Studies of Normal and Exceptional Children.* New York: Grune and Stratton, 1973.

National Assessment of Educational Progress. *Explanatory and Persuasive Letter Writing: Selected Results from the Second National Assessment of Writing.* Denver, CO: Education Commission of the States, 1977.

National Assessment of Educational Progress. *Expressive Writing: Selected Results from the Second National Assessment of Writing.* Denver, CO: Education Commission of the States, 1976.

National Assessment of Educational Progress. *The Second National Assessment of Writing: New and Reassessed Exercises with Technical Information and Data.* Denver, CO: Education Commission of the States, 1978.

National Assessment of Educational Progress. *Write/Rewrite: An Assessment of Revision Skills. Selected Results from the Second National Assessment of Writing.* Denver, CO: Education Commission of the States, 1977.

National Assessment of Educational Progress. *Writing Mechanics, 1969–1974. A Capsule Description of Changing in Writing Mechanics.* Denver, CO: Education Commission of the States, 1977.

National Assessment of Educational Progress. *Writing: National Results—Writing Mechanics, Report 8.* Denver, CO: Education Commission of the States, 1972.

Neal, Edmund R. "Writing in the Intermediate Grades." In A. Burrows, ed., *Children's Writing: Research in Composition and Related Skills.* Champaign, IL: National Council of Teachers of English, 1961. (ED 090 546)

Nebraska Curriculum Development Center. *A Curriculum for English.* Lincoln, NE: University of Nebraska Press, 1966. (ED 161 078)

New, J., and Leyba, R. "Miscue Analysis in Writing." Urbana, IL: National Council of Teachers of English, 1975. (ED 161 078)

Newkirk, T. "The Mass Testing of Writing: How Well Is It Being Done?" Report prepared at the University of New Hampshire, 1977. (ED 158 310)

O'Donnell, R.C., Griffin, W.J., and Norris, R.C. *Syntax of Kindergarten and Elementary School Children, Research Report 8.* Urbana, IL: National Council of Teachers of English, 1967.

O'Hare, Frank. *Sentence Combining: Improving Student Writing Without Formal Grammar Instruction.* Urbana, IL: National Council of Teachers of English, 1973.

O'Hare, Frank. *Sentence Craft: An Elective Course in Writing.* Lexington, MA: Ginn and Company, 1975.

Orton, S. *Reading and Writing and Speech Problems in Children.* New York: Norton, 1937.

Otto, W., McMenemy, R.A., and Smith, R.J. *Corrective and Remedial Teaching.* 2nd ed. Boston: Houghton Mifflin Company, 1973.

Perkins, W.H. "The Picture Story Language Test." In O.K. Buros, ed., *The Seventh Mental Measurements Yearbook.* Highland Park, NJ: Gryphon Press, 1972.

Petty, W.T. "The Writing of Young Children." In Charles R. Cooper, and Lee Odell, eds., *Research on Composing, Points of Departure.* Urbana, IL: National Council of Teachers of English, 1978.

Piaget, J. *The Language and Thought of the Child.* New York: World Publishing Co., 1955.

Poteet, James A. "Characteristics of Written Expression of Learning Disabled and Non-Learning Disabled Elementary School Students." *Diagnostique,* 1979, 4, (1) Winter/Spring: 60–74. (ED 159 830)

Powell, David. *What Can I Write About? 7000 Topics for High School Students.* Urbana, IL: National Council of Teachers of English, 1981.

Pradl, G. *Expectation and Cohesion.* Berkeley, CA: Bay Area Writing Project, 1979.

Pratt-Butler, G.K. *Let Them Write Creatively.* Columbus, OH: Charles E. Merrill Co., 1973.

Progoff, I. *At a Journal Workshop.* New York: Dialogue House Library, 1965.

Rico, G., and Claggett, M. *Balancing the Hemispheres: Brain Research and the Teaching of Writing.* Berkeley, CA: Bay Area Writing Project, 1980.

Rinsland, H. *A Basic Vocabulary of Elementary School Children.* New York: Macmillan, 1945.

Robinson, H., ed. *Reading and Writing Instruction in the United States: Historical Trends.* Newark, DE: International Reading Association, 1977.

Rosenbaum, N.J. "Problems with Current Research Using the Microcomputer." Paper presented at Delaware Valley Writing Council Spring Conference, February 1984.

Rosenthal, J.H. *The Neuropsychopathology of Written Language.* Chicago: Nelson-Hall, 1977.

Rudorf, H.E. "Measurement of Spelling Ability." In T.D. Horn, ed., *Research on Handwriting and Spelling.* Champaign, IL: National Council of Teachers of English, 1966.

Sager, C. "Improving the Quality of Composition Through Pupil Use of a Rating Scale." Paper presented at the Annual Meeting of the National Council of Teachers, 1973. (ED 089 304)

Sealey, L., Sealey, N., and Millmore, M. *Children's Writing: An Approach for the Primary Grades.* Newark, DE: International Reading Association, 1979.

Shaughnessy, Mina P. *Errors and Expectations, A Guide for the Teacher of Basic Writing.* New York: Oxford University Press, 1977.

Shostak, R., ed. *Computers in Composition Instruction.* Eugene, OR: International Council for Computers in Education, 1984.

Siegal, G., Jensen, J., Chittenden, L., and Wall, J. *Sequences in Writing, Grades K–13.* Berkeley, CA: Bay Area Writing Project, 1980.

Smith, J.A. *Creative Teaching of the Language Arts in Elementary School.* Boston: Allyn and Bacon, 1973.

Sommers, E., and Collins, J. "What Research Tells About Composing and Computing." Paper presented to Computer Educators League, Buffalo, NY, September 1984.

Strickland, R. "Evaluating Children's Compositions." In A. Burrows, ed., *Children's Writing: Research in Composition and Related Skills.* Champaign, IL: National Council of Teachers of English, 1961. (ED 090 546)

Taylor, Karl K. "If Not Grammar, What? Taking Remedial Writing Instruction Seriously." Paper prepared at Illinois Central College, 1978. (ED 159 668)

Thorndike, Edward L., and Lorge, Irving. *The Teacher's Word Book of 30,000 Words.* New York: Teachers College, Columbia University, 1944.

Vygotsky, L.S. *Thought and Language.* Cambridge, MA: MIT Press, 1962.

Wallace, G., and Larsen, S.C. *Educational Assessment of Learning Problems: Testing for Teaching.* Boston: Allyn and Bacon, 1978.

Wallace, G., and McLoughlin, J.A. *Learning Disabilities: Concepts and Characteristics.* Columbus, OH: Charles E. Merrill Co., 1979.

Weehawken Board of Education, *Individualized Language Arts.* Weehawken, NJ: Weehawken Board of Education, 1974.

Weiner, Eva. "The Diagnostic Evaluation of Writing Skills (DEWS): Application of DEWS Criteria to Writing Samples." *Learning Disability Quarterly,* 1980, 3, (2), Spring: 54–59.

Weiss, M.J. *From Writers to Students: The Pleasures and Pains of Writing.* Newark, DE: International Reading Association, 1979.

Wiederholt, J.L., Hammill, D.D., and Brown, V. *The Resource Teacher: A Guide to Effective Practices.* Boston: Allyn and Bacon, 1978.

Wiener, Harvey S. *Any Child Can Write.* New York: McGraw-Hill, 1978.

Wituche, V. "The Book Talk: A Technique for Bringing Together Children and Books." *Language Arts,* 1979, 56, (4): 413–417.

Wood, S. *An Evaluation of Published English Tests.* Madison: Wisconsin Department of Public Instruction, 1967.

Zinsser, W. *On Writing Well, An Informal Guide to Writing Nonfiction.* New York: Harper & Row, 1976.

Zinsser, William. *Writing with a Word Processor.* New York: Harper & Row, 1983.

Directory of Publishers

Addison-Wesley Publishing Co., Inc.
One Jacob Way
Reading, MA 01867

Allyn and Bacon
7 Wells Ave.
Newton, MA 02159

American Faculty Press
44 Lake Shore Drive
Rockaway, NJ 07866

Apple Computer, Inc.
20525 Mariani Ave.
Mailstop 23-AX
Cupertino, CA 95014

Art Education
28 E. Erie Street
Blauvelt, NY 10913

Atheneum Publications
115 Fifth Ave.
New York, NY 10003

Avon Books
1790 Broadway
New York, NY 10019

Bantam Books
666 Fifth Ave.
New York, NY 10103

Barnell Loft
958 Church St.
Baldwin, NY 11510

Bradbury Press
866 Third Ave.
New York, NY 10022

Brittanica Computer Based
Learning
625 Michigan Ave.
Chicago, IL 60611

Broderbund Software
17 Paul Drive
San Rafael, CA 94903

COMPress
Division of Wadsworth, Inc.
PO Box 102
Wentworth, NH 03282

Comp-Unique
4615 Clausen Ave.
Western Springs, IL 60558

Conduit
University of Iowa
Oakdale Campus
Iowa City, IA 52242

Thomas E. Crowell Co.
10 E. 53rd Street
New York, NY 10022

CUE Softswap Project
SMERC Library and Microcomputer
  Center
San Mateo County Office of
Education
333 Main Street
Redwood City, CA 94063

Curriculum Associates
5 Esquire Road
North Billerica, MA 01862

D.C.H. Software
D.C. Heath Publishing Co.
125 Spring Street
Lexington, MA 02173

DLM Teaching Resources
P.O. Box 4000
One DLM Park
200 E. Bethany Drive
Allen, TX 75002

Davidson and Associates
3135 Kashiwa St.
Torrance, CA 90505

Delacorte Press
c/o Dell Publishing
One Dag Hammarskjold Plaza
245 E. 47th Street
New York, NY 10017

Dial Press
One Dag Hammarskjold Plaza
245 E. 47th Street
New York, NY 10017

Doubleday and Co., Inc.
245 Park Ave.
New York, NY 10167

E. P. Dutton, Inc.
2 Park Ave.
New York, NY 10016

Eastman Kodak Company
School and Youth Services
343 State Street–2nd floor
Bldg. 16–Dept. 373
Rochester, NY 14650

Encyclopedia Brittanica Education
  Corporation
Brittanica Computer Based Learning
425 North Michigan Ave.
Chicago, IL 60611

Farrar, Strauss and Giroux, Inc.
19 Union Square, W.
New York, NY 10003

Four Winds Press
Grolier Electronic Publishing
Sherman Turnpike
Danbury, CT 06816

Golden Press
c/o Western Publishing Co.
850 Third Ave.
New York, NY 10022

Harcourt Brace Jovanovich, Inc.
1250 Sixth Ave.
San Diego, CA 92101

Harper and Row
10 East 53rd Street
New York, NY 10022

Hayden Book Co., Inc.
Div. of Hayden Publishing
10 Mulholland Drive
Hasbrouck Heights, NJ 07604

Henry Holt & Co.
521 Fifth Ave.–6th floor
New York, NY 10175

Houghton Mifflin Co.
One Beacon Street
Boston, MA 02108

Learning Well
200 South Service Road
Roslyn Heights, NY 11577

Lerner Publications
241 First Avenue N.
Minneapolis, MN 55401

J.B. Lippincott Company
Subs. of Harper & Row, Publishers,
  Inc.
E. Washington Square
Philadelphia, PA 19105

Little, Brown and Company, Inc.
34 Beacon Street
Boston, MA 02108

Lothrop, Lee and Shepard Co.
Div. of William Morrow & Co.,
  Inc.
105 Madison Ave.
New York, NY 10016

MacMillan Publishing Co.
866 Third Ave.
New York, NY 10022

McDougal, Littell and Co.
P.O. Box 1667
Evanston, IL 60204

McGraw-Hill Book Co.
Division of McGraw-Hill,
  Inc.
1221 Avenue of the Americas
New York, NY 10020

MECC
3490 Lexington Ave. North
St. Paul, MN 55126

Microsoft Press
Div. of Microsoft Corp.
6011 E. 36 Way
Redmond, WA 98073-9717

Mindscape, Inc.
3444 Dundee Rd.
Northbrook, IL 60062

Milliken Publishing
1100 Research Blvd.
P.O. Box 21579
St. Louis, MO 63132

Pantheon Books, Inc.
c/o Random House, Inc.
201 E. 50th Street, North
New York, NY 10022

Parent's Magazine Press
Div. of Gruner & Jahr USA,
  Publishing
New York, NY 10017

Prentice-Hall, Inc.
Route 9W
Englewood Cliffs, NJ 07632

Random House, Inc.
201 E. 50th St.
New York, NY 10022

Scarborough Systems, Inc.
25 North Broadway
Tarrytown, NY 10591

Scholastic Book Services
1290 Wall Street West
Linhurst, NJ 07071

Scholastic, Inc.
730 Broadway
New York, NY 10003

Sensible Software
210 S. Woodward
Suite 229
Birmingham, MI 48011

Sierra-On-Line
Sierra-On-Line Bldg.
P.O. Box 485
Coarsegold, CA 93614

Simon & Schuster Electronic Publishing
A Division of Simon & Schuster
1230 Avenue of the Americas
New York, NY 10020

South-Western Publishing Co.
Subs. of SFN Cos., Inc.
5101 Madison Road
Cincinnati, OH 45227

Sunburst Communications
39 Washington Avenue, Room EA
Pleasantville, NY 10570

Spinnaker Software
1 Kendall Square
Cambridge, MA 02139

Springboard Software, Inc.
7808 Creekridge Circle
Minneapolis, MN 55435

Stemmer House Publishers
2627 Caves Road
Owings Mills, MD 21117

Sterling Publishing Co.
2 Park Ave.
New York, NY 10016

Charles C Thomas, Publisher
2600 S. First Street
Springfield, IL 62717

Vanguard Press
424 Madison Ave.
New York, NY 10017

Viking Penguin, Inc.
40 W. 23rd Street
New York, NY 10010

Frederick Warne and Co., Inc.
40 W. 23rd Street
New York, NY 10010

Weekly Reader Family Software (Xerox)
Field Publications
245 Long Hill Road
Middleton, CT 06457

Workman Publishing Co.
One W. 39th Street
New York, NY 10018

Yukon Koyukuk School District
APEL Computer Project
P.O. Box 309
Nenana, Alaska 99760

INDEX

Achievement tests, 7
Add the Ending, activity, 185
Adjectives, judgmental, 13, 33
Alligator Antics, 97
Analytic evaluation, of writing, 5
Ask, Tell, Exclaim, activity, 185
Audience, in writing, 50
Autobiography, activity, 86

Bare Bear, The, activity, 197
Brainstorming, 50
Broad and Narrow, activity, 120

Capital Contest, activity, 180
Capitalization rules, table, 181
Carlson Analytical Originality Scale, 6
Characters I, activity, 87
Characters II, activity, 89
Character Description Worksheet, 88
Character Moods, activity, 90
Checklists (see Informal evaluation)
Cliche, 150–153
Collaboration, in writing, 52, 59
Collections of student writing, 48
Comic Strips, activity, 80
Compare and Contrast, activity, 127
Compare and Contrast Chart, 128
Complain, Complain, Complain, activity, 103
Computer applications, in writing, 62
Computerized writing analyzers, 5
Computer labs, 63
Computer software, 64–74
Computer use, in writing, 59
    prewriting, 60, 68
    writing, 61, 71
    editing, 61, 69
    revising, 62
    publishing, 62
Content editing, of writing, 2
Conversations, activity, 187
Cooperative learning, 7
Count the Izzes and Wazzes, activity, 143
Creative writing, 75

Creatures, Monsters, and Dragons, activity, 96

Descriptive detail, 163
Descriptive Words, activity, 147
Diagnostic tests, of writing, 7
Diagnostic Evaluation of Writing Skills, (Weiner), 7–8
DI-COMP, A Diagnostic System for Teaching Composition, 8
Dogs Eat (Descriptive Detail), activity, 163

Editing, 52
Evaluation, of writing skills (see Analytic evaluation; Holistic evaluation; Informal evaluation; Peer evaluation; Self-evaluation; Teacher evaluation)
Electronic bulletin board, 62
Eye Witness News, activity, 115

Fast-write, 56
Feelings About Words, poem, 138
First Person Point of View, activity, 90
Foolish Questions, activity, 186

Goal setting, in writing, 53
Grocery List, activity, 133

Handwriting
    evaluation of, 38, 46
    levels of performance, 14
        low level, 22
        middle level, 30
        high level, 34
Handwriting Checklist, 46
Happy as a Lark, activity, 151
Hasty Generalizations, activity, 125
Help!, activity, 176
Hidden Sentences, activity, 182
High frequency words, 193 (see also Most frequently used nouns)
Holistic evaluation, of writing, 4
How Do Stories Begin?, activity, 95

Ideas/content
    evaluation of, 39, 40
    levels of performance, 12
       low level, 15–16
       middle level, 22–26
       high level, 31–33
Ideas/Content Checklist, 40
Informal evaluation, of writing
    procedures, 34
    activities, 37–38
    checklists, 35–36, 40–46, 54
Irrelevant Sentences, activity, 131
Is That So? (Fact or Opinion?) 134
It's My Opinion!, activity, 105

Journals, in writing, 76
Jumbled Jokes, activity, 129

Keyboarding/Typing Tutorials, 64

Listen for the Details, activity, 126

Main Ideas, Details, Conclusions, activity, 126
Make It Parallel, activity, 175
Make It Real, activity, 148
Mary Had a Little Lamb, activity, 146
Mixed-Up People, activity, 191
Mixed-Up Stories, activity, 130
Most frequently used adjectives and adverbs, table, 141
Most frequently used nouns, table, 139
Most frequently used verbs, table, 140

New News, activity, 115
Newsleads, activity, 114
Nouns, abstract, 13, 33

Organization, in writing
    evaluation of, 39, 41
    levels of performance, 12
       low level, 17–19
       middle level, 26–27
       high level, 33
Organization Checklist, 41
Outline Match, activity, 126

Parallel structure, 174
Pass It On, activity, 168
Peer evaluation, of writing, 6, 53, 57, 61
Phrase, 158, 164
Picture File, activity, 78
Picture Story Language Test (Myklebust), 7–8
Playing with Words, activity, 138
Pro and Con, activity, 117
Prove It!, activity, 129
Publishing, student writing, 57, 194
Punctuation, 180, 182, 184

Prewriting, 2, 50, 194
Proofreading, 181, 194

Qualitative evaluation, of writing, 3
Quantitative evaluation, of writing, 3
Questions, activity, 124
Questionnaire about Reading, 49

Rating scales, 6
Reading, Writing, and Rating Stories, 6, 57
Repetitive Words, activity, 145
Revising, in writing, 55

Scene I, Scene II, Scene III, activity, 79
Self-evaluation, of writing, 6
Sentence Collage, activity, 162
Sentence combining, 5, 172
Sentence Sort (Main Ideas and Details), activity, 121
Sentence structure, 2, 5, 13, 29, 157
    sentence types
       complex sentences, 5, 158
       compound sentences, 158, 170
       compound-complex sentences, 158
       expanded sentences, 158, 165–168, 183
       fragments, 162
       kernel sentences, 158, 159, 163, 176
       run-on sentences, 183
       simple sentences, 158, 161–162
    evaluation of, 42, 44
    levels of performance,
       low level, 19
       middle level, 29–30
       high level, 33
Settings I, activity, 92
Settings II, activity, 94
Setting Description Worksheet, 93
Six Square Activity, 55
Slide-Tape Show, activity, 83
Spelling
    checkers, computerized, 70
    evaluation of, 42, 45
    levels of performance, 14
       low level, 20
       middle level, 30
       high level, 34
Spelling Checklist, 45
Spelling Interviews, activity, 195
Spotting Details, activity, 128
Sport News (Verb Tense), activity, 191
Storyboard Sequences, activity, 81
Storybooks, activity, 84
Storybooks for Young Children, activity, 100
Story Starters, activity, 99
Student Writing Checklist I, 36
Student Writing Checklist II, 54
Structure editing, of writing, 2

Student Generated Chart, "What Makes
    Good Writing?" 56
Syntactic maturity, of writing, 5

Targets, in ads, activity, 116
Task Analysis, activity, 109
Task analysis, of writing, 2
Teacher evaluation, of writing, 4
Teen Job Ads, activity, 107
Telecommunications, 63

Telephone Messages, activity, 101
Test of Written Language (Hammill
    and Larsen), 7–8
Text analysis, of writing, 5
Time Machine: Past, activity, 110

Verbs, cognitive, 13, 33
Verb tense, 188, 191

Writing process, 47